$29.95

$6.98

D0331138

Who's Who in Roman Britain and Anglo-Saxon England
55 BC–AD 1066

Who's Who in Roman Britain and Anglo-Saxon England
55 BC–AD 1066

RICHARD FLETCHER

Series Editor:
GEOFFREY TREASURE

STACKPOLE
BOOKS

First published in North America in 2002 by
STACKPOLE BOOKS
5067 Ritter Road
Mechanicsburg, PA 17055
www.stackpolebooks.com

Originally published in Great Britain in 1989 by Shepheard-Walwyn
(Publishers) Ltd.

Printed in the United States of America

10 9 8 7 6 5 4 3 2 1

FIRST EDITION

Library of Congress Cataloging-in-Publication Data

Fletcher, R. A. (Richard A.)
    Who's who in Roman Britain and Anglo-Saxon England / Richard
Fletcher.— 1st ed.
        p. cm. — (Who's Who in British history)
    Originally published: London : Shepheard-Walwyn, 1989.
    Includes bibliographical references (p.) and index.
    ISBN 0-8117-1642-2
    1. Great Britain—History—Roman period, 55B.C.–449 A.D.—
Biography. 2. Great Britain—History—Anglo-Saxon period,
449–1066—Biography. 3. Biography—Middle Ages, 500–1500—
Biography. 4. Romans—Great Britain—Biography. 5. Anglo-Saxons—
Biography. 6. Britons—Biography. I. Title. II. Series.

DA145.2 .F55 2002
941.01—dc21
                                                    2001055127

To Eleanor, Humphrey, and Alice

Contents

General Introduction ix

Preface xiii

WHO'S WHO IN ROMAN BRITAIN
AND ANGLO-SAXON ENGLAND 1

Bibliographical Note 235

Glossary 237

Index 241

General Introduction

The original volumes in the series *Who's Who in History* were well received by readers who responded favorably to the claim of the late C. R. N. Routh, general editor of the series, that there was a need for a work of reference that should present the latest findings of scholarship in the form of short biographical essays. Published by Basil Blackwell in five volumes, the series covered British history from the earliest times to 1837. It was designed to please several kinds of reader: the "general reader," the browser who might find it hard to resist the temptation to go from one character to another, and, of course, the student of all ages. Each author sought in his own way to convey more than the bare facts of his subject's life, to place him in the context of his age, and to evoke what was distinctive in his character and achievement. At the same time, by using a broadly chronological rather than alphabetical sequence, and by grouping together similar classes of people, each volume provided a portrait of the age. Presenting history in biographical form, it complemented the conventional textbook.

Since the publication of the first volumes of the series in the early sixties, the continuing work of research has brought new facts to light and has led to some important revaluations. Knowledge of the Anglo-Saxon period has been transformed by recent work, archaeological as well as historical. There has also been intense controversy about certain aspects of Tudor and Stuart history. There is plainly a need for fuller treatment of the medieval period than was allowed for in the original series, in which the late W. O. Hassall's volume covered the years 55 BC to 1485 AD. The time seems also to be ripe for a reassessment of some Tudor and Stuart figures. Meanwhile the continued requests of teachers and students for the series to be reprinted encourages the authors of the new series to think that there will be a warm response to a fuller and more comprehensive *Who's Who*, which will eventually include the nineteenth and early twentieth centuries. They are therefore grateful to Shepheard-Walwyn for the opportunity to present the new, enlarged *Who's Who*.

Following Volume I, devoted to the Roman and Anglo-Saxon period, two further books cover the Middle Ages. The Tudor volume, by the late C. R. Routh, has been extensively revised by Dr. Peter Holmes. Peter Hill and I have revised for republication our own volumes on the Stuart and Georgian periods. The authors' prime concern has been England, with Scotsmen and Irishmen figuring only if they happened in any way to be prominent in English history. In the eighteenth century Scotsmen come into the picture, in the nineteenth Irishmen, in their own right, as inhabitants of Great Britain. It is hoped that full justice will be done to Scotsmen and Irishmen—and indeed to some early Welshmen—in subsequent volumes devoted to the history of those countries. When the series is complete, we believe that it will provide a comprehensive work of reference that will stand the test of time. At a time when so much historical writing is necessarily becoming more technical, more abstract, or simply more specialized, when textbooks seem so often to have little room to spare for the men and women who are the life and soul of the past, there is a place for a history of our country that is composed of the lives of those who helped make it what it was, and is. In contributing to this history the authors can be said to have taken heed of the stern warning of Trevor Roper's inaugural lecture at Oxford in 1957 against "the removal of humane studies into a specialization so remote that they cease to have that lay interest which is their sole ultimate justification."

The hard-pressed examinee often needs an essay that puts an important life into perspective. From necessarily brief accounts he may learn valuable lessons in proportion, concision, and relevance. We hope that he will be tempted to find out more and so have added, wherever possible, the titles of books for further reading. Mindful of his needs, we have not however confined our attention to those who have left their mark on church and state. The man who invented the umbrella, the archbishop who shot a gamekeeper, the real hero of a Shakespearian tragedy, a lady who allegedly rode naked through the streets of Coventry, a successful highwayman, and an unsuccessful admiral find their place among the great and good. Nor have we eschewed anecdote or turned a blind eye to folly or foible: it is not the authors' view that history that is instructive cannot also be entertaining.

With the development of a secure and civilized society, the range of characters becomes richer, their achievements more diverse. Besides the soldiers, politicians, and churchmen who dominate the medieval scene there are merchants, inventors, industrialists; more scholars, lawyers, artists; explorers and colonial pioneers. More is known about more people and the task of selection becomes ever harder. Throughout, whether looking at the medieval warrior, the Elizabethan seaman, the Stuart radical, or the eighteenth-century entrepreneur, the authors have been guided by the criterion of excellence. To record the achievements of those few who have had the chance to excel and who have left a name behind them is not to denigrate the unremarkable or unremarked for whom there was no opportunity to shine or chronicler at hand to describe what they made or did. It is not to deny that a Neville or a Pelham might have died obscure if he had not been born to high estate. It is to offer, for the instruction and inspiration of a generation that has been led too often to believe that individuals count for little in the face of the forces that shape economy and society, the conviction that a country is as remarkable as the individuals of which it is composed. In these pages there will be found examples of heroism, genius, and altruism; of self-seeking and squalor. There will be little that is ordinary. It is therefore the hope of the authors that there will be little that is dull.

GEOFFREY TREASURE
Harrow

Preface

The most renowned historian whose life and writings are discussed in the course of this book was Bede. He dedicated his most famous work to the king of his native Northumbria, Ceolwulf; and we learn from the preface that he had already submitted a draft copy of it to Ceolwulf for his comments. Whatever might have been Bede's intention in so doing, the submission of the draft and the subsequent dedication to the highest secular authority in the kingdom could be interpreted as a means of disarming criticism. I doubt whether Bede had any such motive: neither were the qualities of the work in question such as to tempt an author to a subterfuge at once so craven and so imprudent. The three dedicatees of the present book may greet with mixed feelings a work that contains so few pictures. *That* criticism may be launched from a domestic source; others may be anticipated from different quarters. It is with this apprehension in mind that I offer a few pages of introduction directed at that elusive creature, the general reader, for whom this book is intended, in an attempt to explain some of its odder features.

The expanse of time embraced by this book is long. Our sources of information about most of this period are meager and difficult to interpret. The notion of a national community—"England"—barely existed until the last quarter of the period surveyed. These three considerations have shaped my treatment in important ways of which the reader should be made aware.

Let us start with the last of them. This first volume of the *Who's Who in British History* series is intended as a biographical companion to the history of England before 1066. The political unit known as the kingdom of England did not exist before the tenth century and its boundaries were not finally fixed until after the point at which this volume ends. In making my selection of persons I have tended to think in terms of those whose lives were related to the territories that very gradually came to be thought of as "England." What this means in practice is as follows. First, after a certain point very roughly indicated by the year 600, persons whose lives were primarily concerned with the regions we now call

Wales and Scotland have been excluded (except for the occasional household name such as Macbeth). Welsh or Scottish readers, should there be any, may be pained by the absence of, let us say, Hywel Dda or Kenneth mac Alpin. This at any rate is the reason, palatable or not, why these figures are not treated herein. Second, I have included persons not of native birth whose influence upon the history of "England" has been significant. Such, for example, are Julius Caesar, Pope Gregory I, or Canute. Third, and as a corollary, I have included a number of natives of "England" whose spheres of activity and influence were primarily foreign. Such are, among others, Pelagius, Patrick, and Boniface.

With the possible exception of King Alfred no person who features in the following pages and lived before the eleventh century (when our sources of information start to increase in bulk) can be the subject of a biography in anything approaching the normal sense of the word. Our knowledge is simply too fragmentary. We can be sure that there were formidable personalities among the men and women represented here but we cannot know them as intimately as we can know people of later ages. To take but one example, which may stand for many: among military men we know a fair amount about Agricola from the biography—less than fifty pages long in a modern printed edition—composed by his son-in-law. Famous soldiers of much later centuries, a Marlborough or a Wellington, can be approached through scores of volumes of dispatches, letters, state papers, and memoirs. These were three men of comparable stature and achievement, yet we can know far, far less about the earlier of them than we can about the later two. The point is an obvious one, but it needs underscoring.

A volume entitled *Who's Who* will necessarily be concerned with persons of distinction. It cannot be too strongly emphasized that such persons are the *only* ones of whom we can form any impression when we peer into these remote centuries. The ordinary men and women of Roman Britain or Anglo-Saxon England are elusive. We can reconstruct something of the material environment of their lives. We can make a few ill-informed guesses about their thoughts and beliefs. But as individuals they are lost beyond recall. Here are two examples to illustrate the point.

In the year 83 or 84 AD the Greek philosopher and historian Plutarch met at Delphi a teacher named Demetrius, a native of Tarsus—a slightly younger contemporary and fellow-citizen of St. Paul.

Demetrius had recently returned from Britain where, probably in the year 82, he had taken part in a reconnaissance of the western isles of what is now Scotland; a voyage of exploration commissioned by Agricola into what were for the Romans uncharted waters. Nearly 1,800 years later, in 1840, there was unearthed in York, a town founded by the Romans in 71, a small bronze plaque inscribed in Greek with the words "To Ocean and Tethys, Demetrius." The dedication to the god Ocean and his consort Tethys recalled— and surely deliberately—a similar dedication made by Alexander the Great some four hundred years earlier on the shore of the Indian Ocean. Alexander had reached the uttermost limits of the ancient world in the east. Demetrius had seen in the surge and thunder of a mightier ocean the bounds of the world on its western fringe. Plutarch's chance acquaintance at Delphi and the donor of the votive tablet at York were surely one and the same man. Demetrius was a figure of no significance in Romano-British history. Still, one would like to know more about him. We never shall.

About nine hundred years after Demetrius's day a scribe at Durham recorded that an unnamed lady had "given freedom to Ecceard the smith and Alfstan and his wife and all their children born and unborn, and Arcil and Cole and Ecgferth and Ealdhun's daughter and all those people who had bowed their heads to her (i.e., sold themselves into slavery) in return for food when times were bad." It is a startling glimpse of some of the harsher realities of Anglo-Saxon society. Here again, we should like to know more about these people. What circumstances had led them to the desperate course of selling themselves and their families into slavery? What did this slavery involve? What were the motives of their manumitter? We can only guess at the answers to these questions.

The paucity of our information explains the reiterated expressions of caution with which the following pages are so thickly strewn. Readers who are unacquainted with the period and the evidence may find that this tiresome feature undermines their confidence in the author. Encountering for the umpteenth time the phrase "It is not impossible that," they will doubtless mutter petulantly "This fellow doesn't seem to know his stuff." Other readers, who are so acquainted, are likely to accuse me of not being nearly cautious enough in my treatment of controversial matters. Eyebrows will be raised, tongues clicked in disapproval, breath sharply indrawn. "So he thinks the *Anglo-Saxon Chronicle* was produced under Alfred's sponsorship, does he? Just unsupported assertion too—not a shred of evidence quoted to back it up!" All I can say is that I sympathize with both points of view, and that one cannot please everybody. All historians of distant and ill-documented epochs have to try to steer a course between excessive doubt on the one hand and excessive dogmatism on the other. All know how easy it is to drift away from it.

If we can know so little about these distant ages, why do we bother to study them? The answer is simple. The achievement of these early centuries was an enduring one. It shaped and continues to shape the world in which we live. This view is not fashionable today. But fashion is capricious and ephemeral, and the thesis advanced seems to me solid, self-evident, and irrefutable. That achievement was essentially an *institutional* one. If we can know but little about the people who created them, we are potentially much better informed about the institutions they made, be they legal, administrative, economic, social, military, or ecclesiastical. The best modern work on the Romano-British and Anglo-Saxon periods has been devoted to institutional history, broadly defined. It was my wish to introduce the reader to some of this work, but it does not readily lend itself to exposition in a book whose arrangement is biographical. Accordingly, I decided to slip it in by way of digression in the course of biographical treatment. The reader must judge of the awkwardness or otherwise of the result. Some institutional topics (I should like to think) crop up naturally in this fashion. For example, discussion of the Anglo-Saxon fiscal system is unavoidable in any account of the reign of Ethelred the Unready, which was dominated by immense levies of taxation to pay off the Danes. Other topics are dragged in by the scruff of the neck. I am uneasily aware, for instance, that the shadowy Ingimund serves simply as a peg on whom to hang a few lines about Norse settlement in Cumbria.

A few words must be said about conventions. The entries are in chronological rather than alphabetical order. Cross-referencing is provided by the index. At an entry's end I have suggested where appropriate one, sometimes more than one, item of further reading, to draw the reader's attention either to original sources in translation or to good secondary literature (the latter in book rather than article form). The absence of such items of further reading does not mean that none exists but simply that the career of the person concerned is adequately treated in the works listed in the Bibliographical Note that appears at the end of this volume. In referring to counties I have throughout kept to the administrative map of England as it was before the hateful reforms of 1974. Where spelling is concerned I have kept to the familiar and time-honored, even though it is sometimes incorrect: thus, Boadicea rather than Boudicca, Canute rather than Cnut or Knud.

The reader of a biographical dictionary will expect to see portraits of its subjects. However, we simply do not know what the great majority of these people looked like. It is true that we have some sketchy indications about the physical appearance of a very few of them: Pelagius was fat, Paulinus was dark with an aquiline nose, King Athelstan had fair hair, and Harald Hardrada was tall; but these do not take us very far. It is also true that we have representations of many Anglo-Saxon kings from the eighth century onward on their coins: these, however, are not portraits but stylized images. Perhaps the closest we come to a royal portrait—though here too there are stylized elements—is in the rendering of King Edward the Confessor on the Bayeux Tapestry. I have chosen for illustration a sample of artifacts executed in various media at widely scattered times and places, some of them with personal associations that link them with historical figures who feature in the following pages. I hope that this modest sample of what has survived will stimulate the reader to explore landscapes, buildings, and museums.

The three maps that accompany the text are intended to furnish only the most elementary orientation. If the reader is driven by their inadequacies—and I mean inadequacies of conception not of execution—to search out at the first opportunity the maps listed in the Bibliographical Note, so much the better.

It remains only, and pleasurably, to express my thanks to those who have assisted in bringing this book to birth. Geoffrey Treasure has been a sympathetic and indulgent editor. My publisher Anthony Werner has been unfailingly helpful. Some of the biographical entries have been scrutinized, to their profit, by those who command greater expertise than I: in particular I gratefully acknowledge the help of James Campbell, Eric Christiansen, and Ken Lawson. My greatest debt of all is to my wife.

Nunnington, York
November 1988

Who's Who in Roman Britain and Anglo-Saxon England

PYTHEAS OF MARSEILLES (*fl. c.* 310 BC) was a Greek navigator, astronomer, and explorer to whom we owe the earliest written account of the British Isles by a traveller from the civilized Mediterranean world. His work has not survived, so we are dependent for our knowledge of it upon a summary preserved by the historian Polybius, who was writing about a century and a half after Pytheas's day. Some authorities, both ancient and modern, have been skeptical about the voyage of Pytheas, but others have been more charitable. It seems reasonable to suppose that it did indeed take place, that Pytheas sailed up the Atlantic coasts of Spain and France, visited Cornwall (whose tin-mines he mentioned), explored some at least of the south and east coasts of Britain and heard stories of an island somewhere to the north named Thule (possibly Shetland).

GAIUS JULIUS CAESAR (102–44 BC), the great Roman soldier and statesman, was the first of the Romans to undertake military expeditions to Britain, thus unwittingly providing many generations of schoolchildren with the second most memorable date in British history. Caesar's expeditions in 55 and 54 BC were the earliest military encounters between the Roman state and the native principalities of Britain. They occurred during and in some sense grew out of his conquest of Gaul, which was going forward between 58 and 51 BC. His motives in undertaking them have been much debated. He himself tells us that the expeditions were necessitated because the Britons were harboring anti-Roman refugees from Gaul. Doubtless we should also make allowance for Caesar's desire for glory and booty, and his need for further barbarian conquests, which would improve his position in the intense struggle for power that then dominated Roman politics (and which Caesar was eventually to win after his defeat of Pompey in 48 BC). The first expedition to Britain took place late in the campaigning season of 55 BC. It can scarcely

1

be described as a success. After a landing near Deal in Kent, Caesar's forces won a modest victory over the Britons, which they failed to follow up. Four days later their fleet was severely damaged in a storm. After further indecisive fighting another victory was won but once more left unexploited. Caesar then took hostages and hastily withdrew to Gaul before winter came on.

Caesar had learned his lesson. The campaign of 54 was a much more serious affair. Eight hundred ships transported some 27,000 men to a landfall close to that chosen the year before. The size of this force—about three times the size of William the Conqueror's army in 1066—suggests that Caesar was aiming at conquest and annexation of at least part of the island. Swift advance and initial success near Canterbury was followed by indecisive fighting until Caesar managed to inflict a severe defeat upon the British King Cassivellaunus, ruler of the Catuvellauni, a people whose territory was centered upon what is now Hertfordshire; this victory cleared the country as far as the Thames. Having forded the river, Caesar was able to exploit opposition to the Catuvellauni among other tribes, notably the Trinovantes in what is modern Essex. Cassivellaunus thus isolated, Caesar was able to storm his principal fortress—probably at Wheathampstead—and compel him to sue for peace. Caesar had already decided to return to Gaul and his terms were moderate: Cassivellaunus gave hostages and promised an annual tribute. Caesar then left Britain forever, crossing in haste to Gaul to deal with troubles there that culminated in the rising of Vercingetorix.

If Caesar's motives were simply to deter Britons from assisting Gallic dissidents, his expeditions were successful. If in 54 he were intending conquest, he did no more than demonstrate the feasibility of invasion. Cicero's brother, Quintus, who was serving as an officer in Caesar's army, is on record that the material returns of the expeditions were disappointing. Perhaps the most significant result of Caesar's expeditions was the drawing of southeastern Britain into some sort of Roman orbit. In the century between the invasion of Caesar and that of Claudius trade and diplomacy began to enmesh Britain little by little in a Roman cultural web. Julius Caesar put the conquest of Britain on his dynasty's agenda; and through his efforts that dynasty was soon to command the huge resources of the Roman state.

Caesar's own account of his campaigns can be read in his *de Bello Gallico:* there is a good translation under the title *The Conquest of Gaul* in the Penguin Classics series, revised edition, 1982.

CASSIVELLAUNUS (*fl. c.* 54 BC) was king of the Catuvellauni, a British people settled in what is now Hertfordshire and the adjacent regions, at the time of Julius Caesar's invasions. He was chosen to lead the confederacy of British peoples that opposed the Roman forces in 54 BC. Caesar managed to defeat him in the field, isolate him by diplomacy, and finally storm his principal base, which was probably at Wheathampstead in Hertfordshire. At this point Cassivellaunus sought peace, offering hostages and tribute to the Romans. Nothing further is known of him. He must have died before about 20 BC when Tasciovanus, possibly his son or grandson, was ruling the Catuvellauni.

CUNOBELIN (*fl. c.* 5–41 AD) was the son of Tasciovanus. King of the Catuvellauni, and thereby probably a descendant of Cassivellaunus, the opponent of Julius Caesar, Cunobelin, otherwise known as Cymbeline, ruled the Catuvellauni from about 5/10 AD until his death in about 40/41. During this period they became the most powerful tribal confederacy in southern Britain. It was particularly significant that they absorbed the coastal territories of the peoples to their south and east—Cunobelin ruled from Colchester, formerly the center of the Trinovantes—for this brought them into economic and political contact with the Roman dominions in Gaul. For most of Cunobelin's reign these relations seem to have been peaceful, though there were signs of strain in the late 30s, when the Emperor Gaius (Caligula) planned but never carried out an invasion of Britain. In Cunobelin's later years events may have been moving toward the breakdown of relations, which took place after the accession of his son Caratacus and led to the Roman invasion of 43 AD.

TIBERIUS CLAUDIUS NERO GERMANICUS (10 BC–54 AD), usually known simply as Claudius, ruled as Roman emperor from 41 to 54. In 43 he mounted the second and successful Roman invasion of Britain, following the example set by his forebear Julius Caesar. His motives in doing so were probably mixed. There were diplomatic pretexts for Roman intervention in British affairs; Claudius needed the support of the army and the prestige of victories to buttress his insecure position as head of state; his respect for Roman and family tradition inclined him to emulate Caesar by subduing barbarian peoples; and his government looked to the spoils of foreign wars for profit. Claudius took a keen interest in the expedition and himself visited Britain, accompanied by elephants, at the end of the first campaigning season: he received the surrender of Colchester and, as was later claimed on the triumphal arch erected at Rome in his honor, the submission of eleven British kings. He may personally have drafted some of the arrangements for the administration of the new province, and his clemency in 52 toward the captive British King Caratacus was recorded by Tacitus. By the time of Claudius's death in 54 most of lowland Britain south of the Humber was under Roman control.

G. Webster, *The Roman Invasion of Britain,* 1980, and *Rome against Caratacus,* 1982, give a detailed history of the campaigns of the years 43–58.

CARATACUS (*fl.* 40–52), son of Cunobelin, succeeded his father as king of the Catuvellaunian confederation in about 40/41. His power in Britain and known hostility of disposition toward Rome were among the factors leading the Emperor Claudius to invade Britain in 43. After being defeated early on in the invasion, Caratacus disappears from our sources for a few years: he seems to have withdrawn to those western regions beyond the reach of Roman power. In 47 he reappears, leading first the Silures of south Wales and then the Ordovices of central Wales in their resistance to Roman advance. In 51 he was defeated by the Roman governor Ostorius Scapula, possibly on the southern fringes of Snowdonia, and fled for safety to the Brigantes, the principal people of north Britain between the Humber and the Forth-Clyde line. Cartimandua, queen of the Brigantes, had been a client-ruler in treaty-relationship with Rome for at least four years. As she was bound to do, she handed Caratacus over to the Roman authorities. He was sent to Rome and displayed alongside other captives in 52. His speech and bearing on this occasion so impressed the Emperor Claudius, Tacitus tells us, that Caratacus and his family were released from burdensome captivity and permitted to live out their lives in honorable confinement in Italy. The date of his death is not known.

TIBERIUS CLAUDIUS COGIDUBNUS (*fl. c.* 43–85) is known to us from only one literary reference, a sentence in the biography of Agricola by his son-in-law Tacitus. This establishes that Cogidubnus was a client-king, not necessarily of British birth, charged by the authorities in the early stages of Roman occupation with the rule of certain British communities, by implication near the south coast. A damaged inscription on stone found at Chichester in 1723, referring to him as "king and imperial legate," serves to localize his principality. The palatial villa at Fishbourne, a little to the west of Chichester, excavated since 1961, is likely to have been his principal residence, though it should be emphasized that a connection between Fishbourne and Cogidubnus cannot be demonstrated with certainty. Fishbourne invites comparison with any of the great country houses of eighteenth-century England, in scale certainly (for it covered a larger area than Blenheim Palace), and probably in decoration and appointments as well. If correctly identified as the residence of Cogidubnus, it suggests how far the Roman authorities were prepared to go in rewarding loyal cooperation. This in its turn hints at the high value they set upon their newly acquired province of Britannia.

B. Cunliffe, *Fishbourne: A Roman Palace and Its Garden,* 1971.

BOADICEA (*d.* 61) is the incorrect but time-honored spelling of BOUDICCA (always so rendered in our only contemporary source), the wife of King Prasutagus of the Iceni, a British people settled in what are now Norfolk and Suffolk. Prasutagus may have been established as a client-king under Roman authority—like Cogidubnus—after the suppression of an Icenian rebellion in 47. After his death in 60 his family were maltreated by the Romans— Boadicea was flogged and her daughters raped—and his people were subjected to various oppressions and humiliations, principally, it seems, deprivation of their ancestral lands. Boadicea and the Iceni, assisted by some other tribes including the Trinovantes of Essex, rose in revolt. They sacked Colchester and defeated the Ninth Legion under Petillius Cerealis (later governor of Britain [71–74] and founder of York), then went on to sack Verulamium (St. Albans) and London. A contemporary estimated that about 70,000 Roman citizens and sympathizers were massacred; and archaeology has confirmed the extent of the destruction at the three towns. The governor of Britain, Suetonius Paulinus, hastened back from campaigning in Wales and managed to bring the rebels to battle somewhere in the Midlands. After heavy fighting the Britons were decisively defeated. Boadicea took her own life by poison shortly afterwards. It was the most serious rebellion the Romans ever faced in Britain and came near to ending Roman domination there only seventeen years after the Claudian invasion.

G. Webster, *Boudicca: The British Revolt against Rome*, 2nd ed., 1978.

GNAEUS JULIUS AGRICOLA (40–93) was governor of Britain from 78 to 84. Agricola is the best known of all the governors of Roman Britain, owing to the survival of the very dutiful biography of him by his son-in-law, the historian Tacitus, composed in 97–8. A native of southern Gaul, Agricola first served in Britain under Suetonius Paulinus at the time of the rebellion of Boadicea. After holding administrative posts in Asia Minor and Italy, he returned to Britain for the years 71–3. There followed a spell as governor of Aquitaine (74–7) and then the consulate (77), after which he came back to Britain as governor in 78. Agricola is best remembered for the military operations by which he extended Roman dominion in northern Britain. In successive campaigns he reduced north Wales and Anglesey (78), what is now the northwest of England (79) and the central and eastern Scottish Lowlands as far as the river Tay (80). After a season of consolidation he moved against southwestern Scotland in 82 and contemplated invasion of Ireland. Indecisive fighting against the Caledonii, probably in the region of what is now Perthshire, occupied the campaigning season of 83. In 84 the decisive battle was fought: Agricola advanced far to the northeast and shattered the Caledonii under their leader Calgacus at *Mons Graupius*. (The battlefield has never satisfactorily been identified. The latest suggestion is Durno, near Inverurie in Aberdeenshire.) His fleet meanwhile was circumnavigating the north of Britain, perhaps an indication that further campaigns in the extreme north of Scotland were being contemplated.

Despite these hectic military operations, Agricola found time to be a model governor of the conquered province. When every allowance is made for the subtle partisanship of his son-in-law's narrative, it remains clear that Agricola, himself a man of provincial background and sympathies, and one who had been able to observe at first hand the errors of previous governors, was an exceptionally talented administrator of Britain. His period of office was notable for his attempts to restrain the rapacity and corruption of Roman authority and, by a combination of persuasion and pressure, to educate the Britons in Roman ways of life. This was a process that occasioned one of Tacitus's characteristic epigrams: "the Britons called it civilization, when it was really just part of their servitude."

Agricola's most permanent mark on the British landscape resides in the forts and roads that his engineeers laid out between Cheshire and Aberdeenshire. More than sixty forts of Agricolan date have been identified and more may yet·be discovered; the three-quarters of a million iron nails found at the legionary fortress at Inchtuthil in Perthshire convey vividly the scale and efficiency of his operations; and the 1,300 miles of road, which he laid out, continue today, nineteen centuries later, to mark out the main lines of the road system of northern Britain.

Whether Agricola planned to subdue the whole of the British Isles we shall never know. He was recalled in 84 by the neurotically suspicious Emperor Domitian. What is certain is that Rome was never again to be in a position seriously to consider this option. The subsequent history of Scotland and, especially, Ireland might have been very different if Agricola's command had been prolonged by a few years.

Tacitus's biography of Agricola has been well translated in the Penguin Classics series, revised edition, 1978.

PUBLIUS AELIUS HADRIANUS (76–138) ruled as Roman emperor from 117 to 138. Himself a provincial, a native of southern Spain, Hadrian was the first emperor ever to devote a considerable part of his reign to tours of inspection of the provinces of the empire. It was in the course of one of these that he visited Britain in 122. During this visit he commissioned the construction of the Wall with which his name is associated. The immediate background to the project is reasonably clear. Hadrian himself had a keen interest in military installations; he had recently (in 121) supervised the construction of a timber barrier in the German frontier provinces; shortly before his visit to Britain there had been serious troubles there (whose nature is not made clear in our very meager sources) that demanded some new defensive initiative.

Hadrian's Wall and its associated structures form the most elaborate frontier works ever constructed by the Romans. The Wall runs from Wallsend in the east to Bowness-on-Solway in the west, a distance of some seventy-four miles. Small forts at intervals of one Roman mile, known as milecastles, provided quarters for the troops on patrol duty; larger forts just to the south, such as Chesters and Housesteads, acted as permanent barracks and depots for the garrison. An enormous earthwork, the Vallum, a ditch flanked by banks, accompanied the Wall at a little distance on the south side, thereby defining a "military zone" between Vallum and Wall. There were outpost forts to the north, such as Bewcastle, and a string of fortifications scattered down the west Cumberland coast to the south.

The Wall and its related works constituted a formidable barrier. However, although it could be—often had to be—defended against marauders from the north, it is likely that its original function was not *primarily* defensive so much as divisive. Hadrian apparently wanted to push a wedge through the territories of the restless Brigantian peoples, the better to control them and to encourage more settled and civilized social life in the regions to the south, such as the river valleys of the Eden, the Wear, and the Tees. This, at any rate, is the current conclusion of subtle, painstaking, and sometimes brilliant archaeological research. The design, constructional sequences, purpose, and function of the Wall continue to provoke debate, which cannot be summarized here. What seems clear is that the building history of the Wall is intensely complicated and displays many of the characteristics that we associate with large-scale government works: capricious changes of plan, oscillation between extravagance and parsimony, and a strong dose of muddle. For all this Hadrian's Wall remains a prodigious achievement, which even in its shattered condition retains the power to move the visitor as he contemplates the scale and doggedness of the Roman imperial aspirations and achievement.

D. J. Breeze and B. Dobson, *Hadrian's Wall*, 2nd ed., 1978, is the most up-to-date guide to its subject.

LUCIUS SEPTIMIUS SEVERUS (*d.* 211) ruled as Roman emperor from 193 to 211. He spent the years 208–11 in Britain campaigning against the tribes beyond the northern frontier and died at York in February 211. It was possibly during this imperial visit that Alban, the first British Christian martyr, was executed on the orders of Severus's son Geta, who had been left in charge of the administration of Britain while his father was absent on campaign.

ST. ALBAN (3rd century?) was allegedly the earliest Christian martyr in Britain. According to tradition Alban was a citizen of Verulamium who sheltered a Christian priest during a time of persecution and was converted to Christianity by him. When the authorities came to arrest the fugitive, Alban offered himself up instead. Under interrogation and torture Alban refused to sacrifice to the pagan gods and was executed for blasphemy. This story, though not attested before the fifth century, is in itself not implausible. It is important for the early history of British Christianity to date the episode as precisely as possible, but this is extremely difficult. Three widely differing dates have been proposed: 208–11, 251–59, and 303–11. The last of these seems the least likely. Archaeology may one day provide a more accurate dating. Excavation has shown that the late-Roman cemetery of Verulamium was on a hill outside the town, which later became the site of St. Albans abbey and in due course the focus of the modern town of St. Albans: it may be that this was where the early cult of Alban developed. What is certain from the literary sources is that Alban's cult was flourishing at Verulamium in the early years of the fifth century.

C. Thomas, *Christianity in Roman Britain to A.D. 500*, 1981.

MARCUS AURELIUS MAUSAEUS CARAUSIUS (*d.* 293) ruled as usurping emperor in Britain from 287 to 293. A native of the Low Countries, Carausius commanded a Roman fleet based at Boulogne whose role was to reduce piracy in the Channel. The Emperor Maximian, colleague of Diocletian, became suspicious of his loyalty and ordered his arrest and execution. Carausius's response was to proclaim himself emperor. From 287 (or possibly late 286) he ruled Britain and a northern Gallic outpost at Boulogne in effective independence, repelling an attempt by Maximian to dislodge him in 289. In 293 Maximian's deputy, the Caesar Constantius, father of Constantine, managed to recapture Boulogne. His prestige weakened by this reverse, Carausius was murdered by one of his officials, Allectus, who succeeded him as emperor of Britain. But in 296 Constantius invaded, Allectus was defeated and killed, and Britain was restored to the authority of the legitimate emperor.

The Carausian empire has sometimes been interpreted as an early manifestation of stirrings in favor of British national independence: but this is altogether anachronistic. Carausius has also been credited with the construction of the great defensive forts of the Saxon Shore, which stretch from Brancaster in Norfolk to Portchester in Hampshire. But recent archaeological work has cast doubt on this attribution; it is likely that most of the forts were in existence before the usurpation of Carausius.

S. Johnson, *The Roman Forts of the Saxon Shore*, 1976.

FLAVIUS VALERIUS CONSTANTINUS (*c.* 275–337), better known simply as Constantine I, ruled as Roman emperor from 306 to 337. On the death of Constantius his father, Constantine, was proclaimed emperor at York in 306. It is possible that he revisited Britain on more than one occasion in the subsequent eight years, and it may be that the rebuilding of the fortress walls of York, parts of which still stand, should be attributed to him. Otherwise there were no personal connections with Britain: the myth that his mother Helena was British by birth is medieval in origin. His imperial career may have started in Britain but it was played out on a much larger stage elsewhere. Constantine is remembered as the continuator of the administrative reforms of the Emperor Diocletian, which did so much to provide stability and prosperity for the empire in the fourth century; as the founder of the great city that bore his name, Constantinople, the new Rome of the east; above all, as the ruler who ended the persecution of the Christians and by his patronage made Christianity the most favored religion of the late Roman state. There is much that remains enigmatic about Constantine's character and policies. In particular, his religious convictions have provoked endless discussion and speculation, ultimately inconclusive, from his own day to our own. Though he was baptized a Christian shortly before his death—and at that period it was quite common to postpone baptism until late in life—it is very difficult to gauge the extent to which he had genuinely embraced Christianity beforehand; let alone to discern his thoughts and motives. He did not, as is often said, make Christianity the official religion of the Roman empire; that was a step which was taken later on in the fourth century. But by throwing the whole gigantic weight of imperial favor behind the Christian establishment he hastened the gradual and in many ways mysterious process by which the Roman world was Christianized.

R. MacMullen, *Constantine*, 1969, and *Christianizing the Roman Empire*, 1984.

MAGNUS CLEMENS MAXIMUS (*d.* 388) ruled as usurping Roman emperor from 383 to 388. Of Spanish birth, Magnus Maximus served in the Roman army in Britain from 367 and rose to high military command. In 383 he proclaimed himself emperor, crossed the Channel with an army, and established his rule over Gaul and Spain. In 387 he moved into Italy but in 388 was defeated by the rightful Emperor Theodosius I and executed at Aquileia. His significance in British history is twofold. First, his withdrawals of troops from Britain made the province even more vulnerable than it already was to Pictish, Irish, and Saxon marauders. Secondly, he was remembered (under the name Macsen) in medieval Welsh tradition as the ancestor of several British princely dynasties. Precisely what significance this may have is not clear, but it is possible that Maximus established reliable native subordinates for defensive purposes in positions of authority that later became hereditary. On both counts his unwitting contribution to the confused process called, for convenience, "the end of Roman Britain" was considerable.

J. Matthews, *Western Aristocracies and Imperial Court, A.D. 364–425*, 1975.

PELAGIUS (*fl. c.* 380–420) was a Christian teacher, theologian, and heretic. A native of Britain, where he received what was clearly a very good education—a point of some importance for our understanding of the intellectual culture of Roman Britain—Pelagius settled in Rome about 380, lived there until about 409, and then moved by way of North Africa to Palestine where he is last heard of in 418. It was in the course of his long residence in Rome, where he was taken up by the high-minded, pious, Christian aristocracy, that he developed the views that the ecclesiastical authorities, notably Augustine of Hippo, were to condemn. Pelagius's teaching, often misrepresented, was that man's God-given nature permitted and indeed obliged him to achieve perfection; and that this should be sought by the layman through living a life of stern, austere, ascetic Christian rectitude. In developing his ideas he was led to question the doctrine of Original Sin and it was this that attracted the condemnation of the church. In the land of his birth Pelagian ideas became sufficiently widespread to bring St. Germanus twice to Britain in the second quarter of the fifth century to combat them. In some form or another Pelagius's teaching has remained influential from his day to our own. He is the first native of Britain to have made an enduring contribution to the intellectual and religious culture of Europe. He is also, coincidentally, the first native of Britain of whose physical presence we can form some idea. Pelagius was a great big man, fat and bull-necked; oddly enough, in defiance of all subsequent changes of race and custom, the first "John Bull" figure in British history.

P. Brown, *Augustine of Hippo*, 1967, and *Religion and Society in the Age of Saint Augustine*, 1972.

CONSTANTINE III (*d.* 411), usurping Roman emperor from 407 to 411, was a soldier of unknown antecedents in the Roman army in Britain who was proclaimed emperor in 407. Like his precursor Magnus Maximus in the years 383–88 he stripped Britain of troops, crossed to the continent, and attempted to establish his authority in Gaul and Spain. In 411 he was captured at Arles by the army of the Emperor Honorius and executed. Constantine's usurpation had different consequences for Britain from that of Maximus, for three reasons. It may have permanently denuded Britain of regular units of the Roman army. It coincided with a major invasion of barbarians—Vandals, Sueves, and Alans—across the Rhine frontier and into Gaul, which isolated Britain from the seats of Roman authority in southern Gaul and northern Italy. It also coincided with a serious attack on Britain, probably in 408, by the Saxons. In these circumstances the Britons were thrown back on their own resources. They expelled Constantine's administrators, set up their own government, and took successful steps for their own defense against the invaders; a state of affairs that was recognized by the imperial government in 410. Although this was less apparent to contemporaries than to later generations, it may be said that Constantine III's usurpation led directly to the formal end of Roman rule in Britain.

FLAVIUS AUGUSTUS HONORIUS (384–423) ruled the western half of the Roman empire from 395 to 423. He was a man of feeble intellect and character, who presided over the empire during a period of unexampled humiliation in its fortunes, most vividly represented by the Gothic siege and sack of Rome. Honorius is important in British history only as the emperor who in 410 instructed the cities of Britain "to look to their own safety." The text of this famous document does not survive as such: it is preserved only in a summary in the work of the historian Zosimus who was writing nearly a century later, though it is likely that Zosimus was dependent on the now lost work of Olympiodorus who wrote in about 425, not long after the events in question. Much controversy surrounds the interpretation of Honorius's letter. It may simply have been intended to indicate that, with Constantine III still at large and considerable areas of Gaul and Spain overrun by barbarians, the government could do nothing *for the moment* to reestablish Roman imperial authority in Britain. On this showing, Honorius was not intending a final severance of Britain from the western empire; something that would in any case, one may suspect, have been practically unthinkable for an emperor and his advisers in the early fifth century. However, if plans *did* exist for a recovery of the temporarily abandoned province, they were never implemented. With the passage of time Honorius's decision acquired an air of finality, which it was probably never intended to have. In retrospect the year 410 does indeed mark the end of Roman rule in Britain. As the historian Procopius, writing in the middle of the sixth century, put it, "the Romans never succeeded in recovering Britain, but it remained from that time on under tyrants."

ST. GERMANUS (*c.* 375–437) was bishop of Auxerre in Gaul, probably from 407 until his death. Like many bishops of the late-antique world Germanus was not by training an ecclesiastic. Born into a wealthy Gallo-Roman family, he enjoyed a successful career as lawyer and civil servant until in 407 the bishopric of Auxerre was virtually forced upon him. In troubled times urban communities needed forceful and well-connected personalities as their bishops, equipped to fulfill an expanding role as the patrons and defenders of their flocks. The biography composed by Constantius of Lyons in the 480s was carefully designed to show how magnificently Germanus had performed. It also casts a little light on the affairs of Britain in the almost impenetrable obscurity of the post-Roman period.

Germanus visited Britain twice, in 429 and again in about 435/6. (The date of the second visit is hard to establish. It, and the date of Germanus's death, have traditionally been placed some ten years later. Persuasive arguments for an earlier date have recently been put forward.) These visits were occasioned by the need to combat the heresy of Pelagius, which had recently taken root in Britain. On his first visit Germanus confuted the heretics, worked miracles, visited the shrine of St. Alban, and led a British army in the bloodless "Alleluia" victory over a force of marauding Saxons and Picts. On his second visit he likewise routed the heretics by a combination of vigorous preaching and supernatural aid. These passages, for all that they conform to the literary conventions governing the composition of saints' lives, are important as indicating that a generation after the formal end of Roman rule Britain still remained in some sense a part of the Roman world. It was experiencing intermittent barbarian attack but it had not yet succumbed.

Germanus may have had further contacts with the Christian communities of the British Isles. It is possible that Palladius, who was sent in 431 to be the bishop of a Christian community in Ireland, had been a member of Germanus's circle at Auxerre. It is just conceivable that Patrick spent a little time at Auxerre after escaping from captivity in Ireland.

F. R. Hoare, *The Western Fathers*, 1954, contains a translation of the life of Germanus by Constantius of Lyon.

VORTIGERN (*fl. c.* 425–50?) was the name of a British ruler of the sub-Roman period, remembered in later Welsh legend as a scapegoat: the man who had invited the Saxons to Britain and thus precipitated their conquest of the island. We may suspect that the truth was a little more complicated than this. Our trouble is that we possess scarcely any reliable information about Vortigern. Gildas, who does not mention him by name, seems to refer to him as a "proud tyrant." Bede supplements the account of Gildas by naming Vortigern and referring to him as a king. By the time that Nennius was writing in the early ninth century many doubtful stories had gathered about Vortigern's doings. This is not much to go on, but it is very nearly all that there is.

Modern historians for the most part accept that Vortigern existed and that he exercised political authority over a part—perhaps a large part—of what had been Roman Britain. The period in which he ruled is perhaps most probably placed in the second quarter of the fifth century. It is entirely credible that he should have summoned Germanic mercenaries to Britain, settled them in bases "in the eastern part of the island" (in the words of Gildas), and employed them to defend his territories from the attacks of other enemies, notably the Picts. Such a course of action was in line with standard late-Roman policy, well-attested in several areas of the late empire. Indeed, there is every likelihood that the Roman authorities had been following this practice in Britain in the latter part of the fourth century. These people were difficult to control. It is therefore equally credible that the mercenaries should have revolted against their paymaster, broken out from their bases, defeated Vortigern's forces, and seized large tracts of British territory for themselves. Something like this may have happened, perhaps in the 440s: we shall never know for certain.

AMBROSIUS AURELIANUS (5th century?) was a military leader among the Britons in the sub-Roman period. He is the only fifth-century personage named, albeit casually and allusively, by Gildas. Gildas tells us that he was of high birth and Roman descent; presumably, though not necessarily, Roman-British. It was appropriate to describe him as holding high military rank as a general (*dux*). Gildas identifies him as the leader of the Britons against the Saxon mercenaries who had revolted against the "proud tyrant," assumed to be Vortigern, and had laid waste much territory. This would suggest that Ambrosius flourished about the middle years of the fifth century. He fought and won battles against them "with God's help"; so he was evidently a Christian. The most tantalizing piece of information furnished by Gildas is that relatives of Ambrosius had "worn the purple." This can only mean that more than one among them had been Roman emperors but whether these emperors should be sought among the Constantinian or Theodosian dynasties of the fourth and fifth centuries, or among the many usurpers of the same period, none may say.

Later Welsh tradition represented in the work of Nennius adds a thick layer of legendary encrustation to further obscure the figure of Ambrosius, but also preserves the unsurprising information that he was an enemy of Vortigern, and the much more surprising claim that Ambrosius had been "king among all the kings of the British nation." One may make what one will of this. It is at least possible that Ambrosius Aurelianus exercised political authority as well as military command in post-Roman Britain. Historians of the British Dark Age are prone to set generous limits to their view of the possible. Valiant and ingenious attempts to locate the zone of his authority on the basis of place-names conceivably derived from his name—for example, Amberley in Sussex—have been made: the best one may say is that the case remains unproven.

HENGIST (*fl. c.* 450?) was remembered in later Anglo-Saxon tradition as the first Germanic king of Kent. Bede records that he was invited to Britain as a mercenary leader by Vortigern between 449 and 455. The annals in the *Anglo-Saxon Chronicle,* which in their present form date from the end of the ninth century, record four battles that he fought against the Britons and appear to place his death in 488. Cryptic references to a certain Hengist in the old English epic *Beowulf* and in the fragmentary poem about a fight at *Finnsburh* may be to the same man. Precisely when Hengist lived and what he achieved will always remain obscure, but there is no good reason for doubting his existence. Archaeological evidence suggests that Germanic settlement in Kent was already fairly plentiful by the period when Hengist is alleged to have lived. The artifacts recovered from Dark Age Kent are distinct from those of other early Anglo-Saxon kingdoms. This supports the belief of eighth-century witnesses such as Bede and his informants at Canterbury that the Germanic settlers of Kent were of different stock from others. They called themselves not Angles or Saxons but Jutes, and believed that their original homeland had been in Jutland. Who the Jutes were, where they came from, and what was distinctive about the Jutish culture of Kent, are difficult questions that have stimulated a great deal of discussion. Where so much is uncertain, one thing seems tolerably clear. Whatever the ethnic origin of the Germanic settlers in Kent, the culture of Kent during this period—as indeed during others—was much affected by proximity to the continent, in particular by proximity to the Franks who were settling in Roman Gaul. Franco-Kentish contacts, possibly of no great density in the time of Hengist, thickened in the course of the sixth century. Appreciation of them is essential to an understanding of the age of Ethelbert and Augustine.

AELLE (*fl. c.* 480?) was remembered in later Anglo-Saxon tradition as the first Germanic king of the South Saxons, who gave their name to Sussex. The annals in the *Anglo-Saxon Chronicle* record some very dubious traditions of his military exploits, which were assigned dates between 477 and 491. It is not impossible that his alleged conquest of Sussex bore some relation to the contemporary movement of Frankish expansion under King Clovis in northern Gaul. Bede tells us that Aelle was the first English king to exercise what he termed *imperium* (literally "empire," but perhaps "overlordship" is the most fitting translation) over all English rulers south of the river Humber. The concept was expressed in the ninth-century Old English vernacular of the *Chronicle* as *bretwalda* or *brytenwalda* ("ruler of Britain" or "wide ruler"). Bede does not tell us, perhaps because he did not know, what Aelle's *imperium* had meant, if anything. A plausible guess by modern scholars sees Aelle as the leader of a temporary military confederacy of Germanic warlords directed against the southern Britons. On this argument Aelle would be comparable to leaders of similar character thrown up among other Germanic peoples, for instance the Visigoths, in the course of war with the Roman empire. It may have been so.

ARTHUR (5th century?) is the most elusive of all the figures who flit about in the obscurity of post-Roman Britain, and the one who has provoked the most voluminous and much of the silliest writing on the British Dark Age. The case for believing that Arthur existed rests on the following pieces of early testimony, and on these alone. First, there is a reference in a British poem known as *Gododdin*, composed *c.* 600, to a hero who "glutted black ravens (i.e., killed many men) on the rampart of the stronghold, though he was no Arthur." Unless the phrase is a later insertion into the text (which is possible) this is by far the earliest reference to Arthur, and indicates that he was remembered as a famous warrior. Second, we possess a list in the work attributed to Nennius of twelve battles fought and won by Arthur against the Saxons. Arthur is described as fighting "alongside the kings of the Britons, but he himself was commander in the wars (*dux bellorum*)." This passage has analogies with other "battle-listing poems" in early Welsh literature and is unlikely to have taken shape before the first half of the seventh century at the earliest. The last battle listed by Nennius, that of Mount Badon, is assumed to be identical to "the siege of the Badonic hill" to which Gildas alludes, though without naming the commander on the British side. The site of Badon cannot be identified, neither can the battle be dated except with reference to the time when Gildas was writing, which itself is far from certain. Third, there are two entries in a series of annals that appear to date the battle of Badon to 516 and Arthur's death to 537. These annals were not put together in the form in which we have them until the tenth century and it is unwise to assume that the information they provide about fifth- and sixth-century affairs is in any way reliable.

The irreducible minimum with which we are left is that from the late sixth century onward British poetic tradition celebrated a heroic warrior of the past named Arthur who fought successfully against the Saxons. Additional evidence that this was so is provided by the appearance of the name Arthur—which is derived from the rather unusual Roman name Artorius—under various Celtic guises in diverse but always princely contexts of the late sixth and early seventh centuries. For example, King Aedan of Dalriada, who was killed by Ethelfrith of Northumbria in 603, named his son Arthur.

This is as far as it is prudent to go. That Arthur was a king, that he had a retinue of knights, that he kept chivalric court—all this derives from the brilliant fiction of Geoffrey of Monmouth, the *History of the Kings of Britain,* composed in the 1130s. The Arthurian scholarship of our own day is patchy: some of it muscular and austere, much of it mushy and credulous. The reading and viewing public appears to prefer the latter. Twentieth-century people are as engagingly bent on believing rubbish as the forebears whose gullibility they affect to ridicule.

The literature on Arthur is vast. L. Alcock, *Arthur's Britain,* 1971, is sensible and moderate, especially strong on the archaeological side. J. Morris, *The Age of Arthur,* 1973, is learned, imaginative, stimulating, wild, and infuriating. Both works range widely over the period *c.* 350–*c.* 650.

ST. NINIAN or **NYNIA** (5th century?) was a British bishop of the sub-Roman period. Our information about Ninian is extremely fragmentary, the only faintly reliable early sources being two sentences in the *Ecclesiastical History* of Bede and a tortuous Latin poem of the eighth century known as "The Miracles of Bishop Nynia." Modern scholars are prepared to accept that Ninian was a Briton who became bishop of a Christian community established in what is now Galloway; in Bede's day his cult was celebrated at Whithorn. It is impossible to date his episcopate precisely. The literary evidence, such as it is, suggests that Ninian flourished about the middle of the fifth century. The surviving archaeological evidence is congruent with such a dating: that is, the remains of an early Christian cemetery beneath the medieval Whithorn priory church, the inscribed stone commemorating a Christian named Latinus at Whithorn, and the comparable stone erected in memory of two bishops (successors of Ninian, perhaps) at Kirkmadrinc in the Rhinns of Galloway. Bede reported—somewhat cautiously ("as they say")—that Ninian had converted the southern Picts to Christianity. Whom he meant by the southern Picts is by no means clear; possibly he intended the peoples living about the Firth of Forth. It is not impossible that Ninian preached Christianity to them. We simply do not know.

C. Thomas, *Christianity in Roman Britain to A.D. 500,* 1981.

ST. PATRICK (*c.* 415?–93?) was a British missionary bishop in Ireland, commonly though not very accurately termed the "apostle of Ireland." Patrick is the earliest native of Britain who can still speak to us directly, so to say, about himself. We possess two documents, undoubtedly genuine, of his own composition: the *Epistola,* or "Letter," addressed to a British king named Coroticus and the *Confessio,* or "Declaration," a justification of his career and conduct. The *Confessio* is a kind of spiritual autobiography and is the prime source of evidence about his life. It is short, simple, awkward, and oddly moving. Anyone who seeks to understand Patrick should start (and finish) by reading the *Confessio.*

Patrick was born into a well-to-do landed Romano-British and Christian family, probably somewhere in the northwest of the province of Britannia and perhaps not far from Carlisle, at some point in the first quarter of the fifth century. (The chronology of his life has generated long and sometimes fierce controversy. I follow the reconstruction suggested by Professor Thomas (see below) whose arguments I find persuasive.) He evidently received some schooling, though of a fairly rudimentary kind: throughout his life he remained pathetically ashamed of his lack of learning, which is evidenced in the very simple Latin that was all that he could command. At the age of sixteen he was captured by raiders from Ireland and spent six years in captivity there working as a herdsman for his master "near the forest of Foclut which is near the western sea," an area tentatively identified as the region of Killala in County Mayo. At the end of this period he escaped and managed to take ship to Gaul. It is possible that he spent some time at an ecclesiastical center in Gaul such as Tours or the Auxerre of St. Germanus, though all he himself tells us is that after a few years he returned to his family in Britain. This may have been somewhere about the year 440.

It was then that Patrick saw a vision in which he was summoned to return to Ireland: a man from Ireland appeared to him proffering a letter headed "the voice of the Irish," and as he read it he heard voices crying, "We beg you, holy boy, to come and walk again among us." That Patrick experienced some sort of call is in no doubt. But there may have been rather more prosaic reality behind his mission as well. Patrick was consecrated a bishop before his return to Ireland, so we must allow further time in Britain for ecclesiastical training; he can hardly have gone back to Ireland before c. 450 at the earliest. Furthermore, it is likely that he was dispatched by the British church authorities, answerable to them, not with a roving commission to convert the heathen but as the bishop of an existing Christian congregation. Where this group was we do not know, though it is more likely to have been in the northern than in the southern half of Ireland. (The connection with Armagh is not claimed before c. 700 and must be regarded as unproven.)

Patrick spent the rest of his life as a bishop in Ireland, ministering to his congregation and also enlarging it by evangelization. Of his activities in detail we know very little. We hear of large numbers of converts drawn from all ranks of the Irish social hierarchy; of the ordination of clergy; of travels to remote parts hitherto untouched by Christianity; of the foundation of religious communities. We also hear of dangers and tribulations; among these, criticisms levelled at Patrick and his conduct of the mission by the clergy in Britain, whose accusations the *Confessio* was seemingly designed to rebut. Undeterred by difficulties, Patrick worked on in

Ireland to the end of his life, in his own words "a slave in Christ to a foreign people." We do not know where he was buried, though his cult was later based at Armagh. The fine hymn known as "St. Patrick's Breastplate" is a later composition incorrectly attributed to him. To strip his career of its accretion of legend and to deprive him of the "Breastplate," as modern scholarship has done, is in no way to diminish his achievement. Patrick and his anonymous fellow-workers and successors laid the foundations on which the justly acclaimed achievements of early medieval Irish culture were raised.

The most recent translation of the relevant texts may be found in A. B. E. Hood, *Saint Patrick: His Writings and Muirchu's Life*, 1978. There is an excellent commentary upon them in the final chapters of C. Thomas, *Christianity in Roman Britain to A.D. 500*, 1981.

GILDAS (*fl. c.* 490–520?) was a British priest, probably not a monk, who was the author of a treatise entitled *De Excidio Britanniae* (The ruin of Britain.) Gildas intended it as a "tract for the times": it is a long-winded castigation of the shortcomings of the British clergy and of five named secular rulers. This is preceded by a short introduction that surveys, albeit very allusively, the history of Britain from the later fourth century down to the time of writing. Gildas adopted the stance of the Old Testament prophets whose words he quoted so freely. He wrote to denounce the sinner and to warn of the wrath to come. He used a convoluted Latin style that renders his work at times almost incomprehensible. However, his tract is the only surviving near-contemporary account of its period by a British author, and as such a historical source of considerable importance. (It is somewhat as though a single sermon by a Puritan divine constituted our principal source of knowledge for the history of Britain in the seventeenth century.)

Gildas is a very important witness, not simply in what he says but also in what he *was:* a well-educated cleric, able to take for granted an established Christian church, thinking of the Britons as "Roman citizens" and addressing secular princes in rhetorical Latin. Though there were barbarians settled within its frontiers the once-Roman province had not relapsed into barbarism at the time he wrote. It is therefore desirable to fix that time as precisely as possible. Until recently most historians would have asserted confidently that Gildas was writing in the 540s. However, there is reason to suppose that this date is too late. It is not impossible that Gildas wrote early in the sixth century or even in the last quarter of the fifth. Certainly the British church whose shortcomings he denounces so violently seems to have much in common with the church that Germanus had visited in the second quarter of the fifth century and of whose learned leaders Patrick was so painfully in awe about a generation later.

M. Winterbottom, *Gildas: The Ruin of Britain and Other Documents,* 1978, contains an edition and annotated translation of Gildas's work.

CERDIC (*fl. c.* 490–530?) was remembered in later Anglo-Saxon tradition as the first Germanic king of Wessex. The annals in the *Anglo-Saxon Chronicle* record some very dubious traditions of his military exploits, which are assigned dates between 495 and 534. The most intriguing thing about this shadowy personage is his name, which is not Germanic but Celtic: compare, for example, the King Cerdic of the British kingdom of Elmet in the early seventh century. Whatever may be the implications—and the possibilities are manifold—the presence of this anomalous name in the genealogies did not embarrass those who claimed to be his descendants: "his kin goes back to Cerdic" was a regular boast of the chroniclers who recorded the doings of later kings of Wessex.

If the *Anglo-Saxon Chronicle* is to be believed, Cerdic's operations occurred in that area of Hampshire and south Wiltshire extending northward from Southampton toward Winchester and Salisbury. The rather meager archaeological record of the early Anglo-Saxon period confirms that this region was one nucleus of the later kingdom of Wessex. Archaeology reveals much thicker Germanic settlement of the upper Thames valley, notably round Dorchester-on-Thames, which was later, significantly, to be the site of the first West Saxon bishopric under Birinus; but on the early traditions of this region the literary sources are silent. It is a reminder (if one were needed) that the origins of the political entity later known as the kingdom of Wessex were more complex and diverse than we shall ever know.

ST. COLUMBA or **COLUMCILLE** (*c.* 522–97) was the founder of the monastery of Iona, often termed, somewhat misleadingly, the "apostle of Scotland." He was a native of Ireland, a member of the northern branch of the princely family of Ui-Neill or O'Neill. From an early age he was prepared for a career in the church and it was probably from his teacher Finnian—either St. Finnian of Clonard or St. Finnian of Moville—that he acquired his commitment to the monastic life. His first monastic foundation was at Derry (550s?). In 563 he left Ireland for Britain. The reasons for his departure have been much debated. There is a possibility that it was not entirely voluntary, that Columba might have been sent into an exile that was at once political and penitential.

During the previous two or three generations the Irish—during this period, confusingly, known as Scots—had been drifting over the North Channel to settle the coastline and islands of western Scotland from Kintyre and Islay in the south to Ardnamurchan and Coll in the north. The principality that they established there was known as Dalriada. In founding a monastery at Iona therefore, which he did soon after his arrival in Dalriada, Columba was settling among people of his own race and language. Nevertheless, the act of renunciation involved in abandoning his homeland and settling upon this inhospitable islet for a life of austerity and prayer was intended by Columba and perceived by his contemporaries as an act of specially intense Christian devotion. It was called *peregrinatio,* "pilgrimage." Columba had become a "pilgrim (*peregrinus*) for Christ." This was an ideal of Christian living that was to be widely diffused by the Irish, in Britain and on the continent, during the seventh and eighth centuries.

Pilgrimage merged insensibly into mission. The act of founding monasteries in remote places helped to diffuse Christianity among peoples who were little or not at all acquainted with it. Columba, like other monastic leaders of this age, founded a whole confederation of monasteries. Apart from Iona itself, there were Derry and later Durrow in Ireland; and in Dalriada there were communities on Tiree and Hinba and probably elsewhere as well. The confederation continued to grow after his death: Lindisfarne, founded by Aidan from Iona in 635, was immensely influential in the conversion of Northumbria.

Columban monasteries were also established among the Picts of eastern Scotland, though probably not until after Columba's day. Columba certainly had dealings with the Picts. He visited their king, Bridei, near the shores of the Moray Firth and is known to have made a few Christian converts among them. But his earliest surviving biography, composed by Adomnan *c.* 690, claims no general conversion of the Picts for him, and Columba's reputation as their apostle is based on later and much less reliable evidence. Adomnan's account of Columba's visits to Pictland is chiefly remarkable for containing the earliest reference to the Loch Ness monster.

Columba died and was buried on Iona in 597. The house that he had founded there remained a center of spirituality, learning, and culture for the next two centuries: it is one of several places at which the great manuscript known as the Book of Kells might have been produced toward the end of the eighth century. Iona suffered terribly from Viking attacks early in the ninth century and though it was restored soon afterward it never quite recovered the preeminence it had enjoyed earlier on.

A. O. and M. O. Anderson have edited and translated *Adomnan's Life of Columba*, Edinburgh, 1961. For a recent treatment of his career see A. P. Smyth, *Warlords and Holy Men: Scotland A.D. 80–1000*, 1984, chapter 3.

IDA (*d. c.* 560) was the first recorded king of Bernicia, the northern half of the Anglo-Saxon kingdom of Northumbria. Bede states that he ruled from 547 for twelve years. Northern annalists add that his power was based at Bamburgh on the coast of Northumberland. Traditions preserved by Nennius of fighting between the sons of Ida and the northern Britons in the late sixth century also suggest that at that date Bernician rule did not extend far inland. The extreme scarcity of archaeological finds of Anglian type and sixth-century date from inland sites is consistent with this. It was Ethelfrith, grandson of Ida, who first significantly extended Bernician power westward to the hinterland.

AELLE (*d.* 588?) was the first recorded king of Deira, the southern half of the Anglo-Saxon kingdom of Northumbria. According to Northumbrian tradition reported independently by Bede and by the anonymous author of the "Whitby" life of Pope Gregory, it was during the reign of Aelle that Gregory encountered Deiran boys for sale in the slave-market at Rome and was thereby moved to excruciating puns ("Not Angles but angels") and missionary endeavor. Whether the story is true or not, it is of some interest to the economic historian. It is significant that early eighth-century commentators such as Bede thought that there was nothing surprising about the presence of Anglo-Saxon slaves for sale in a Mediterranean city. This is only one of several surviving pieces of evidence that suggest that slaves were an important commodity of trade in early Anglo-Saxon England.

CEAWLIN (*d.* 593) was king of Wessex, according to the *Anglo-Saxon Chronicle*, whose chronology however is not reliable for this period, from 560 to 593. The annals in the *Chronicle* relating to his career are cast in a tone that suggests that they may derive from a lost Old English epic poem. For what they are worth, they conjure up a Germanic warlord of the sort celebrated in the surviving epic *Beowulf*. They show Ceawlin engaged in warfare with his neighbors both Anglo-Saxon and British, winning battles as at Dyrham in 577, capturing towns such as Bath, acquiring booty, and perishing probably by violence. Bede allotted him an *imperium*, or overlordship, like that attributed to Aelle of Sussex: whatever this may have meant to Bede, to us Ceawlin's *imperium* is as opaque as Aelle's. It is possible that Ceawlin was responsible for the construction of some or all of the great earthwork known as Wansdyke. If this were so, he might have had a greater degree of ordered power at his disposal than the bloody record of the *Chronicle* suggests.

ETHELFRITH (*d.* 616), grandson of Ida of Bernicia, was king of Northumbria from 593 to 616 and the first ruler significantly to extend Anglian power in northern Britain westward from its original bases on the eastern coastline. Bede remembered him as "a very strong king and most eager for glory, who harried the Britons more than any other English ruler." It was probably he who shattered a British army at Catterick about the year 600, a defeat mourned in the British poem *Gododdin*. It was certainly he who defeated the army of Aedan, king of the Irish-Scottish kingdom of Dalriada, at the unidentified place *Degsastan* in 603, and some ten years later was victorious over a British army from Wales near Chester. These victories did not necessarily result in any permanent gains of territory west of the Pennines: tribute and plunder, slaves and livestock probably mattered more than land to an early Anglo-Saxon war-lord. While it is likely that Anglian settlement east of the Pennines, between the Humber and the Tweed, thickened during Ethelfrith's lifetime, there is every probability that his expanding kingdom embraced many communities of British stock. Early Northumbrian institutions, in so far as they can be discerned through the medium of later evidence, have an Anglo-Celtic look rather than a purely Germanic one. Northumbria may not have been unusual in this respect. Historians today are more ready than they used to be to allow for a degree of British survival and continuity in such matters as settlement patterns and agrarian organization.

At some stage of his reign Ethelfrith managed to extend his power over the southern Northumbrian kingdom of Deira. Nothing is known of the circumstances in which this occurred, though we do know that he married a daughter of King Aelle of Deira. We also know that other members of the Deiran dynasty, notably Edwin, were scattered in exile. Edwin spent the latter part of his exile at the court of Redwald, king of the East Angles. It was in battle with Redwald's army that Ethelfrith was defeated and killed in 616, as a result of which Edwin became king of Northumbria.

ETHELBERT (*d.* 616) was king of the Jutish kingdom of Kent and the earliest English royal convert to Christianity. According to Bede, King Ethelbert was the third English ruler after Aelle of Sussex and Ceawlin of Wessex to exercise *imperium,* overlordship, over all the Anglo-Saxon kingdoms south of the river Humber. The stages by which he achieved this position and the period during which he exercised it are alike obscure. Bede also tells us that Ethelbert reigned for the impossibly long period of fifty-six years (560–616). This would seem to be one of Bede's very rare chronological mistakes: it is likely that Ethelbert became king of Kent *c.* 590.

Ethelbert married a Frankish princess named Bertha, daughter of King Charibert (*d.* 567), himself a grandson of Clovis (*d.* 511), the first Christian king of the Franks. When the marriage took place (perhaps *c.* 580), Bertha was accompanied to Kent by a Christian entourage, which included a bishop named Liudhard, and she had a Roman building just outside Canterbury restored for her use as a church. So, as Bede says, "some knowledge of the Christian faith had already reached" King Ethelbert before the arrival of missionaries sent by Pope Gregory I. There may have been more to it than this. Ethelbert's marriage may have indicated a degree of subjection to Frankish overlordship. Bertha and Liudhard may have been pressing for the king's conversion to his overlord's faith. Ethelbert may have given some sort of commitment to Christianity, even if it did not go as far as conversion and baptism, before the arrival of the Roman missionaries. Indeed, knowledge of the king's interest may have been among the factors impelling Pope Gregory to dispatch the mission at the time he did.

These are speculative matters, but it is at least worth pondering the proposition that the background to Ethelbert's conversion may have been a little more complicated than Bede's informants at Canterbury let on (or even realized). What we can be sure about is that the dynastic connections between the Jutish and Frankish royal houses formed only one strand in a network of contacts that bound sixth-century Kent closely to her neighbors across the Channel. There may have been Frankish settlers in Kent and Jutish communities in the Rhineland under Frankish rule. Artifacts of Frankish type (e.g., weapons, glassware, jewelery) have been found in Kentish graves, jewelry of Kentish manufacture in Frankish ones. Exotic objects were reaching Kent from the distant Mediterranean, and among the commodities exchanged for them were almost certainly slaves such as Pope Gregory saw in the Roman slave-market. Late sixth-century Kent was rich. It may be that this wealth had had far-reaching effects upon the social structure, among them the dislocation involved upon the hold of traditional paganism upon people's minds and hearts: so at least anthropologists like to explain barbarian conversion. Certainly the king and his court would have known of a world of richer, more powerful and imposing rulers elsewhere; would have known that all of them were protected and upheld by the Christian God.

Augustine arrived at Thanet, then an island, in eastern Kent in 597. After a preliminary meeting with him there, Ethelbert granted him permission to proceed to the seat of the royal court at Canterbury. It was thus that Canterbury became, as it has remained, the chief seat of the Christian church in England. Ethelbert himself was converted and baptized—in view of speculations above, perhaps we should say *definitively* converted—at a date unknown. The little that we know of his actions as a Christian king suggests that he took his new role very seriously. He gave Augustine sites in Canterbury for the foundation of his cathedral church and outside the town for the establishment of a monastery (later known as St. Augustine's). He endowed the new church with additional properties, probably having the grants recorded in written form. He assisted in the foundation of bishoprics at Rochester and London. He strongly encouraged the conversion of his subjects. He issued a code of laws for his people, whose opening clause makes it unambiguously plain that the new church was to enjoy royal protection. He helped Augustine in difficult negotiations with the British clergy of Wales.

Though temporary setbacks were to occur after Ethelbert's death in 616, the king had taken positive steps to ensure the establishment of the Christian church in Anglo-Saxon England. Very far-reaching consequences for the development of English civilization were to flow from this commitment. In a letter to Ethelbert in 601 Pope Gregory welcomed him into the community of Christian rulers. Ethelbert was another Constantine; his name would live forever: how right the Pope was. What Ethelbert thought about it all we do not know. He could rejoice in the protection of a God whom he was encouraged to believe more powerful than his ancestral gods. He had been introduced to techniques of rulership, notably the use of writing, which might dignify and enhance his authority. He was the friend and patron of clergy who commanded potent rituals. Christianity could make a king more imposing. Its coming was to transform Anglo-Saxon kingship in the course of the seventh century.

J. M. Wallace-Hadrill, *Early Germanic Kingship*, 1971.

ST. GREGORY THE GREAT (*c.* 540–604) was pope as Gregory I from 590 to 604, and the most commanding figure in the history of the early medieval papacy. Of his many-faceted personality and activities—aristocrat, monk, diplomat, politician, administrator, biblical commentator, hagiographer, moral theologian, and liturgist—the English remember chiefly his role as the initiator in 596 of the Roman mission to the pagan Anglo-Saxons under the leadership of Augustine. A famous story records that an encounter between Gregory and some Anglian slave-boys for sale in the market of Rome had implanted in him the desire to convert the English to Christianity. Whether the story is historical or not, what is plain is that Gregory felt keenly a missionary responsibility toward pagan barbarians. This is rather more surprising than it might seem. The traditional view of Christians within the civilized Roman and Mediterranean world was that Christianity and civilization were coterminous. Despite the clear precepts of the Gospels, extraordinarily few attempts were made to preach Christianity to barbarian peoples outside the imperial frontiers: they were beyond the pale; the faith was not for them. The occasional fringe figure like Patrick, who undoubtedly did possess a strong missionary vocation, was regarded by his contemporaries as eccentric and vaguely troublesome; a common fate of missionaries. Gregory's initiative was therefore an unusual one. But it was also an influential one. The surge of missionary activity in seventh- and eighth-century Europe was largely the result of his example.

Gregory's surviving correspondence enables us to witness the care with which he planned the mission to England, his guidance of it during the early years, and his keen pleasure at its success. Letters to Frankish kings and bishops made smooth the journey. Advice on missionary tactics was proffered. Plans for the organization of the nascent English church were laid down. Practical advice in answer to Augustine's queries was provided on topics ranging from the arrangements for episcopal consecrations to the marriage customs of the new converts. Books, relics, plate, and vestments were supplied, as well as human reinforcements. Congratulatory letters of masterly tact were sent to the royal convert Ethelbert of Kent and his consort. The letters give an insight into Gregory's practical talents and his rare spiritual gifts as a Christian teacher.

The earliest biography of Gregory was the work of an unknown monk of Whitby (c. 710). But it was above all Bede who by allotting to Gregory so prominent a place in his *Ecclesiastical History* ensured that the English would never forget their apostle. King Alfred translated some of his works into Old English. Church-dedications to him, attested from the seventh century, remained frequent throughout the Anglo-Saxon period and beyond. From at latest the year 747 his feast day on 12 March was observed in all English churches—the only commemoration of a medieval pope in the English ecclesiastical calendar to survive the scrutiny of sixteenth-century reformers. For many centuries from the seventh onward the English retained a strong sentimental attachment to the see of Rome, their mother church; somewhat to the embarrassment of later Protestant scholars and divines. The instinct was a correct one. Christianity did not reach the English only from a Roman source, as later entries under Aidan and others will show. But Roman influences upon the shaping of the English church proved the strongest in the long run. Gregory's initiative held out to the Anglo-Saxons the fruits of a civilization that as well as Christian was Mediterranean, classical, literate, and urban. Acceptance of this legacy was perhaps the most decisive of all turning-points in the history of—to use a phrase first coined by Gregory himself—the *gens Anglorum*, "the English people."

J. Richards, *Consul of God*, 1981, is the most recent study of Pope Gregory I.

ST. AUGUSTINE (*d.* 604–9) was the leader of the Gregorian mission to England and first archbishop of Canterbury. Augustine is too often remembered as the man who lost heart on his way to England and had to have his resolution stiffened by a strong letter from Pope Gregory: a timid and vacillating character, who was not really up to the task imposed upon him. This is unjust. Augustine was a monk of Gregory's own monastery of St. Andrew's in Rome and before 596 had risen to be its prior. This was a position of considerable responsibility and it marks Augustine out as one in whom Pope Gregory—no mean judge of men—placed great trust both as spiritual guide and as practical administrator. Gregory's choice of Augustine to lead the mission to England was a mark of his confidence and there is no reason to suppose that it was misplaced. Augustine's achievements were, in fact, quite remarkable. Within seven years of his arrival in England in 597 he and his fellow-missionaries had converted two kings (Ethelbert of Kent and Sabert of Essex) and thousands of their subjects, established three bishoprics (Canterbury, London, Rochester), founded a monastery and a school at Canterbury, secured endowments for their foundation, sought and received guidance from the Pope on various problems involved in setting up a new church, attempted (unsuccessfully) to cooperate with the British clergy of Wales, and schooled their most distinguished convert, Ethelbert, in the rudiments of Christian kingship. This is a record of which any missionary might be proud. Yet there is a sense in which Augustine *does* remain somewhat indistinct. As so often, this is largely the result of the nature of our sources. For all that concerns the conversion of the Anglo-Saxons we are overwhelmingly dependent on the *Ecclesiastical History* of Bede; and Bede in his turn was dependent on *his* sources. Bede's main informants about the early history of the church of Canterbury were Albinus and Nothelm. They seem not to have passed on to him much early tradition about the Kentish church; possibly because not much tradition had survived: for example, they evidently did not even know the date of Augustine's death and we are left to work out that it must have occurred somewhere between 604 and 609. Canterbury passed on to Bede no anecdotes about Augustine that might have brought him vividly to light. And it is his peculiar misfortune that the only two anecdotes about him that we do possess—neither of which reached Bede from Canterbury—show him in an unflattering light: the stories of his hesitation on the way to England and of his arrogant treatment of the British clergy. There was much more to Augustine than this: he must have been a man of great energy and many-sided talent.

II. Mayr-Harting, *The Coming of Christianity to Anglo-Saxon England,* 1972.

REDWALD (*d.* 627?) was king of East Anglia and according to Bede the fourth English ruler to exercise overlordship over all the Anglo-Saxon kingdoms south of the Humber. In 616 he defeated and killed Ethelfrith of Northumbria and thereby assisted Edwin, whom he had harbored as an exile, to gain power there. Redwald was converted to Christianity, apparently at the court of Ethelbert of Kent, but on his return to East Anglia had been led away from the faith "by his wife and by certain evil teachers." Bede tells us that in his temple he set up a Christian altar alongside a pagan one. For him, Christianity meant the acceptance of an additional god, not the abandonment of his ancestral heathen ones, a not uncommon phenomenon in barbarian "conversions" of the early Middle Ages.

It is likely, though not certain, that it was Redwald who was interred in the magnificent ship-burial at Sutton Hoo discovered in 1939. There he was deposited in the ship that was to convey him to the next world (with money to pay the steersman and the rowers), with all the equipment he would need: helmet, armor, and shield; weapons and jewelry; silver spoons and plate; bronze cauldrons, drinking horns, wooden buckets, and cups; a harp and a lamp; and more mysterious objects whose significance is not clear, such as a large whetstone in mint condition, decorated at each end with carved and painted human faces, one end surmounted by a bronze statuette of a stag. These treasures are of a splendor unparalleled in the early medieval archaeology of Europe. Like the remains of Edwin's great hall at Yeavering they convey something of the magnificence of seventh-century kingship. Most interesting is their revelation of the cosmopolitan world in which Redwald lived. His helmet and shield were Swedish; possibly his ancestors too. The great silver dish came from Constantinople; a bronze bowl from Alexandria; the coins from Gaul; the hanging bowl perhaps from Ireland. How these objects were acquired can only be a matter for conjecture. Most of them were too luxurious to have been the fruit of mundane commerce. Heirlooms? plunder? tribute? presents acquired in the course of diplomacy? we cannot say. But it is not irrelevant to bear in mind that Redwald's East Anglia, like the Kent of Ethelbert, was rich in part at least because of trade. Recent excavations at Ipswich, only seven miles from Sutton Hoo, have revealed a thriving emporium with trading connections across the North Sea with the Rhineland and a native pottery industry whose products—the consumer goods of the seventh century—were widely distributed in eastern England.

The Sutton Hoo finds are superbly displayed in the British Museum, whose booklet, *The Sutton Hoo Ship-Burial,* is the best introduction to them.

EDWIN (585–633) was the son of Aelle of Deira, king of all Northumbria from 616 to 633, and its first Christian ruler. Bede says of Edwin that not only was he the fifth English king to exercise overlordship over other Anglo-Saxon rulers but also that his power extended farther than any English king before him. "He ruled over all the inhabitants of Britain, English and Britons alike, saving only the people of Kent, and also subjected Anglesey and Man to English rule." This is a grandiose claim, but Bede was a sober scholar who was careful in his choice of words. One of Edwin's residences, not necessarily an important one, has been excavated at Yeavering in Northumberland. In size, construction, and perhaps (though this has to be conjectural) in fittings and decoration too, the great hall of Yeavering was a fit setting for a ruler whose sway extended from Berwickshire to Cornwall, from London to Holyhead. No doubt the king who kept court there was arrayed as gorgeously as his contemporary Redwald of East Anglia.

Yeavering and Sutton Hoo conjure up a world of raids and warfare, plunder and tribute. They are as "barbaric," as has often been pointed out, as the world of the Old English epic *Beowulf*. But another aspect of Edwin reveals him keeping state in the Roman city of York, quite possibly in the pretorian building of the Roman fortress, which was still standing in good repair in his day, as recent excavations beneath York Minster have shown. Edwin spent most of his childhood and early manhood in exile, a refugee from the long and bloody reach of Ethelfrith. Part of this exile was spent at the court of a Christian prince of north Wales; part at that of Redwald, where he may have met the missionary Paulinus. He married a Christian princess from Kent, and during his reign incorporated into his own kingdom the Christian principality of Elmet. Like Ethelbert of Kent a generation earlier, Edwin knew something of Christianity before it was formally preached to him in Northumbria by Paulinus.

Bede's account of Edwin's conversion is elaborate, carefully designed to teach lessons and to move; a great set piece about a royal conversion, which owes something to the account of the conversion of Clovis by Gregory of Tours, though it has greater literary artistry. Though Bede's account presents some chronological problems, what is certain is that Edwin was baptized at York on 12 April 627. Like Ethelbert, again, he showed himself an enthusiastic convert. He established a bishopric for Paulinus at York and started to build a stone church there. He assisted Paulinus in his work of evangelization in Northumbria and in the kingdom of Lindsey (roughly, Lincolnshire), which was then subject to him. It was also through Edwin's influence that Eorpwald, king of East Anglia, the son of Redwald, was converted in about 628.

Edwin's supremacy was as short-lived as that of any other seventh-century Anglo-Saxon king. In 633 Cadwalla of Gwynedd and Penda of Mercia rebelled against him. Edwin was defeated and killed at Hatfield Chase, near Doncaster.

PAULINUS (*d.* 644) was a missionary to Northumbria and the first bishop of York. A native of Rome, he was sent by Pope Gregory in 601 along with other Italian ecclesiastics to reinforce the Kentish mission of Augustine. After the partial conversion of King Redwald of East Anglia at the court of Ethelbert of Kent it seems likely that Paulinus accompanied the king back to his kingdom; he probably encountered the exiled Edwin there. When Redwald relapsed into paganism we may assume that Paulinus returned to Kent. In about 619 he accompanied the Kentish princess Ethelburga to Northumbria when she was betrothed to King Edwin, and remained at his court slowly working toward his conversion, which finally came about in 627. Paulinus had been consecrated a bishop in 625 and Edwin established an episcopal see for him at York. During the remainder of Edwin's reign we catch glimpses of Paulinus preaching and baptizing at Yeavering, Catterick, Lincoln, and elsewhere. When Edwin was defeated and killed in 633 the church nurtured by Paulinus in Northumbria was almost blotted out. Leaving ecclesiastical direction there in the hands of his assistant James the Deacon, Paulinus withdrew to Kent with the Queen and what remained of the royal family. There he was given charge of the vacant see of Rochester, which he administered until his death in 644.

COIFI (*fl. c.* 627) was the pagan high-priest at the court of King Edwin of Northumbria. It was into the mouth of Coifi that Bede inserted two speeches (doubtless his own composition) in his account of the debate of Edwin's council, which preceded the king's conversion. Coifi, persuaded of the truth of Christianity by the preaching of Paulinus, ritually profaned and then burned down a pagan shrine at Goodmanham, about eighteen miles east of York. Coifi's main contention was that his position as a pagan priest had brought him little worldly profit. The fact that Bede regarded such materialistic arguments as "wise words" gives us some clue as to how Christianity was presented to pagan audiences. There is some kinship with the missionary tactics advocated by Bede's contemporary, Bishop Daniel of Winchester, in a celebrated letter to Boniface.

It is very difficult indeed to discover what Christian missionaries were up against. Our secure knowledge of Anglo-Saxon paganism could be written on a postcard. What Bede tells us of Coifi shows that heathen cult involved a priesthood, temples, idols, and taboos. We know the names of certain gods and goddesses, for example, Eostre, whose name was transferred to the central festival of the Christian year, Easter. We hear of sacrifices and fertility rituals. We can draw a few hazardous inferences from the archaeology of graves about belief in an afterlife. A handful of place-names indicate heathen cult-sites; for instance, Harrow in Middlesex, recorded in an eighth-century document as *Gumeninga hearg*, "the holy place of the Gumenings." And that is all. There were still pagan kingdoms (in Sussex and the Isle of Wight) in the England of Bede's childhood, and even in the years of his maturity there were almost certainly large areas of the country that had been touched only superficially by Christian teaching. Bede could have told us a great deal about Anglo-Saxon paganism but he chose not to. To try to understand why is one step on the labyrinthine journey to the heart of his concerns as Christian teacher and historian.

ST. OSWALD (*d.* 642) was the son of King Ethelfrith and king of Northumbria from 634 to 642. During the reign of Edwin he lived in exile among the Irish and the Picts. In the course of this exile he was converted to Christianity through the agency of the Irish-Scottish churchmen of Columba's monastery of Iona. In 634 he returned to Northumbria and defeated and killed Edwin's slayer, Cadwalla of Gwynedd, near Hexham.

According to Bede, Oswald exercised an overlordship even more extensive than Edwin's. To the peoples under Edwin's sway he added lordship over the Irish settled in western Scotland and over the Picts. His authority in Wessex is indicated by his cooperation in the establishment there of Bishop Birinus in about 635. But Bede presented Oswald as much more than just a powerful king. He was "beloved by God," a saint as well as a king, the model of what a Christian ruler should be. Not only was he active in the spreading of the faith—for example, by bringing Aidan to Northumbria—but he was notable also for his exercise of Christian virtues, humility, charity, piety. He won victories under the sign of the cross. It was because he was so good a Christian, Bede seems to urge (no doubt with an eye to the somewhat less than godly kings of his own day), that he was so great a king. Bede could present his death in battle at the hands of Penda, probably near Oswestry in Shropshire, as a kind of martyrdom.

After his death his cult was promoted partly under the influence of Wilfrid, partly through the actions of King Oswy of Northumbria and his daughter Osthryth. The cult mattered to the family: a royal saint could shed luster on a dynasty. Oswald's miracle-working relics became a focus of eager interest. His head was buried at Lindisfarne; the skull found inside the coffin of St. Cuthbert when it was opened in 1827 was probably his. His hands and arms were buried at the royal residence of Bamburgh. The rest of his body was laid in a shrine at the monastery of Bardney in Lincolnshire. Early in the tenth century the Bardney relics were removed by Ethelflaed, the daughter of King Alfred, to Gloucester, where the church of St. Oswald, which she built in the saint's honor, has recently been excavated. Meanwhile the cult of Oswald had been exported to the Continent by English missionary churchmen such as Willibrord. Throughout the Middle Ages and beyond Oswald remained a popular saint in Germany and Italy.

ST. AIDAN (*d.* 651) was bishop of Lindisfarne from 634 to 651. Of Irish-Scottish birth, Aidan became a monk at Iona and was invited to Northumbria by King Oswald shortly after his accession. Oswald settled him at Lindisfarne or Holy Island, off the coast of Northumberland and significantly close to the royal residence of Bamburgh, where a monastery was founded and the seat of a bishopric established. The coming of Aidan and his followers opens the second phase in the conversion of Northumbria to Christianity: the "Celtic," or Irish-Scottish, phase as opposed to the "Roman" phase under Paulinus.

Bede provides a carefully drawn and deservedly famous account of Aidan's conduct as bishop, stressing his pastoral energy, his abstinence, humility, and charity. In doing this Bede intended to rebuke the bishops of his own day whose shortcomings he castigated in his letter to Egbert of York. We may suspect that there was more to Aidan than gentle saintliness alone. Bede himself tells us that he was no respecter of persons, and would correct the sins of the great "with sharp rebuke"; a characteristic that Aidan shared with other Irish missionary churchmen active in Anglo-Saxon England and Frankish Gaul.

Bede's only reservation about Aidan and his followers was that they celebrated Easter at the wrong time. The so-called Paschal controversy between the Roman and Celtic churches occupies an enormous amount of space in Bede's *Ecclesiastical History:* a disproportionate amount, we might be tempted to think, but we should be wrong. For early medieval churchmen—not just for Bede—the proper calculation of the movement of Easter was not a trivial thing. It mattered very much because it was charged with theological significance. Divergence on this issue was schism: a rent in the seamless robe that was the church, the society of all Christians; displeasing to God, and thereby perilous to humankind, His people, not just in this world but through all eternity. To grasp this is to begin to understand something of the passion with which this issue, now long-forgotten, was debated in the seventh century. For a generation after Aidan's coming it divided the churchmen of Northumbria until the dispute was settled in favor of the Roman party at a council, the Synod of Whitby, presided over by King Oswy in 664.

ST. BIRINUS (*d. c.* 648) was a missionary to and the first bishop in the kingdom of Wessex. His origins are unknown. He came to England on the advice of Pope Honorius I (625–38), at whose instance he had been consecrated a bishop in Italy, "promising to sow the seeds of the faith in the remotest regions of England where no Christian teacher had been before." Finding that the West Saxons, the first people he encountered, were pagan, he chose them as his mission field: this was in about 635. He converted Cynegils, king of Wessex (611–43). Oswald, king of Northumbria and at that time overlord of Cynegils, was present at the king's baptism. The two kings jointly gave Birinus the former Roman town of Dorchester-on-Thames as the seat of a bishopric. Birinus used it as a base for his work of evangelization until his death in about 648.

ST. FURSA or **FURSEY** (*fl. c.* 620–45) was an Irish monk and ascetic who spent some time, probably in the 630s, in East Anglia where he established a monastery in the remains of a Roman fort (probably Burgh Castle, Suffolk). Later he moved on to Gaul where he founded another monastery at Lagny, a little to the east of Paris. Fursa is an obscure figure but he is representative of a number of Irishmen who cut loose from their homeland and travelled abroad as "pilgrims for Christ" during this period. We hear of a few others in seventh-century England: for example, Maeldubh who founded the monastery of Malmesbury—later to be the home of Aldhelm—and Dicuil who established a monastery at Bosham. There may have been many others and it is not impossible that they played a larger part in the evangelization of the Anglo-Saxons than we shall ever know. Fursa serves as a reminder that early missionary enterprise did not emanate exclusively from the centers about which we happen to be well-informed, such as the Canterbury of Augustine or the Lindisfarne of Aidan. His career also shows, as does Columba's, how the practice of pilgrimage and ascetic monasticism merged into mission.

PENDA (*d.* 655) was king of Mercia from 633 to 655, a lifelong heathen, at a time when the conversion of the English to Christianity was proceeding apace, and a formidable ruler who rivalled the power of the Northumbrian kings. In 633 he defeated and killed Edwin and in 642 Oswald. It was only with great difficulty that Oswy managed to serve Penda the same way at the battle of the river *Winwaed* (unidentified, probably one of the tributaries of the Humber) in 655. Bede never refers to Penda as enjoying an overlordship of the type he attributes to these three Northumbrian kings; but he reveals that Penda had power, at least from time to time, over Wessex and East Anglia, and Welsh tradition recorded by Nennius recalled that British kings could be counted among Penda's subjects.

Penda's power might have been based in part upon peaceable relations with his British neighbors in Wales. It is significant that he threw off the overlordship of Edwin and established himself as king of Mercia in alliance with Cadwalla, king of Gwynedd. Mercia's westward expansion under Penda may have been a matter of diplomacy as much as of war. Early Mercia could have been as "Anglo-Celtic" as the Northumbria of Ethelfrith or the Wessex of Ine.

Penda is notorious, thanks to Bede, for his heathenism. He did not forbid Christian missionaries such as Cedd to preach in his dominions and he even tolerated the conversion of his son Peada in 653. But for himself, he preferred to stick by his ancestral gods and did so until his death. The conversion of Anglo-Saxon kings to Christianity was not a walkover.

OSWY (*d.* 670) was the son of King Ethelfrith and king of Northumbria from 642 to 670. According to Bede, Oswy was the seventh Anglo-Saxon ruler to exercise overlordship; like his brother Oswald he held sway over English, Britons, Picts, and Irish-Scottish. It was a supremacy for which, like other seventh-century kings, Oswy had to fight hard, not only against neighbors like

Penda of Mercia whom he defeated and killed in 655, but also against princes of his own Northumbrian dynasty. In 651 he was guilty of what Bede called the shameful murder of Oswin of Deira at Gilling, where he subsequently founded a monastery in expiation for his crime in which Ceolfrith first experienced the monastic life. Oswy founded several other monasteries, notably Whitby in 657. Whitby was closely associated with the Northumbrian royal family: its first abbess was a Northumbrian princess, Hilda; it served as a royal mausoleum—the body of King Edwin was removed there; and in 664 it was the meeting-place of the council under Oswy's presidency at which the issues between Roman and Irish churchmen, which had troubled Northumbria since the time of Aidan, were debated and resolved in favor of Rome. Oswy's Roman allegiance was pleasing to Bede, who tells us that the king had intended to lay aside his kingdom and travel to Rome, accompanied by Wilfrid, there to end his days; though his death in 670 prevented this. Bede also approved of Oswy's active propagation of Christianity. The king was instrumental in the conversion of Sigebert, ruler of the East Saxons, and of Peada, the son of Penda of Mercia; he took counsel with the king of Kent about the appointment of an archbishop of Canterbury. But in the last resort Bede had his reservations. Careful as always in his choice of words, for him Oswy was a "most noble" King but not a "most Christian" one: Oswy was not an Oswald.

AGILBERT (*d. c.* 675?) was bishop successively of Dorchester-on-Thames and of Paris. He was of Frankish origin and had studied in southern Ireland—a reminder of the renown of Irish centers of learning in the seventh century. Coming to Wessex afterward he was given the bishopric of Dorchester by King Cenwealh in succession to Birinus in about 649–50. In about 663 the king divided the West Saxon bishopric and established an additional see at Winchester. Agilbert, offended, departed. In 664 he is traceable at the Synod of Whitby as the leading representative of the Roman party, closely associated with Wilfrid. He then returned to Gaul, where we next encounter him as one of the bishops who assisted at Wilfrid's episcopal consecration at Compiègne in 664. He subsequently became bishop of Paris (shortly after 666?) and in this role entertained Archbishop Theodore on his way to England in the winter of 668–69, and doubtless gave him much information about

English conditions. It must have been about this time that Cen-wealh invited him back to Wessex. Agilbert was unwilling to leave the bishopric of Paris and sent his nephew Leutherius (or Hlothere) in his place, who ruled the undivided see of Wessex from 670 to 676. Agilbert himself probably died about 675 or slightly later. His splendid tomb may still be seen in the monastery of Jouarre, to the east of Paris, which had been founded by one of his relatives.

Agilbert's career focuses attention upon a theme until recently little explored by historians of the early Anglo-Saxon church: its close connections with the Frankish church of Gaul. This was something about which Bede either knew little or did not care to say much. Frankish influence can be seen in the foundation of monasteries in seventh-century England, in the diffusion of texts, in the form of official documents, and in early Anglo-Saxon art and architecture. Perhaps most important of all, it can be sensed in a certain style and tone. The Frankish church was an aristocratic one: its example may have powerfully influenced the nobility of Anglo-Saxon England into throwing the weight of their support behind the new Christian establishment. The Frankish bishops tended to be rich and powerful: men like Agilbert may have pro-vided an example of episcopal might that was not lost upon his protégé Wilfrid.

J. M. Wallace-Hadrill, *The Frankish Church*, 1983, is a superb ac-count of its subject.

ST. CEDD (*d.* 664) was a monk, missionary, and bishop of the East Saxons. A native of Northumbria and a monk of Lindisfarne under Aidan, he went to work as a missionary among the Middle Angles in 653 and then, probably in the following year, was transferred to the kingdom of the East Saxons, whose bishop he became. The surviving church at Bradwell-on-Sea in Essex is probably that built by him for the monastery that he founded there. He retained his links with Northumbria, where he founded the monastery of Last-ingham (Yorkshire), probably in 655–56. He attended the Synod of Whitby in 664 where he acted as interpreter between the Roman and Irish parties. He died during a visitation of the plague shortly afterward. His brother Chad succeeded him as abbot of Lastingham.

ST. CHAD or **CEADDA** (*d.* 672) was bishop successively of York and Lichfield. A native of Northumbria, he received his training in the monastic life partly in Ireland and partly at Lindisfarne. In 664 he succeeded his brother Cedd as abbot of Lastingham. Later in the same year he was appointed bishop of York by King Oswy. Now Wilfrid had already been nominated to the see of York by Oswy's son, and had gone to Gaul to be consecrated. There were thus two contending claimants to the bishopric of York when Archbishop Theodore arrived in England in 669. Owing to irregularities in Chad's consecration he apparently resigned from York at the prompting of Theodore and retired to Lastingham. Wilfrid got York, but Chad was soon afterward compensated with the bishopric of Mercia, whose seat he established at Lichfield. During his Mercian episcopate he founded a monastery at Barrow-on-Humber in Lincolnshire. He died in 672. Bede had a personal link with Chad, for one of his teachers, named Trumberht, had been a monk in one of Chad's monasteries (probably Lastingham).

ST. THEODORE OF TARSUS (602?–90) was archbishop of Canterbury from 668 until 690 and a figure of major importance in the history of the English church. A native, like St. Paul, of Tarsus in Cilicia, Theodore was born in or about 602. The first sixty-five years of his life—in the early Middle Ages a much longer than average life span—are almost a blank to us. We know only that he had studied at Athens at some period, and evidently become an extremely learned man; and that he was a monk. In 667 he was in Rome, though we do not know why. Not long before this the archbishop-elect of Canterbury had come to Rome for consecration at the hands of Pope Vitalian but had died of the plague before he could receive it. Vitalian offered the vacant see to the African monk Hadrian, who declined it, suggesting Theodore's name instead. The offer was made, Theodore accepted, was consecrated (March 668), and journeyed to England in the company of Hadrian and Benedict Biscop. In the course of a leisurely journey through Gaul he spent some time at Paris with Agilbert who presumably briefed him on conditions in England. He reached Canterbury in May 669.

Theodore's appointment must on any showing be judged the most surprising in the whole history of the English church. An old man, he was taking up an office that was bound to be physically as well as mentally demanding. A Greek-speaking intellectual from the civilized Mediterranean, he was being sent to minister to barbarians barely converted to Christianity, whose language he could not speak, whose climate and food would almost certainly be uncongenial, whose social customs and political organization he would find unfamiliar and uncouth. The English church to which he was going was in a state of disarray. It had until recently been divided by the Paschal controversy, and the sores of that confict had not yet healed. It was lacking in structure and organization, and it was desperately short of manpower: at the time of Theodore's arrival there was only one properly constituted bishop in England, namely, Wilfrid. Furthermore, England had recently been ravaged by plague, and it is likely that its inhabitants were frightened and demoralized. Part of the kingdom of Essex had reverted to paganism during the plague and the same could well have happened elsewhere.

The extraordinary thing is that despite these obstacles Theodore's archiepiscopate was a resounding success. He gave the English church an administrative shape that endured with little essential change for nearly nine hundred years. He introduced routines and disciplines for the day-to-day ordering of the church. As a teacher and patron of learning he built up a school at Canterbury that played an important part in introducing the Anglo-Saxons to the learning of Mediterranean Christendom. In short, he provided leadership, direction, and inspiration. It was an astonishing achievement for a man in his seventies and eighties.

His first few years set the tone. Soon after his arrival he conducted a general visitation of all the English churches, a tour of inspection to acquaint himself with the country and its clergy. By 672 he had established a diocesan framework by appointing or confirming bishops in East Anglia, Northumbria, Mercia, and Wessex. In 673 he held the first council of the whole English church, at Hertford. Its decrees were of the utmost significance in regulating the affairs of the church in England; for instance, in clarifying the relations between bishops by insisting that each had a distinct jurisdiction in his own diocese. Two of them were of special moment. The seventh decree laid down that annual ecclesiastical councils were to be held at a place named *Clovesho*. (This place has never satisfactorily been identified. It has been suggested that it might have been Brixworth in Northamptonshire, which is reasonably central and where there is an imposing Anglo-Saxon church that as it stands is probably of *c.* 840 but may overlie a building of Theodoran date.) What little evidence we have—for instance, casual references to councils in the letters of Aldhelm—suggests that Theodore's decree was not a dead letter and that regular church councils were indeed held. These councils were intended for the proper ordering of English church life but they had a further importance. The sense of unity and common purpose induced in those who attended them gradually served to wear down the barriers of tribe and region. The notion of "the English church" slowly gained over the idea of a scatter of separate churches for the Kentishmen, or the Mercians, or the West Saxons, or the Northumbrians. And it was in some sense owing to Theodore's efforts that Bede could make a still more daring leap and give general currency to the idea—which he may have picked up from the writings of Pope Gregory—that the Anglo-Saxon inhabitants of Britain were all one *gens Anglorum,* one "English people."

The ninth decree at Hertford laid down "that more bishops should be created as the number of believers increases," but the record continues darkly, "however we passed over this matter for the present." Theodore came from a Mediterranean world where dioceses were small. In England they were enormous: Wilfrid's bishopric of York embraced the whole area between the Humber and the Firth of Forth. Theodore was determined to reduce their size by multiplying the number of bishops, so that in a diocese of manageable size the diocesan could effectively discharge the pastoral duties that were his prime responsibility. His thinking was in line with that of Pope Gregory on this matter. The fact that the Hertford decree was not implemented shows us that Theodore had run into opposition. It presumably came from those bishops of big dioceses who were unwilling to submit to a reduction in their status, wealth, and power. (There is plenty of evidence to suggest that English bishops were already rich and powerful. One of the reasons why Cuthbert was so reluctant to become a bishop in 685 was because he wished to shun these temptations.) Theodore was determined that this reform should take effect. He implemented it gradually by a tactic of prudent opportunism: whenever a bishopric fell vacant he moved in and divided it up. Theodore could usually rely on the cooperation of the local king; for example, it was at the request of King Ethelred that he divided the huge diocese of Mercia into five, probably in 679–80. In this Theodore showed tact. But he was also a tough man, perhaps not always altogether scrupulous, possibly not untouched by a streak of megalomania. He may too have been driven by the sense of urgency imparted by old age: an old man in a hurry. In trying to implement his plans he may vastly have extended the power of Canterbury over the English church beyond the limits laid down by Pope Gregory. This was how he was perceived at York. Theodore's most bitter opponent was York's Wilfrid. The quarrel between them is examined elsewhere. But we can note here that Theodore got his way. In 678 he divided the Northumbrian diocese into three and in 681 increased this to five. East Anglia was also divided (673) and Wessex followed a few years after Theodore's death (704–5). The diocesan structure created by Theodore survived with only small modifications, such as the twelfth-century creation of sees at Ely and Carlisle, until the 1540s.

The council of Hertford had also legislated on the subject of marriage. Theodore's teaching on moral and pastoral issues—the attempt to provide the basic essentials of Christian discipline for the laity—is preserved in a work known as his *Penitential*. (The book was put together in the form in which we have it by an anonymous editor after Theodore's death, but there is general agreement that the rulings it embodies do derive from his teaching.) A penitential is a kind of handbook for confessors, listing various sins and prescribing appropriate penances for them. Theodore's *Penitential* is of the greatest interest in showing what sort of pastoral problems he encountered among the Anglo-Saxons and what solutions he proposed to them. The claims made for the ecclesiastical guidance of daily life show Theodore's characteristically robust determination to Christianize his barbarous new converts. But the *Penitential* also reveals a mind broad and humane. Within certain limits Theodore was prepared to adapt Christian moral teaching to meet the customs of the English. It was an important condition of the successful follow-up to the age of conversion that the English church should have been directed by a man so wisely liberal in outlook.

The anonymous compiler of the *Penitential* may have been educated in the school at Canterbury established by Theodore and Hadrian. Aldhelm allows us a glimpse of Theodore in class, "hemmed in by a mass of Irish students like a savage wild boar checked by a snarling pack of hounds." One can sense an atmosphere at once genial and boisterous. In the 1950s a German scholar identified some materials in an eleventh-century manuscript at Milan as fragments of biblical commentaries composed by Theodore. It thus became possible to characterize the method of scriptural exegesis practiced at Canterbury, which was rather different from that employed by Bede at Jarrow; and to get a glance, in the surviving fragments, of Theodore expounding the flora and fauna of a Middle Eastern holy book to a rapt audience on the shores of the North Sea. The curiosity about the Holy Places that we meet in such eighth-century travellers as Willibald of Eichstätt may have been stimulated directly or indirectly by Theodore's teaching. In the field of ecclesiastical law, Theodore's reputation stood high. This is attested not simply by the survival of his *Penitential* but also by the judgment of some of the most distinguished men of a slightly later date, such as Archbishop Egbert of York and Pope Zacharias in a letter to Boniface in 748. Theodore's intellectual attainments were evidently diverse: Bede tells a story that shows he was regarded as an authority on medicine too.

Theodore died on 19 September 690 at the age of about eighty-eight. The sober judgment of a nineteenth-century scholar on his achievement is still the best epitaph to his career: "It is difficult, if not impossible, to overstate the debt which England, Europe and Christian civilization owes to the work of Theodore."

There is as yet no full-scale modern treatment of Archbishop Theodore. In its absence, H. Mayr-Harting, *The Coming of Christianity to Anglo-Saxon England*, 1972, is probably the best book.

HADRIAN (*d.* 709 or 710) was a monk, scholar, and abbot of Canterbury. He was a native of North Africa who had crossed the Mediterranean to Italy, possibly as a refugee from the Islamic advance in Africa, and become a monk in a monastery near Naples. In 667 Pope Vitalian invited him to become archbishop of Canterbury but he declined, suggesting Theodore in his place. He accompanied Theodore to England in 668–69 and became abbot of the monastery of St. Peter and St. Paul (later known as St. Augustine's) at Canterbury, probably in 671. He spent the remainder of his life in this office, devoting himself mainly to teaching. The life of a teacher is usually uneventful and Hadrian's was no exception. But his influence was very considerable. He numbered among his pupils Aldhelm, the greatest English scholar of his day; Albinus, the friend and correspondent of Bede who succeeded Hadrian as abbot; and the learned Bishop Tobias of Rochester (*d.* 726). Theodore and Hadrian—for it is impossible to separate their individual contributions to learning—made Canterbury into an intellectual center that played a very important role in diffusing the accumulated learning of the Mediterranean world among the Anglo-Saxons. In addition to biblical and patristic studies, law, mathematics, astronomy, poetry, rhetoric, and medicine were among the disciplines studied. Theodore was a native speaker of Greek, Hadrian was skilled in Greek as well as Latin. The school of Canterbury under their direction was one of the very few places in Europe north of the Alps where Greek could be studied.

ST. HILDA (614–80) was a Northumbrian princess and abbess of Whitby. She was the daughter of Hereric, the nephew of King Edwin of Northumbria, and was born while her parents were in exile in the British kingdom of Elmet during the reign of King Ethelfrith. Hilda was baptized a Christian with her great-uncle by Paulinus at York in 627. In 647 she decided to become a nun and went to East Anglia, intending to follow her sister Hereswith, until recently the wife of King Ethelhere of East Anglia, to the Frankish monastery of Chelles, near Paris. But in 648 she was recalled to Northumbria by Bishop Aidan who settled her with her companions in a small community beside the river Wear. Shortly afterward she was transferred to be abbess of Hartlepool, the earliest nunnery to be founded in the kingdom of Northumbria. When King Oswy founded the monastery of Whitby in 657, Hilda was appointed its first abbess. She held this office until her death in 680.

Hilda's career is one illustration of the important part played by women in the early days of Anglo-Saxon Christianity. Clearly, she was a woman of formidable presence and organizing ability besides possessing the spiritual talents that Bede stressed in his account of her. We are not surprised to learn from him that "kings and great noblemen used to seek her counsel." Whitby was a "double house": that is to say, the community was composed of both men and women living in segregation but coming together for daily worship. The idea of the double monastery was an importation from Gaul—another sign of the importance of Frankish influence upon the early English church—but a peculiarity of the

English houses was that their superior was always an abbess. Considerable numbers—probably more than we shall ever know about—of these communities were founded in seventh-century England and they were often established by ladies of princely rank. Apart from Whitby we might cite Ely, founded by Ethelthryth, the daughter of an East Anglian king and wife of Ecgfrith of Northumbria; or Wimborne, founded jointly by the sisters of King Ine of Wessex. At Whitby, Hilda was herself succeeded as abbess by Eanflaed, daughter of Edwin and widow of Oswy, and she in turn by her daughter Elflaed.

Whitby was, then, an important house, richly endowed, closely linked to the Northumbrian dynasty, impeccably aristocratic in its direction. Perhaps we should not be surprised that the finds excavated at the site suggest that the inmates lived in some style and comfort. Significantly, Bede never tells us that asceticism was a virtue practiced at Whitby.

Whitby was influential too. It was the setting for the council that settled the Paschal controversy in 664. It was a nursery for bishops in the next generation of English Christianity—no less than six of them between about 680 and 730. It was there that Caedmon was encouraged to compose vernacular religious poetry. And it was there that learning was cultivated, as Bede tells us, and as is confirmed by the earliest surviving piece of Anglo-Saxon hagiographical writing we possess, a life of Pope Gregory I, the work of an unknown monk of Whitby who was writing soon after the year 700. This is an impressive achievement and much of the credit for it should go to Abbess Hilda.

CAEDMON (*fl. c.* 660–80) was a monk of Whitby and Christian poet, the subject of one of the best-known of all the stories told by Bede in his *Ecclesiastical History*. Caedmon—it is of great interest that the name is Celtic rather than Germanic—was a layman in the service of the monastery of Whitby. He is often described or represented as a cowherd, but a close reading of Bede's text does not indicate that he was necessarily of menial status. Caedmon's problem was that he could not sing. At feasts, when songs were sung in turn by the guests to the music of the harp—perhaps just such a harp as was found in the tomb of Redwald at Sutton Hoo—Caedmon would get up and leave when he saw his turn approaching. On one such occasion he had a dream in the night following. A man appeared to him and told him to sing about the creation of the world. To his astonishment Caedmon found himself doing so. In the morning he remembered his dream and the words he had sung. He was taken before Abbess Hilda and examined by the more learned among the monks, who decided that the gift of song had been miraculously granted to him by God. At Hilda's bidding he became a monk of Whitby and during the remainder of his life he composed much more verse on biblical themes. Of this poetry, only nine lines that may with near-certainty be regarded as his survive. They were copied into the so-called Moore manuscript of Bede's *History,* now in Cambridge University Library, in or soon after the year 737. In prose translation they run as follows:

> Now we must laud the heaven-kingdom's Keeper, the Ordainer's might and his mind's intent, the work of the Father of glory: in that he, the Lord everlasting, appointed of each wondrous thing the beginning; he, holy Creator, at the first created heaven for a roof to the children of men; he, mankind's Keeper, Lord everlasting, almighty Ruler, afterwards fashioned for mortals the middle-earth, the world.

Whatever may have been the historical circumstances in which Caedmon became a poet, his achievement essentially was to adapt the conventions of secular vernacular poetry to Christian themes and ends. Caedmon's initiative was to bear fruit, in time, in some of the most moving religious poetry in the English language, such as the poems attributed to Cynewulf or the anonymous *Dream of the Rood.* There is rather more to this achievement than meets the eye. The more rigorous Christian churchmen, among them Bede himself, regarded secular poetry with disgust. It smacked too much of the pagan past; its ethic was frankly martial and violent; it was best avoided by the godly. But Bede could approve of Caedmon's verses: "By his songs the minds of many were often fired to despise the world and to seek the heavenly life." It was not by chance that this experiment occurred at Whitby. Willingness to adapt secular literary conventions presupposes familiarity with them. The Whitby of St. Hilda was less concerned than the Jarrow of Benedict Biscop to close its doors to the values of the secular world.

S. A. J. Bradley, *Anglo-Saxon Poetry*, 1982, from which the above extract is taken, contains a generous selection of verse, admirably translated and introduced.

ECGFRITH (645–85) was the son of Oswy and succeeded him as king of Northumbria over which he ruled from 670 to 685. We first meet him, aged ten, as a hostage at the court of Penda, king of Mercia: presumably he returned to his father's realm in the wake of Penda's defeat and death in 655. In 670 he succeeded Oswy, probably not without a struggle. Ecgfrith's reign was as full of warfare as that of any other seventh-century king. The Picts rebelled against him (*c.* 672) and were crushed; Ecgfrith's establishment of a new bishopric at Abercorn on the Firth of Forth in 681 was intended to reinforce Northumbrian rule in the north. He continued to expand his kingdom toward the west at the expense of the Britons of Cumbria and Strathclyde. In 674 he defeated an invasion led by King Wulfhere of Mercia, as a result of which he extended Northumbrian rule over Lindsey; in 679 he was defeated by Wulfhere's successor Ethelred and his control of Lindsey faded. In 684 he mounted an attack on Ireland in the teeth of opposition from leading churchmen such as Egbert of Iona and Cuthbert, possibly because the Irish were harboring British refugees: evidently—like his grandfather Edwin, the conqueror of Man and Anglesey—he had at his disposal an effective fleet. In 685 he led an expedition far into Pictland, where he met his end: he was defeated and killed at the battle of *Nechtansmere*, probably Dunnichen in Forfarshire. After this, says Bede, "the hopes and strength of the English kingdom began to ebb and fall away." Northumbrian power over the Picts crumbled forever, the see of Abercorn was abandoned, the Irish of Dalriada and some of the (Strathclyde?) Britons recovered their independence. The great days of Northumbrian royal power were over.

Bede strongly condemned Ecgfrith's attack on Ireland in 684, which he regarded as an act of unprovoked aggression against a Christian people. Elsewhere he could refer to Ecgfrith as a "most pious" ruler. In the ecclesiastical politics of his reign the king's quarrel with Wilfrid from 678 onward looms large for the historian; perhaps rather larger than it did for contemporaries. Ecgfrith was a dutiful Christian king. He attended church councils (673,

684), furthered the policy of Archbishop Theodore by creating new dioceses (Lindsey, Hexham, Abercorn), was a generous patron to Cuthbert, whom he persuaded to accept a bishopric in 684–85, and lavishly endowed the twin monastic foundations of Benedict Biscop at Wearmouth and Jarrow.

ST. WILFRID (634–709) was a monk, bishop of York, and the most prominent figure alongside Theodore in the history of the English church in the second half of the seventh century. Wilfrid's career can be known to us in unusual detail owing to the survival of a biography composed shortly after his death by his devoted chaplain Eddius at the request of Bishop Acca of Hexham. Eddius's *Life of Wilfrid* is full of detail, remarkably frank about the controversial aspects of a stormy career, and passionately partisan. Bede also has much to say about Wilfrid in his *Ecclesiastical History*. Bede had met Wilfrid, knew a good deal about him from friends such as Acca, and was probably familiar with Eddius's *Life*. His treatment of Wilfrid's career is much more discreet than that of Eddius. The resultant differences between our two major sources have given rise to much discussion and puzzlement. Wilfrid continues to be a controversial figure thirteen centuries after his lifetime.

Wilfrid was born into a Northumbrian family, almost certainly of noble rank, in 634. At the age of fourteen he experienced some kind of religious conversion and with the patronage of Eanflaed, the queen of King Oswy, he was placed in the monastery of Lindisfarne, then still under the rule of its Irish founder, Aidan. In about 652 he formed the ambition of going to Rome on pilgrimage. With the recommendation, once again, of Queen Eanflaed he went to Kent where he spent a year at the royal court. In 653 he set off for Rome in the company of Benedict Biscop. They travelled together as far as Lyons, where they parted company for reasons that remain unclear. Biscop went on to Rome while Wilfrid remained behind in Lyons where he had struck up a friendship with the bishop, Annemundus, and his brother Dalfinus, count of Lyons. Annemundus indeed wanted to adopt Wilfrid as his son, offered him the hand of his niece in marriage, and undertook to launch him upon a distinguished secular career in Gaul. Wilfrid resisted— though he may have been tempted: might this have been the occasion of his breach with Biscop?—and went on his way to Rome.

This first visit to Rome was of decisive importance in Wilfrid's life. He learned of Roman ecclesiastical usages, especially in the matter of the calculation of Easter, of which he was ignorant: this was to have important repercussions on his return to England. Perhaps even more significantly, in a Rome still mindful of Pope Gregory, Wilfrid was touched by a missionary impulse—as other visitors had been in the seventh century, notably the great Gallic missionary-bishop Amandus, of whose evangelization of the Low Countries Wilfrid may already have heard something—this too was to bear fruit later on. Furthermore, Wilfrid had an audience with the pope. Pope Martin I was engaged at the time in a fierce theological dispute with the authorities in Constantinople. Toward the end of 654 he was to be kidnapped by emissaries of the Byzantine emperor and exiled to the Crimea. His death there in 655 was to be widely regarded as martyrdom. It is not fanciful to suppose that Wilfrid's witnessing of this unseemly conflict between church and state was to affect the stance he adopted in his later quarrels with successive kings of Northumbria. Wilfrid's whole-hearted devotion to all things Roman never again wavered after the months he spent in Rome as an impressionable young man of twenty in the year 654.

After leaving Rome Wilfrid returned to Lyons where he spent the next three years with Bishop Annemundus. It was during this period that he received the monastic tonsure. Annemundus was murdered in 658. Wilfrid narrowly escaped the same fate and made his way back to England. Returning to Northumbria he attached himself to Alchfrith, son of Oswy, who was then ruling as a subking in Deira, the southern half of Northumbria. Alchfrith expelled the Irish monks whom he had recently established at Ripon and gave the monastery to Wilfrid instead. It was at Ripon that Wilfrid was ordained priest, probably early in 664, by Agilbert, the Frankish bishop of Dorchester whom Wilfrid had probably already met in Wessex, who was visiting the Northumbrian royal court. Together Agilbert and Wilfrid attended the Synod of Whitby in 664. Wilfrid was the principal spokesman for the Roman party, which carried the day in the question of the observance of Easter.

Shortly after the synod Wilfrid was promoted to the bishopric of York. At this time the see of Canterbury was vacant, and since Wilfrid could not be consecrated by schismatic British or Irish bishops he went to Gaul. He received consecration at Compiègne at the hands of Agilbert, who was magnificently (and symbolically) assisted by eleven other bishops. Wilfrid tarried some time in Gaul afterward. During his absence from Northumbria, and in circumstances at which we can only guess—not improbably to be connected with a quarrel between King Oswy and his son Alchfrith—Oswy gave the bishopric of York to Chad. Wilfrid regarded this as illegal usurpation of his see. Moreover, Chad made matters worse by being consecrated by the simoniac Bishop Wine of Winchester and two of the schismatic British bishops. Wilfrid returned to Northumbria probably in 666, after shipwreck and battle with looters on the coast of still pagan Sussex. (It is some indication of the state he kept that he had a retinue of 120 men. The single ship in which they all travelled must therefore have been considerably larger than the forty-seater in which King Redwald had been buried at Sutton Hoo a generation earlier.) Finding Chad in possession of York, Wilfrid retired to his monastery of Ripon, which formed his base for the next three years. During this period he occasionally discharged episcopal functions in Mercia and in Kent. Eddius also tells us that he founded more than one monastery in Mercia (one of them perhaps at Oundle) during this period, on the strength of landed endowments granted by King Wulfhere.

Archbishop Theodore reached England in May 669. In the course of the general visitation of the English churches that he conducted soon afterwards, Theodore removed Chad from York and replaced him with Wilfrid; Chad was soon afterward compensated with a Mercian see at Lichfield. Wilfrid held the bishopric of York in peace from 669 until 678. These were busy years. Wilfrid rebuilt his cathedral church at York; he built a church at Ripon and another at his northernmost monastic foundation, Hexham. (The crypts that underlay the two latter churches still stand.) He was an active diocesan in the vast Northumbrian bishopric subject to him.

In 678 King Ecgfrith picked a quarrel with Wilfrid and enlisted the support of Archbishop Theodore. Grasping this opportunity to further his plans for the division of over-large dioceses, Theodore consecrated three new bishops for Northumbria. Wilfrid, incensed, set off for Rome to appeal to the pope. He spent the winter of 678–79 in Frisia preaching the gospel to the heathen, and then proceeded to Rome. His case was heard in a council presided over by Pope Agatho, and the decision went in his favor. So he returned to England in 680 armed with papal letters designed to effect his reinstatement in the see of York. But King Ecgfrith disregarded the papal decision, refused to reinstate Wilfrid, and flung him into prison for nine months. In 681 he was released, but only on condition that he leave Northumbria.

Wilfrid's exile lasted five years (681–86). Most of this period he spent in the kingdom of Sussex, preaching to the heathen under the patronage of its recently converted king and founding a monastery at Selsey. He also spent some time in Wessex where he was active in the conversion of the inhabitants of the Isle of Wight, recently conquered by King Cadwalla. The king granted Wilfrid a quarter of the island and of the booty he had acquired by conquering it. Wilfrid gave these endowments to one of his nephews. It is an intriguing glimpse of the way in which from a certain aspect Wilfrid's operations were a kind of joint-stock enterprise bringing substantial benefits to his kin.

King Ecgfrith was killed in battle in 685. This marked a turning point in Wilfrid's fortunes. He and Theodore were reconciled and the new king of Northumbria, Aldfrith, allowed Wilfrid to return as bishop of York (late 686 or early 687). But he returned to a much diminished diocese. York was now the seat of the bishopric of Deira alone; Bernicia was divided between bishoprics at Lindisfarne, then under Cuthbert, and Hexham. Wilfrid administered the see of York for about five years. However, in 691 or 692 King Aldfrith quarrelled with him and he was again expelled. This time his exile was even longer, and we know less of it. We can trace him from time to time in Mercia, East Anglia, and Kent. In 703 (probably) Aldfrith summoned Wilfrid to a council in Northumbria and made it clear that he intended to ruin him by depriving his churches and monasteries of all their endowments. Wilfrid, now in his seventieth year, at once set out for Rome to appeal against this treatment. Pope John VI upheld Wilfrid's case and in 705 he returned to England. Aldfrith of Northumbria died shortly afterward and his successor Osred allowed Wilfrid back to Northumbria and to the custody of his monasteries. Wilfrid seems to have spent the last four years of his life in Northumbria, but it was at one of his Mercian monasteries, Oundle, that he died in 709.

It is customary to regard Wilfrid's career as turbulent. So indeed it was. But that we think of it thus is mainly because Eddius adopted the *tone* that he did in composing Wilfrid's biography. Other Anglo-Saxon bishops of this period may have had careers as stormy as Wilfrid's, but of which we know nothing. (It is salutary to consider what we might make of Wilfrid if we had only Bede's account of him.) We should resist the temptation—hallowed though it is by a long tradition of English, and especially Anglican historiography—to regard Wilfrid himself as touchy, self-centered, and impetuous. When strong personalities come into conflict, hasty words will be uttered, violent actions ensue; of course they will. But the conflicts were not simply those of personality. The controversies in which Wilfrid engaged were genuine controversies. There were hard questions at issue. They had to be thrashed out. They would not just go away.

That conceded, it remains curiously difficult to be sure precisely what the successive controversies were actually about. (This may seem odd; but it arises from the divergences, already mentioned, between our two principal sources, Eddius and Bede.) The initial quarrel with Ecgfrith of Northumbria was partly caused, we may suspect, by Wilfrid's encouragement of the queen in a vow of virginity. It was hardly calculated to endear him to a king who wanted an heir. The concentration of great landed wealth and ecclesiastical power in Wilfrid's hands aroused the envy of both Ecgfrith and Aldfrith; and behind this lurked knotty legal issues about the terms on which the church held its endowments. Wilfrid's friendship with successive rulers of Mercia was bound to cause apprehension to the rulers of Northumbria whose neighbors and rivals they were. And they were right to be apprehensive. Wilfrid was a kingmaker. In 676 he had supplied Dagobert II, then in exile in Ireland, with an army with which he won his way to the kingship of Austrasia (or east Francia). Wilfrid's chain of monasteries scattered from Hexham to Selsey, housing communities intensely loyal to their founder, constituted a following outside the control of kings whose authority was territorially circumscribed. Neither was it only kings who were envious and apprehensive. Eddius makes it clear that Wilfrid had enemies among the higher clergy of Northumbria, and behind these men (and women) we can sense the network of aristocratic clans from which they came. It was not that Wilfrid was a "political" bishop; for that is what all bishops necessarily and usually unrepentantly were. But what we call "politics" in the seventh century were compounded of family and feud, grievance and graft, and frequent violence. Wilfrid did not dictate the terms on which he lived. They were the common currency of a society of aristocratic warriors slowly adapting themselves to Christianity—and Christianity to themselves.

Important issues of principle lay behind Wilfrid's quarrels with two successive archbishops of Canterbury, Theodore and Brihtwold. Pope Gregory had laid down a plan for the organization of the English church. Theodore's laudable desire to divide big bishoprics into more manageable units seemed, to a bishop of York, to involve an assertion of the claims of Canterbury that went far beyond what Gregory had stipulated. This was offensive to a cleric of Wilfrid's Roman loyalties and Frankish experience; and when he appealed to Rome, Rome upheld him, though perhaps more hesitantly than he would have wished. Eddius saw these issues as clearcut. But they were not. This troubled Bede, and it has troubled many lesser historians of those conflicts ever since.

Conflict bulks large in contemporary accounts of Wilfrid. But to dwell on this facet of his career is to run the risk of laying insufficient stress on Wilfrid's other doings. He was perhaps the most important agent in the introduction of St. Benedict's monastic Rule to England and in its diffusion there. His perception of its potential as an adjunct to evangelization, as for instance at Selsey, may not have gone unnoticed by the young Boniface. He was a patron of scholarship: it is Bede, not Eddius, who tells us that Wilfrid was "very learned." His missionary work in Frisia blazed a trail that others were soon to follow, notably his pupil Willibrord. He was the first prominent western churchman to make it his practice to appeal to the pope in the course of litigation; his example was to have very far-reaching effects upon the government of Latin Christendom. His building and embellishment of churches, at Ripon, York, Hexham, and elsewhere—like Biscop's at Monkwearmouth and Jarrow—helped to familiarize the English with the dignified aesthetic of the Mediterranean world. The might and magnificence of his episcopal style, which he had learned from his Frankish mentors Annemundus and Agilbert, may have occasioned anxiety to the stricter sort of churchman such as Bede; but it was an important element in the process of attracting the Anglo-Saxon elite into the church and thus furthering the Christianization of the English.

At every point in his career Wilfrid touched the religious life of his countrymen with a current of creative vitality. This was how he was remembered at York. Some eighty years after his death Alcuin wrote that "his fame shone far and wide by virtue of his achievements." It was a just assessment.

After Wilfrid's death his body was carried by his grieving followers from Oundle to Ripon for burial. There his relics remained, the focus of a cult, for nearly two-and-a-half centuries. Then, probably in 948, they were removed to Canterbury by Archbishop Oda and reinterred there. By one of history's ironies Wilfrid's mortal remains ended up as one of the most precious possessions of the cathedral church with whose archbishops he had spent so many years locked in conflict.

Eddius's biography of Wilfrid is available in two translations: one by B. Colgrave, *The Life of Bishop Wilfrid by Eddius Stephanus*, 1927, reprinted 1985, and the other by D. H. Farmer in a volume called *The Age of Bede*, 1983.

BENEDICT BISCOP (628?–89) was the founder and first abbot of the twin monastic houses of Wearmouth and Jarrow. Biscop was a Northumbrian nobleman who spent his early manhood as a thane in the service of King Oswy and then at the age of about twenty-five experienced religious conversion and abandoned his secular career. In 653 he visited Rome, travelling in the company of Wilfrid as far as Lyons. After returning to England for a stay of some years, he again departed to the continent for a more prolonged visit (664–68). He twice visited Rome, and spent two years as a monk at the island monastery of Lerins off the south coast of France near Marseilles. In 668–69 he travelled back to England in the company of Theodore and Hadrian. He settled with them at Canterbury where for about two years (669–71) he was abbot of the monastery of St. Peter and St. Paul (later St. Augustine's). After another journey to Rome (671–72) he returned to his native Northumbria where in 673 he founded the monastery of Wearmouth with the help of a generous landed endowment from King Ecgfrith. The next few years were occupied in building and equipping the new monastery. Masons and glaziers were brought over from Gaul, and Biscop returned from yet another visit to Rome (678–80) with books, paintings, relics of the saints, a choirmaster, and a papal privilege designed to protect his monastery from secular encroachment. In 681 Biscop founded a twin monastery at Jarrow, over which he appointed Ceolfrith abbot: the church at Jarrow, much of which still stands, was consecrated in 685. A last trip to Rome to acquire more books and paintings took place in 685–86. Benedict Biscop died after a long illness in 689.

We know a good deal about Benedict Biscop and his monastic foundations at Wearmouth and Jarrow, partly through the writings of Jarrow's most distinguished inmate, Bede, and partly through recent excavations at the two sites. Biscop's monastery—he seems to have envisaged it as a single community though existing on two separate sites a few miles apart—was marked by several unusual characteristics. The principal buildings were of sophisticated design, construction, and decoration. Stone-built and roofed in lead, with plastered and painted walls and colored glass in some of the windows, they would have contrasted sharply with the simple wooden buildings at Lindisfarne and elsewhere. In an age when monastic founders were not necessarily interested in learning, Biscop was determined that his community should be a learned one. He grasped the simple but fundamental point—apparently lost on modern patrons of learning such as the University Grants Committee—that you cannot have learning without books. He went to enormous trouble and expense to equip his monastery with books collected in Italy and Gaul, and assembled what was probably one of the best libraries in western Europe; hence the ample learning of Bede. It also seems that Biscop held ideals about the monastic life that differed significantly from those held by many of his contemporaries. Although Biscop was on good terms with King Ecgfrith, a frequent visitor to the royal court and dependent on royal patronage for endowments, he did not wish his community to be tarnished by overmuch contact with the world outside. The distinctions of rank in the secular world were to count as nothing inside the monastery. The founder's noble kinsmen were not to be permitted to interfere in the life of the community. All its members were to be equal in the sight of God. In thus following scriptural precept—as Bede noted with approval—in cutting loose from family and social ties, Biscop was challenging some of the most cherished values of his contemporaries. The privilege that he acquired from the Pope was designed to uphold his ideals in a world that, as Bede (who shared them) makes very clear, was often indifferent or even hostile to them.

The principal source for the life of Benedict Biscop is Bede's "Lives of the Abbots," translated in D. H. Farmer, *The Age of Bede*, 1983.

ST. CUTHBERT (*c.* 634–87), monk, anchorite, and bishop of Lindisfarne, has always been one of the best-loved saints of the early Anglo-Saxon church. This is mainly owing to the survival of two remarkable biographies of him: the first, by an anonymous monk of Lindisfarne, composed between 698 and 705; the second, closely based upon the first yet differing subtly from it, by Bede, composed shortly before 721.

The facts of Cuthbert's life are soon told. He was born in Northumbria, probably in what is now the Border country, in about 634. In 651 he became a monk at Melrose. From about 659 he was at the short-lived colony of Melrose at Ripon, but returned to the motherhouse when the Melrose monks were expelled from Ripon to make way for Wilfrid in about 661. In 664 he moved to Lindisfarne, or Holy Island, and became prior of the community there. Later on, perhaps about 675 or 676, he went to live as a hermit on Farne Island, about seven miles south of Lindisfarne and about a mile and a half from the mainland. In 684, much against his will, he was chosen bishop of Lindisfarne and consecrated at York in 685. In 687, foreseeing his death, he retired again to Farne where he died on 20 March.

Saints are by definition distinctive persons. Furthermore, we can only see them as our authorities have chosen to present them to us. Those authorities were not biographers as we understand the term. They wrote a particular form of biography, what is technically known as hagiography, the life of a holy person, or saint. The hagiographer was concerned not simply to relate but to venerate, to satisfy not curiosity but pious devotion, to present an ideal, sometimes just a stereotype, of holy living. It follows that it is peculiarly difficult to discover what a seventh-century saint—perhaps a saint of any period—was *actually like*. These obstacles admitted, it does nevertheless seem to be the case that Cuthbert impressed his contemporaries as a man of altogether exceptional qualities and of powers quite beyond the natural. Their witness, recorded by the anonymous monk and by Bede, has communicated itself to later generations. On a famous occasion at Carlisle in 685 Cuthbert saw by second sight the defeat and death of King Ecgfrith at distant Nechtansmere. This was witnessed by many responsible people: the incident cannot have been invented. Once on the shores of the North Sea at Coldingham an observer whose presence was unknown to Cuthbert witnessed otters drying and warming his feet after he had waded in from the sea where he had been standing waist-deep to pray. It is one of several stories about Cuthbert's intimate relationship with animals and birds that contemporaries took to be indicative of his sanctity. Cuthbert crossed the frontiers of normal human expectation and experience.

Cuthbert's posthumous history has been as remarkable as his earthly life. The miracles that he worked during his lifetime continued at Lindisfarne after his burial there. In 698 the monks exhumed his body and found it to be incorrupt—one of the signs of sanctity. The body was reburied in a new coffin. Further miracles occurred. The anonymous *Life*, and then Bede's *Life*, were composed. A cult was born. It was a cult with which the royal family of Northumbria became associated: it was to St. Cuthbert's monastery that King Ceolwulf retired when he resigned the kingdom in 737. Cuthbert may have become something like a patron saint of Northumbria in the course of the century following his death.

In 793 the monastery of Lindisfarne was sacked by the Vikings; its monks were killed or carried off into slavery but Cuthbert's shrine survived. It was the opening of nearly a century of turbulence and peril for the community. Viking raids continued, culminating in the Danish conquest and settlement of Northumbria from 867 onward. In 875 the monks of Lindisfarne took evasive action. Bearing with them the body of St. Cuthbert, they wandered from place to place in Northumbria, in search of permanent safety, for seven years. In 883 the community, and with it the bishopric of Lindisfarne, settled at Chester-le-Street. There they remained for a little over a century until moving to Durham in 995. It is at Durham that Cuthbert has rested ever since. In 1104 a new shrine was constructed for him next to the high altar of the new Norman cathedral, which was then rising about it. Throughout the Middle Ages and beyond St. Cuthbert remained the most tremendous presence in the north of England: the goal of pilgrims, the worker of miracles, the protector of the dwellers in "Saint Cuthbert's Land" against the Scots, the sustainer of the wealthiest ecclesiastical corporation in the north. Henry VIII's commissioners dispersed his monks, broke up his shrine, rifled his tomb, but dared not touch his mortal remains. There at Durham they still remain. And there may still be seen such of his relics as have survived the thirteen centuries that separate us from him: the wooden coffin made in 698, Cuthbert's small silver-plated portable altar, and the magnificent pectoral cross that he wore, as bishop, round his neck.

B. Colgrave, *Two Lives of Saint Cuthbert*, 1940, reprinted 1985, edits and translates the texts. C. F. Battiscombe (ed.), *The Relics of Saint Cuthbert*, 1956, contains elaborate art-historical studies of the surviving relics.

C. W. Jones, *Saints' Lives and Chronicles in Early England*, 1947, is an excellent introduction to hagiography.

ALDFRITH (*d.* 705) was king of Northumbria from 685 to 705. He was an illegitimate son of King Oswy who was perhaps intended for a career in the church since he was given a first-rate education. We know that he studied in Ireland, and it is not impossible that among his fellow students there was Aldhelm (who was his godfather too). Aldfrith succeeded Ecgfrith as king of Northumbria in 685 and in the words of Bede "nobly restored the shattered state of the kingdom, although within narrower bounds." Northumbrian ascendancy over the Picts had gone forever. Aldfrith continued his predecessor's quarrel with Wilfrid; this apart, his reign was remembered as a time of peace. He married Cuthburh, sister of King Ine of Wessex. Their son Osred succeeded his father in 705.

All authorities are agreed about Aldfrith's learning. To Bede he was "very learned"; to Eddius, the biographer of Wilfrid, he was "a most wise king"; and Alcuin commented that he was "at once both king and teacher." Poems in Irish attributed to him have survived. Adomnan, abbot of Iona and biographer of Columba, was his friend: on one of his visits to the Northumbrian court Adomnan presented Aldfrith with a copy of his book on the Holy Places. Aldfrith is known to have bought from Benedict Biscop a book that the latter had acquired in Rome. Aldhelm addressed to him a treatise mainly devoted to metrics and written in highly elaborate Latin. Aldfrith was probably the most learned king to rule in England before James I. It was fitting that such a man should have presided over the kingdom during the golden age of Northumbrian intellectual culture.

CADWALLA (*c.* 659–89) was king of Wessex from 685 to 688. He was a descendant of Cerdic—and like him had a British name—

and Ceawlin. In the course of a youth spent in exile as the leader of a war band, like his near contemporary Guthlac, we hear of his ravaging Sussex and killing its king (684?). In 685, according to the *Anglo-Saxon Chronicle,* he "began to contend for the kingdom" of Wessex and had won his way to power there by 686. His reign was short and violent. He ravaged Kent in 686 and 687. He conquered the Isle of Wight in 686. He again invaded Sussex and made it tributary to him. He had power, how acquired we can only guess, over Surrey. Yet though his life was devoted to warfare he was also a generous patron of the church, the friend of Wilfrid, and a founder of monasteries. It is significant that Bede apparently saw no contradictions in Cadwalla's career: he ruled "most effectively." Above all, Bede approved of his end. In 688 Cadwalla resigned his kingdom and went on pilgrimage to Rome. There he was baptized in 689—and it is remarkable that he had not been baptized before—and died ten days later.

We may find Cadwalla's career more extraordinary than Bede did. A warrior cast in the heroic mold so well described in the epic poem *Beowulf,* as barbarian a king as one could wish for, he yet could perform "Roman" regal acts, such as the issue of charters in Latin and, probably, the striking of coin. The man who could perpetrate acts of savagery in his conquest of Wight died in the odor of sanctity less than three years later and was commemorated in a fulsome Latin epitaph composed by an archbishop of Milan. Of such paradoxes and surprises was the impact of Christianity on Anglo-Saxon kings made up.

INE (*d.* after 726) was king of Wessex from 688 to 726. His long reign is illuminated for us by a larger and more diverse body of evidence than can be brought to bear upon the reign of any earlier English king. In particular a code of laws and a number of charters—the formal written record of grants of land—issued by Ine have survived. Historians are duly grateful for this, but their gratitude should be tinged with awareness of certain hazards. Not only does the new evidence present knotty technical problems of interpretation; there is the more insidious danger that its very existence may affect the way we look at King Ine. It is tempting to draw a contrast between the barbaric Cadwalla and the statesmanlike Ine who succeeded him. But Ine's reign may have been quite as violent as Cadwalla's. Bede tells us that he ruled Sussex just as oppressively.

He laid Kent under massive tribute. We hear of dynastic conflict within Wessex, of civil strife, of the banishment and slaying of a rival. Above all, Ine was active against the still independent British kingdom of Dumnonia in the southwest.

Ine's father had been a subking in Wessex, possibly in Dorset. It is likely that Ine came from rather farther west than Cadwalla, and this might explain his preoccupation with western affairs. During the seventh century, and especially in the reigns of Cenwalh (643–74) and Centwine (676–85), the kingdom of Wessex had been expanding westward at the expense of the Britons of Dumnonia. Although the process cannot be traced in confident detail it is likely that by about 700 much of Devon was under West Saxon domination. We hear of wars between Ine and the Britons in 710 and 722, and there may have been more fighting of which we know nothing. At one stage of his reign Ine was able to dispose of land to the west of the river Tamar, in Cornwall. Although he did not do away with the kingdom of Dumnonia—which seems to have lingered on until the last quarter of the ninth century—Ine consolidated the West Saxon presence in Devon and perhaps to some degree in eastern Cornwall. A glance at a map will show that English place-names predominate in Devon and eastern Cornwall, Celtic ones farther west.

In 705 the vast West Saxon bishopric of Winchester—for the see established by Birinus at Dorchester had lapsed at some point in the second half of the seventh century—was divided. A new bishopric was set up at Sherborne under Aldhelm with ecclesiastical responsibilities for the new western districts. There is some likelihood that a community of British clergy already existed at Sherborne. It is probable that there were other communities of monastic or quasi-monastic type that experienced similar continuity; for instance, at Stoke, near Hartland in Devon. The most abundantly documented of them is Glastonbury, where it is almost certain that there was a British monastery before the arrival of the West Saxons. Ine was a generous benefactor to Glastonbury, as he also was of monasteries established farther east such as Malmesbury and Abingdon.

This willingness to integrate British communities into the West Saxon establishment is also displayed in Ine's code of laws, the earliest such code issued by a ruler of Wessex, promulgated in about 694. Ine's laws also show the king throwing the weight of his authority behind the church. For example, he enforced the payment of the tax known as church-scot, an annual payment in kind, probably quite a heavy one, rendered by all free men to the church. Ine's ability to enforce the church's claim to tax is indicative of a degree of ordered power at his disposal. This is borne out by other clauses in his laws. We can dimly make out an apparatus of government for the peaceful administration of justice and the economic support of the royal establishment, operating upon a diverse and not uncomplicated society. It is likely, for example, that already in Ine's day the West Saxon kingdom was divided for administrative purposes into shires, each of them centered upon an important royal estate and presided over by an *alderman* who was in some sense the king's deputy in his shire.

Ine's laws have something in addition to tell us of the economic activity which underpinned this institutional superstructure. They suggest a wealthy economy, predominantly agrarian yet one accustomed to the use of coin, in which trading and merchants were sufficiently important to be the subject of legislation. Recent archaeological discoveries have fleshed out the skeleton revealed by the written sources. At *Hamwih,* the ancestor of the modern Southampton, excavation has shown the remains of a big and prosperous trading settlement that was active during this period. Ine may have been instrumental in developing the port. The tolls that he could levy there were probably an important source of royal revenue. It is significant that by the year 755 (at latest) the place-name *Hamtun,* the royal estate immediately adjacent to *Hamwih,* had given its name to one of the administrative divisions of Wessex: *Hamtun-scir,* Hampshire.

Ine was the most formidable king of his day in northern Europe. In 726 he resigned his throne, like Cadwalla before him, and went on pilgrimage to Rome, there to end his days at some date unknown. Even the Romans he impressed: after his death they regarded him as a saint.

S. M. Pearce, *The Kingdom of Dumnonia,* 1978, is useful on the southwest. R. Hodges, *Dark Age Economics,* 1982, is stimulating on towns and trade but needs to be used with caution.

ST. ALDHELM (*d.* 709/710) was a monk, scholar, and first bishop of Sherborne. Most of Aldhelm's career is shrouded in obscurity.

We do not know from what part of England he originated. Wherever he may have received his early education—and it is not impossible that he spent some time in Ireland—he was clearly given a very good grounding in Latin. The first certain fact in his career is that he studied at Canterbury under Hadrian, perhaps in the early 670s. At some point he became abbot of Malmesbury; it is assumed, though on no very good grounds, that this was in about 674. He founded at least two other monasteries, one possibly at Wareham and the other at Bradford-on-Avon. (The surviving Anglo-Saxon church at Bradford-on-Avon, long thought to date from Aldhelm's day, is now considered to have been built about three centuries later; an instructive example of the difficulties of dating Anglo-Saxon buildings.) At some point in his life he is known to have visited Rome. When the bishopric of Wessex was divided in 705 Aldhelm was given the new diocese of Sherborne. As a bishop of a see in a sensitive frontier area that had only recently passed under West Saxon control, it is fair to assume that Aldhelm was a trusted servant of King Ine of Wessex. His tenure of the see was short: he died late in 709 or early in 710.

It is for his writings rather than his public life that Aldhelm is remembered today. Unfortunately for his reputation he chose to write in a Latin style of extraordinary complexity and obscurity—in his own words, "a dense forest of Latinity"—and this has meant that until the recent publication of reliable translations his works have remained literally a closed book to all except the most dedicated of scholars. This is a pity, for Aldhelm was the most learned Englishman before Bede. His works have much to tell us of the remarkable achievements of Anglo-Latin Christian culture in the age of Archbishop Theodore; not simply in themselves, but also in what they imply about the Latin learning of their readers. They are also an important source of information about the state of the church in Wessex, an area about which Bede was not well informed.

Aldhelm's most ambitious works were two treatises, one in verse and the other in prose, in praise of virginity. The verse treatise was dedicated to an otherwise unknown abbess named Maxima, the prose one to the nuns of Barking where one of his relatives was a nun. To King Aldfrith of Northumbria he dedicated an elaborate treatise on metrics. To the British king Geraint of Dumnonia he addressed a long letter on the Paschal controversy. Nine other of his letters and three letters to him have survived in whole or in part. His correspondents were widely scattered. They included an Irish monk at Péronne in Gaul and Englishmen who had studied or were proposing to study in Ireland. They embraced local correspondents such as Wynbert, abbot of Nursling and patron of Boniface, and more far-flung acquaintances such as his teacher Hadrian at Canterbury and the abbots of the monastic confederation stretching from Northumberland to Sussex founded by Wilfrid. There also survive five short Latin poems by him celebrating the dedication of churches or altars. A plausible report by a twelfth-century chronicler tells that Aldhelm also composed vernacular poetry on biblical themes—like his contemporary Caedmon at Whitby—though none of this survives (or has yet been identified) among the vast corpus of Old English religious verse.

We get other glimpses of Aldhelm. On his visit to Rome—and of course he may like Benedict Biscop have visited Italy more than once—he acquired vestments and a marble altar. We hear of him bargaining for a Bible with Frankish merchants at Dover—a revealing glimpse of the seventh-century book trade. A twelfth-century transcript of Aldhelm's own copy of a Spanish law-book, the so-called *Breviary of Alaric*, still survives in the Bodleian Library in Oxford; and it is possible that Aldhelm was in direct touch with the scholars of Spain, at that date the most important focus of learning in western Europe. We see him building churches, using his contacts with the royal court to enlarge the landed endowments of Malmesbury, attending ecclesiastical councils.

For posterity, Aldhelm has always tended to be overshadowed by Bede. It is worth reflecting that if Bede had not been a writer, Aldhelm's works would be our principal source of knowledge about English ecclesiastical history in the seventh century. He emerges, if somewhat indistinctly, as a notable abbot, an active bishop, but above all as a man of vast learning, a scholar and a patron of scholars, a gifted teacher. Surviving manuscripts suggest that in the later Anglo-Saxon period his works were studied as attentively as those of Bede. It was only later that he suffered neglect. It is high time that he was given his due and acclaimed as one of the most influential of all Anglo-Saxon churchmen.

M. Herren and M. Lapidge have translated *Aldhelm: The Prose Works*, 1979, and *Aldhelm: The Poetic Works*, 1984.

ST. GUTHLAC (*c.* 675–714) was successively warrior, monk, and hermit. Like many early Anglo-Saxon saints Guthlac was of aristocratic birth; he was connected to the royal family of Mercia. His earlier career was that of a secular nobleman. He gathered a warband about him and for nine years lived a life of adventure, fighting, laying waste, and plundering, of the sort that is described in the epic *Beowulf.* We do not know where these exploits took him—probably they were widespread—but we can be sure that he spent some time in Wales, for his biographer tells us that he had learned some British there. At the age of twenty-three he suddenly threw over this life and became a monk at Repton: the sudden conversion and precipitate response to it somewhat reminiscent of King Cadwalla of Wessex. After two years he left Repton to become a hermit at Crowland in the Fens: this must have been in or about the year 700. Guthlac's biographer, Felix, tells how he wrestled with demons, communicated with birds and fishes, and worked miracles of healing. Like Cuthbert he was also visited by the great. Ethelbald, then an exile, later to be king of Mercia, was a frequent visitor. Guthlac comforted him by prophesying the downfall of his rival, King Ceolred of Mercia (709–16), and his future greatness. Bishop Headde of Lichfield was another friend. So was Ecburga, daughter of King Aldwulf of East Anglia (*d.* 713), who had a leaden coffin made for him. A year after Guthlac's death in 714 his body was found to be incorrupt and translated to a splendid shrine provided by Ethelbald.

Guthlac's career is of great interest because it furnishes a perspective on the conversion of the Anglo-Saxons that is absent from the writings of Bede. Guthlac's acts of spiritual heroism as a hermit mirrored his adolescent career of secular heroism. The earthly warrior became the soldier of Christ. Religious conversion blended the old man into the new. It was not a hurdle in the crossing of which all former attitudes and habits had to be jettisoned. Here was an ideal of sanctity that Anglo-Saxon kings and noblemen could understand and admire. Perhaps significantly, Felix's biography was composed at the request of a king, Alfwald of East Anglia (*d.* 749). In the record of Guthlac's turbulent life we can see something of how Christianity was presented to aristocratic audiences, and of how they reacted to it.

B. Colgrave has edited and translated *Felix's Life of St. Guthlac,* 1956, reprinted 1985.

WIHTRED (*d.* 725) ruled as king of Kent from 691 to 725. He was remembered in later Kentish tradition as "the glorious king, and as with his contemporary Ine of Wessex one can sense that he was an imposing ruler. The early years of his reign were confused. More than one king claimed rule in Kent in the years 690–94, and it was probably not until after a settlement with Wessex in 694 to atone for the Kentish murder of Mul, the brother of Cadwalla, that Wihtred could feel secure. A charter of 694 records the stabilization of the frontiers of the kingdom along its earlier boundaries. In 695 Wihtred issued a code of laws: that one clause was identical to a clause in Ine's code suggests some cooperation between the two rulers.

Wihtred's law-code is chiefly remarkable for its evidence of the privileged position accorded to the church. Its first clause, for example, granted the church immunity from taxation. Royal authority was used to back up ecclesiastical precept on such matters as fasting, abstention from work on Sundays, and the canonical rules governing marriage. It is surely permissible to see in this the influence of Kentish churchmen, most prominent among them Archbishop Brihtwold of Canterbury (693–731). Wihtred was a generous patron of monasteries: the houses at Canterbury, Minster-in-Thanet, and Lyminge received grants of land from him.

The compensation paid to Ine of Wessex for Mul's death took the form of a very large sum of coin. Recent work by numismatists has demonstrated that Wihtred minted coin on a large and hitherto unsuspected scale. Trade with Franks and Frisians on the other side of the Channel played an important role in the economy of Kent. Wihtred's kingdom was wealthy and powerful. Kent had not yet declined into the status of a satellite of Mercia or Wessex.

CEOLFRITH (642–716) was abbot of Wearmouth and Jarrow during the formative years of the life of Bede. By origin a Northumbrian nobleman, Ceolfrith became a monk at Gilling as a young man (*c.* 660) and at the invitation of Wilfrid transferred to the monastery of Ripon in about 664–65. After his ordination as priest in 669 he visited Kent, where we may presume that he met Benedict Biscop, and East Anglia for the purpose of further experience of the monastic life. In about 673 he was summoned by Biscop to assist in the foundation of Wearmouth and accompanied him to Rome in 678–80. After the establishment of the twin house at Jarrow in 681 Ceolfrith was appointed its abbot, and added to this the abbacy of Wearmouth in the last year of Biscop's life, 688. Ceolfrith presided over the twin communities until 716, when he resigned and resolved to end his days with a pilgrimage to Rome. He never reached his goal, but died on the road, at Langres in Burgundy, in September 716.

As abbot of Wearmouth-Jarrow Ceolfrith was a public figure of some importance in the affairs of Northumbria, the friend of King Aldfrith and the man who was responsible for persuading Nechtan, king of the Picts, to adopt the Roman method of calculating the date of Easter. But it was above all for his "domestic" achievements that Ceolfrith was celebrated by Bede and by the anonymous monk who composed a biography of him. He increased the endowments of Wearmouth-Jarrow. He encouraged the growth in numbers, so that by the time of his departure in 716 there were about 600 monks; a larger body of monks by far than was ever again to be assembled in an English religious house. He negotiated a confirmation of the papal privilege that Biscop had received in the 670s—testimony at once to Ceolfrith's inheritance of Biscop's very special monastic ideals and, perhaps, to his awareness of the difficulties of maintaining them in practice. He encouraged the production of books. It was under his patronage that the manuscript of the Bible known as the Codex Amiatinus, now in Florence, was written; it is one of the world's great calligraphic masterpieces. Finally, it was under Ceolfrith's guidance that Bede received his monastic training and his education. Bede always wrote of Ceolfrith with affection and respect, and in the introduction to one of his biblical commentaries composed in 716 he allows us a poignant glimpse of his sense of loss. "The departure of my most revered abbot . . . (brought) to the minds of those who had been entrusted to his care a sense of stunned confusion."

P. Hunter Blair, *The World of Bede*, 1970.

ST. BEDE (*c.* 673–735) was a monk, scholar, and teacher; the most learned man of his day; the earliest and the most influential of all English historians. Practically everything that we know of Bede's life is contained in a short autobiographical notice at the end of his most famous work, *The Ecclesiastical History of the English People*. He was born near the monastery of Wearmouth at about the time that it was founded by Benedict Biscop. When he was seven his kinsfolk placed him in the monastery to receive his schooling. He moved to the twin house of Jarrow shortly after its foundation in 681, and there he became a monk. In about 692 he was ordained deacon and in about 703 priest. He is known to have visited Lindisfarne and he may have travelled as far afield as York. However, as he tells us himself, nearly all his life was lived out at Jarrow:

> Spending all the time of my life living in that monastery,
> I have wholly applied myself to the study of scripture;
> and amid the observance of regular discipline and the
> daily care of singing in the church, I have always
> delighted in learning, teaching and writing.

Benedict Biscop had endowed his monastic foundations lavishly with books and his successor Ceolfrith further enlarged the library. Bede profited from daily access to one of the best libraries in western Europe to become a very learned man. The character of his learning was almost exclusively Christian. Though he was acquainted with some of the Latin classics he regarded pagan literature with suspicion and distaste. By far the greatest part of his learning lay in the Bible, the works of the four Fathers of the Western Church—Ambrose, Jerome, Augustine of Hippo, and Pope Gregory—writers of ecclesiastical history such as Eusebius, and the lives of the saints.

For Bede the teacher therefore there were two priorities: instruction in Latin, the language of the church, and understanding of God's word by means of close scrutiny of and rumination on holy scripture. The Anglo-Saxons spoke the Germanic language known as Old English. Latin was not a vernacular tongue for them as it was for the Italian missionaries to England such as Augustine and Paulinus; it had to be learned as a foreign language. Bede's perception of this need led him to compose works of basic instruction in Latin grammar, spelling, and verse. The excellence of these textbooks is indicated by their unusually long life; they were still being copied and used four hundred years after Bede's death. These works, not widely studied today, throw some light on Bede's methods and motives as a scholar. In the first place they were largely dependent on earlier Latin grammatical works, but Bede reworked his authorities with intelligence and skill. It is characteristic of Bede's literary output as a whole that he did not seek to be original but to preserve the heritage of the past, suitably adapted to present purposes. Second, this adaptation often took the form of giving a new—a Christian—slant to the materials available. The grammarians of late antiquity on whose work Bede built had illustrated the points they made by quotation from respected classical authors, frequently Virgil. Bede to a great extent replaced these citations by quotations from scripture or eminent Christian authority. For example, when discussing the use of the verb *ausculto* ("to listen or hear with attention"), Bede explains that it governs either the dative case or the accusative according as to whether the subject is listening to a person or hearing a thing. To illustrate the latter usage Bede offers the phrase *ausculto praecepta magistri:* "I hear attentively the precepts of the master." Nothing could seem more straightforward. Yet there is an inwardness here that is not immediately obvious. The opening words of the Rule of St. Beedict are *Ausculta, fili, praecepta magistri:* "Hear attentively, my son, the precepts of the master." St. Benedict's Rule was certainly known at Wearmouth and Jarrow, for it was one of the influences upon the monastic rule devised for his houses by Benedict Biscop. Bede's words do not simply illustrate a point about correct Latin usage. They also echo a famous Christian text, which would carry reminders for the pupil of the monastic virtues of humility and obedience. So far as lay within his power Bede was determined that his pupils should be educated in a self-contained, uncompromisingly Christian intellectual environment.

It would be wrong to leave the reader with the impression that Bede's learning was exclusively Latin. He made serious efforts to learn Greek—one of the manuscripts that he used to do so, a copy of the Acts of the Apostles with parallel Greek and Latin texts, still survives—and he put his knowledge of Greek to good use in his commentaries on the New Testament. He was also keenly aware of the importance of the vernacular in Christian instruction. He translated the Lord's Prayer and the Creed into Old English, and in a famous letter to Archbishop Egbert of York—of which more later—he insisted on the necessity for the laity to learn these by heart. On his deathbed he was engaged in the translation of St. John's Gospel into Old English. He approved the vernacular Christian verse composed by Caedmon and he was said to have been skilled in such composition himself.

Knowledge of Latin equipped a man for study of the Bible. Bede composed many works of commentary (or "exegesis") on books of the Bible. Here too he did not claim to be doing original work:

> From the time I became a priest, until the fifty-ninth year of my age, I have made it my business to compile brief commentaries on the scriptures from the works of the venerable Fathers, and to add something about their meaning and interpretation, so meeting my own needs and those of my brethren.

His commentaries were a mosaic of pieces from other men's work but the overall design was Bede's own. The purpose of the exercise was to elucidate the layers of meaning in a given text. The literal meaning was held to be but a small part of its total meaning. Beneath the literal sense of scripture there lay hidden mysteries, which it was the task of the exegete to uncover and expound. allegories of the divine purpose, moral precepts for devout Christian living, mystical meanings concealed in the mathematics of chronology and measurement. This manner of elucidating scripture will seem odd to most—though by no means to all—twentieth-century Christians; certainly the commentaries that Bede composed make tedious reading today. It is important to bear in mind, however, that exegesis of this sort was a serious, coherent, and exacting intellectual discipline. Bede was a master at it.

Exegesis could be turned to other ends. In Bede's hands it became a vehicle for chiding and warning his contemporaries. Here is an example, drawn from Bede's commentary on the books of Ezra and Nehemiah, composed soon after 725. The books concern the rebuilding of the walls and temple of Jerusalem after the end of the Babylonian captivity. Nehemiah 4, verses 1–4 read as follows (in the New English Bible):

> There came a time when the common people, both men and women, raised a great outcry against their fellow-Jews. Some complained that they were giving their sons and daughters as pledges for food to keep themselves alive; others that they were mortgaging their fields, vineyards

and houses to buy corn in the famine; others again that they were borrowing money on their fields and vineyards to pay the king's tax.

Bede comments on this passage as follows:

The people indeed wanted to build the city wall but were prevented from the holy work by great famine. This famine had been brought about not only by shortage of foodstuffs but also by the greed of the rulers who were exacting from the people heavier taxes than they could pay . . .

and it is important to observe that at this point Bede changes *tense,*

For there are many among God's people who sincerely wish to observe His Commands but are held back from doing what they wish not only by poverty but also by the actions of those who appear to be clothed in the garments of religion. For they exact from those committed to their care a huge weight of worldly goods in tribute, and do nothing in return toward the eternal salvation of their flock by teaching, by living exemplary lives or by undertaking acts of charity. Would that another Nehemiah might arise in our days to correct our ways.

These are stern words. Whom did Bede have in mind? Plainly, the Northumbrian bishops of the day. His words are firm and exact; specific abuses are identified. As we shall see, he was not always so temperate. We should remember too that this was not a public document: like his other commentaries it was composed "for the needs of my brethren" in the monastery. Other works were to achieve wider circulation. Passages such as this—for more could be cited—show us something of Bede's standards in matters of ecclesiastical conduct and reveal his anxieties about the state of the church in England. They indicate his loyalty to the high ideals enunciated by his master Benedict Biscop and they cast a perhaps unexpected light upon his character. Bede was not the simple unworldly monk portrayed by a long tradition of English historical writing. He looked hard and sternly at his world and disapproved of much that he saw. The standards by which he judged it were exacting; and his enormous literary output was devoted to sustaining them.

Perhaps the part of exegesis that most taxed and delighted Bede was the study of number. The Bible contains a vast amount of numerical data, from the seven days of creation in Genesis to the seven churches of Asia in Revelation, with some positive numerical orgies in between, such as the measurements of Solomon's temple recorded in relentless detail in I Kings. For Bede these materials, properly sifted and meditated upon, could furnish important truths about God's purposes in and for the world. Preoccupation with number was one route by which Bede came to the study of chronology. Another lay in what was known as *computus*, that is to say, all the operations connected with the understanding of the Christian calendar. Central to *computus* was an understanding of the movement of the date of Easter. This was a particularly sensitive matter in Bede's lifetime. The Irish missionaries to Northumbria under Aidan had calculated the date of Easter differently from the Roman missionaries based at Canterbury. This was a schism in the church and as such a cause for the gravest concern. These differences had been settled in favor of the Roman side at the Synod of Whitby presided over by King Oswy in 664; but this decision affected only the kingdom of Northumbria. During Bede's lifetime the kingdom of the Picts accepted the Roman Easter in about 710, and to his great delight the monks of Iona accepted it in 716 on the teaching of the Northumbrian monk Egbert.

Bede composed two works devoted to exposition of the Christian calendar: *De Temporibus,* an early work composed in 703, and the more elaborate *De Temporum Ratione* of 725. To the latter work Bede appended a chronicle: it was the study of number and chronology, which led Bede on to the composition of chronicles. A chronicle was an elementary device for recording the events of the past—a list of dates, with the corresponding events of the year in question entered against each date. To describe such works as elementary is all very well provided we bear in mind that their preparation involved exacting labor in the correlation and reconciliation of different systems of dating, especially that used by the Jews with that used by the Romans. For example, Bede was able to show that Samson lived about the time of the siege of Troy. One practical device of supreme importance he was responsible not indeed for inventing but for popularizing was the use of the Christian Era, the habit of classifying dates either *x* BC or *y* AD. It is mainly owing to Bede that we still use this system.

To a modern understanding the laborious process of correlating secular and sacred history in this manner may seem pointless. But to Bede and to the many other compilers of chronicles in early medieval Europe, as to their audiences, it was not. In the first place, to arrange all the data of the past in an orderly form was one way, it was believed, of grasping the coherence of God's purposes: a chronicle displayed divine providence at work in history. Secondly, a chronicle would show that sacred history went farther back than secular and that it had permanence in a way that secular history could not match. Bede's chronicle showed that sacred history had advanced as far as Abraham before the Egyptian empire was even founded; it showed that the city of Rome was not founded until the reign of Ahaz II, king of Judah; it showed worldly principalities and powers—Egypt, Persia, Greece, and Rome—foundering and falling while God's purposes ripened and his people grew from strength to strength. From one aspect a chronicle was a kind of manifesto of Christian triumph. Thirdly, a chronicle might teach important lessons for the edification of Christians. Consider, for example, these consecutive entries:

> A persecution arose in Asia: Polycarp and Pionius suffered martyrdom. In Gaul as well many shed their blood gloriously for Christ.
> Shortly afterwards a plague came to avenge these crimes: it laid waste many provinces and especially devastated Italy and Rome.

Such was the fate of persecutors of the church; such the avenging providence of God. Or consider this entry:

> Lucius king of Britain sent a letter to Eleutherius bishop of Rome, asking that he might be made a Christian.

As it happens, the information is historically worthless: we know that, but Bede did not. For Bede it was the record of the be-

ginning of the faith in Britain, and it came to Britain from Rome.
Bede was passionately loyal to Roman authority in the church.
The composition of chronicle was one path by which Bede
came to the writing of history. Another was by way of hagiography,
the composition of lives of holy men and women, the saints. Hagiography was a very different literary genre from chronicle. The
lives of the holy were written to celebrate and to edify; to teach lessons of godly living and holy dying; to record miracles worked and
visions seen and triumphs won over Satan; to preserve the memory
of converts made and churches founded, of pilgrimages undertaken and books acquired. Bede composed several works of this
type, of which the two most famous are his *History of the Abbots* of
Wearmouth and Jarrow and his *Life of St. Cuthbert.*

These different strands—chronicle and hagiography; orderly
arrangement and moral edification—met and mingled in the work
for which Bede is most famous, *The Ecclesiastical History of the English People,* which he completed in 731. Here as elsewhere in his
works Bede had a model to guide him: the *Ecclesiastical History* of
Eusebius (*d.* 340), Bishop of Caesarea, the friend of the emperor
Constantine I and one of his principal advisers on ecclesiastical affairs. Eusebius's work was—as the author emphasized—a new type
of history that marked a sharp break with the historical writing of
antiquity. It was conceived as a record of salvation. The growth of
the Christian church—the record of persecutions and martyr-
doms, of bishops and saints, of insidious heresy and truth triumphant—was God at work in the world. Eusebius celebrated the
faith of the past and fortified the faith of the present. He demonstrated the rewards of the righteous and the fate of the ungodly.
Eusebius pioneered new methods as well as a new content and a
new purpose. His most important innovation was his careful citation of sources, many of which he quoted word for word.

Eusebius did his work outstandingly well. His *History* was deservedly popular and circulated widely. Bede knew it in a Latin
translation and may possibly have had access to a text in the original Greek. Bede's *Ecclesiastical History* followed the Eusebian model
closely. Like Eusebius he wrote providential or salvation history,
but applied to the English church rather than to the Christian
community at large. Like Eusebius he was scholarly in his citation
of sources and careful in his verbatim reproduction of documents.

Bede was indeed very scholarly. The reader who opens the book for the first time at its beginning will at once be struck by this, for Bede's preface reads like the preface to any modern work of scholarship. In it he listed his main informants and modestly expressed his indebtedness to them: the learned Abbot Albinus of Canterbury; the priest Nothelm who provided him with transcripts of documents from the papal archives; Bishop Daniel of Winchester who furnished him with materials relating to the history of the church in Wessex; and so on. These qualitites of care, honesty, and sobriety were maintained throughout the *History.* They assisted Bede to produce what is by any standards a work of remarkable technical accomplishment—an ordered, coherent, and readable account of the growth of the English church assembled with unobtrusive literary skill from scattered and fragmentary sources.

Bede's scholarship makes the *Ecclesiastical History* seem modern. This is deceptive. From what has already been said it should be clear that Bede's concerns were far removed from ours. It would be reasonable to expect that these concerns would be apparent in the *History* as they are in all Bede's other works. There is a passage in the preface that offers a clue to his motives and methods as a historian:

> If history relates good things of good men the hearer is touched, and incited to imitate that which is good. If it records evil things of wicked men, nevertheless, the religious and pious hearer or reader in shunning that which is hurtful or perverse is fired more earnestly to perform those things which he has learned to be good and worthy of God.

These words deserve careful consideration. They show that Bede had a didactic purpose. The *Ecclesiastical History* was meant to teach lessons. Furthermore, it would do so by dwelling on what Bede considered to be good. This implied a measure of selection. Men may be good but they cannot, theologically speaking, be perfect. To highlight their good qualities while playing down their imperfections is to be selective; to be discreet. Discretion was one of the keynotes of Bede's methods.

He was not always discreet. In the last year of his life he wrote a long letter to Egbert, who had recently been appointed to the see of York. In it he released all his pent-up anxieties about the shortcomings of the church in Northumbria, pointing to worldly bishops, bogus monasteries, and ignorant priests. Bede's *Letter to Egbert* is a document of the first importance for the understanding of the *Ecclesiastical History*. The abuses that he castigated so vehemently had sprung up, he believed, in the course of the previous thirty years, since the death of the godly King Aldfrith—a period about which he had had strikingly little to say in the last book of the *History* (a characteristic example of Bedan discretion). By contrast, the Northumbrian church of the seventh century had been free of them; at any rate, as Bede chose to present it. His portrait of St. Aidan in book III, chapter 5, is an instructive example of his method. As Bede offers him to us, Aidan was distinguished by every virtue that was lacking a century later. The reader is given a discreet pointer: Aidan's manner of life as a bishop was "different from the slothfulness of our own times"; but only the *Letter to Egbert* reveals Bede's candid views of what was going wrong.

There were, thus, lessons for the bishops of his own day embedded in the *Ecclesiastical History*—thickly strewn, indeed, on practically every page. There were also lessons for kings. The work was dedicated to King Ceolwulf. In it Bede's royal patron could find instruction in the duties of kingship and take comfort from the example of good kings in the past. Edwin both led his people to Christianity *and* enjoyed unprecedented power. Bede explicitly connected the two: "this king's sway on earth grew as a sign of his attaining the faith and the kingdom of heaven" (book II, chapter 9). Christian virtue was rewarded, vice punished. King Ecgfrith carried out an unprovoked attack on Ireland in 684; in the following year he was defeated and killed by the Picts "as a punishment for his sins" (book IV, chapter 26). The good end happily and the bad unhappily: this is the lesson that Bede taught.

It was a lesson that could only be taught effectively by some adjustment of the materials; another facet of discretion and selection. Very occasionally we have access to the written sources that Bede used, and by comparing them with his text we can see what he did with them. For example, in his account of the Irish monk Fursey who settled in East Anglia (book III, chapter 19) Bede tells us that he preached the gospel there. But his source, an independent biography of Fursey, does not say this: it simply tells us that Fursey founded a monastery. Why the discrepancy? Did Bede have access to additional information about Fursey's sojourn in East Anglia that enabled him to supplement his source? Or did he insert the phrase about preaching because he thought it the sort of work in which monks should engage? Are we being offered historical fact or a pastoral sermon? We cannot tell; but the questions remain disquieting.

Sometimes Bede omitted materials. His treatment of Wilfrid is particularly thought-provoking. Bede probably used the biography of Wilfrid composed by his chaplain Eddius. This has survived independently so that as in the case of Fursey we can compare Bede's text with his source. Eddius dwelt in admiring detail on Wilfrid's quarrels with successive Northumbrian kings and archbishops of Canterbury. Bede did his utmost to minimize conflict in his account of Wilfrid (mainly in book V, chapter 19) and to pour oil on the troubled waters of English ecclesiastical politics. Eddius gloried in his hero's might and state, his retinue of followers, and his ample treasure of gold, silver, and jewelry. Bede omits all mention of this. No reader of the *Ecclesiastical History* could guess that early Anglo-Saxon bishops had retinues and amassed treasure. But Bede was well aware that they did: the evidence is to be found in the *Letter to Egbert.*

One wonders how much else Bede chose not to record about the English church and its setting in the seventh and eighth centuries. He could have told us much about Anglo-Saxon paganism, but he offers us practically nothing. He has much to say about kings and bishops, curiously little about monasteries and absolutely nothing about the secular aristocracy. Yet the adhesion of the Anglo-Saxon aristocracy to Christianity and the growth of aristocratic piety, frequently expressed in monastic foundations, were important conditions for the Christianization of the English. He has much to say about English ecclesiastical contacts with Rome, little about such contacts with Frankish Gaul. Yet it is likely that these latter connections were close and that there were important resemblances between the Frankish and the Anglo-Saxon church.

The list of his silences could be prolonged. Those indicated here are sufficient additional evidence to show that Bede's *Ecclesiastical History* is not a straightforward work—for all its appearance of simplicity and for all its charm. In the words of a leading modern scholar, "The task Bede set himself was not to describe the history of the English church just as it had happened. It was to describe it in such a way as to illustrate and support the principles of faith and conduct in which he believed."

Perhaps no work of history that has ever been written is quite straightforward. Bede's *Ecclesiastical History* was a work of dense texture and subtle design, obedient to conventions of historiography very different from those to which we are accustomed, and moved by purposes and anxieties that lie concealed beneath its tranquil surface. It is a great work of art.

Bede's influence cannot be exaggerated. The *Ecclesiastical History* was quickly recognized as a work of outstanding merit and authority. Through the agency of the English missions to Germany under Boniface and Lul, and by means of émigré scholars such as Alcuin, the corpus of Bede's works was rapidly diffused on the Continent. King Offa of Mercia possessed a copy of the *History*. In the reign of King Alfred it was translated into Old English. It has since been translated into many other languages; most recently, into Japanese. In two directions Bede's *History* has been enormously influential. Living in an age of warring tribal kingdoms, he was the first Englishman to commit to writing the idea that the English were all one people. English unity, which we accept as part of the natural order of things, was for many centuries not a foregone conclusion. It owes more to Bede than to any other single agent. In the second place, Bede has permanently colored our vision of early Anglo-Saxon history. By his uncanny narrative power, above all by adopting the *tone* that he did, he launched an image of the early English past that has proved a major constituent of national mythology, especially in the era of the Reformation and in the Victorian age. His influence is still pervasive, as is most justly due. Bede was not simply the most remarkable intellect of the period of astonishing creativity with which the English responded to their conversion. He is one of the brightest stars in the whole firmament of western civilization. Those who value that civilization neglect Bede at their peril.

Bede's *Ecclesiastical History* is most easily accessible in translation in the Penguin Classics series, but the translation is something less than completely reliable. The most convenient collection of translated texts is that of J. Campbell, *Bede,* 1968, which includes the *Life of St. Cuthbert,* the *History of the Abbots,* and the *Letter to Egbert,* as well as the *Ecclesiastical History;* the whole prefaced by a first-rate introduction. For serious study of Bede the commentary by C. Plummer that accompanied his edition of the Latin text, 1896, and many reprints, is indispensable: although now nearly a century old it has never been bettered. G. Bonner (ed.), *Famulus Christi*, 1976, contains a collection of papers delivered at a conference held in Durham in 1973 to celebrate the thirteenth centenary of Bede's birth: it provides a good conspectus of modern Bedan scholarship.

ALBINUS (*d.* 732?) was abbot of Canterbury and a friend of Bede. He was an English pupil of Abbot Hadrian whom he succeeded as abbot of St. Peter and St. Paul (later St. Augustine) at Canterbury in 709 or 710. Bede, who described him as "very learned," recorded in the preface that it was chiefly through the urging of Albinus that he had undertaken to compose his *Ecclesiastical History of the English People*. We know from a surviving letter of Bede's that he sent a copy of the work to Albinus soon after its completion in 731—important evidence for the early circulation of the *History* in southern England.

NOTHELM (*d.* 739) was archbishop of Canterbury from 735 until 739. While he was a priest in London Nothelm was employed by Albinus of Canterbury to convey to Bede information about the early history of the church in Kent. Afterward Nothelm visited Rome, probably between 715 and 725, and transcribed letters from the papal archives, which also he took to Bede for use in the preparation of the *Ecclesiastical History*. Bede recorded his gratitude to Nothelm in the preface. In 735 Nothelm was consecrated archbishop of Canterbury. Little is known of his brief archiepiscopate. He visited Rome again in 736. He held a church council, probably in 737. Boniface, leader of the English mission to Germany, corresponded with him. He is remembered chiefly for the assistance he rendered to Bede.

EGBERT OF IONA (639–729), monk and bishop, was a Northumbrian who lived a life of "pilgrimage" in exile from his native land but yet exerted great influence there. As a young man he went to Ireland to study—like his friend Chad and many others—and it was there during a visitation of plague, probably in 664, that he took a vow never to return to his homeland but to live a life of self-imposed exile, the better to dedicate himself to the service of God. This did not mean living as a recluse. Egbert was an extremely influential man. We glimpse him vainly trying to dissuade King Ecgfrith of Northumbria from his attack on Ireland in 684; attending an important Irish church council at Birr in 697; advising on the establishment of a Northumbrian monastery early in the eighth century; and—what earned him the special approbation of Bede—converting the monks of Iona to the Catholic observance of Easter in 716 and entering their community for the remainder of his very long life. Another of his initiatives was to be of the utmost significance. Bede tells us that in about 687 Egbert formed the plan of leaving Ireland in order to go as a missionary to the heathen peoples of Germany. In the event, he was prevented by a vision from undertaking this task, but he communicated the impulse to his pupils. Among these, Willibrord was the most outstanding. Egbert's influence lies behind the astonishing activities of English churchmen in eighth-century Germany.

ST. WILLIBRORD (658–739) was a Northumbrian monk who became a missionary to Frisia and archbishop of Utrecht. He was educated under Wilfrid at Ripon, where he became a monk. In 677–78 he went to Ireland, where he remained for twelve years as a pupil of the Northumbrian exile Egbert. It was from Wilfrid and Egbert that he derived his vocation to work on the Continent as a missionary. In 690, accompanied by eleven companions, he crossed to the mouth of the Rhine to begin preaching Christianity to the pagan Frisians. For this he needed the support of the secular authorities and turned to Pippin II, who was at that time the effective ruler, though not actually king, of the Franks. Frankish authority was being pushed gradually eastward into Frisia and it is likely that Pippin saw Willibrord and his fellows as a potential adjunct of Frankish dominion. He willingly extended his protection to them. Willibrord took a further initiative that was to be very important for the future of the Frankish church. As might have been expected from a disciple of Wilfrid, he turned to Rome and obtained the sanction and encouragement of Pope Sergius I for the work he was intent on. A few years later, in 695, Willibrord paid a second visit to Rome at the insistence of Pippin, on which occasion Sergius consecrated him archbishop of the Frisians. When he returned Pippin established him at Utrecht as his base of operations. It was Pippin and his family, again, who were the very generous patrons who helped

Willibrord to establish a monastery farther south, at Echternach in modern Luxembourg.

We know little in detail about the work that Willibrord accomplished during the long remainder of his life. Any correspondence that he kept—so illuminating in the case of his slightly younger contemporary Boniface—has not survived, and the biography composed about a generation after his death by his kinsman Alcuin is not very revealing about his missionary achievements. Bede, who was keenly interested in his work, tells us that Willibrord consecrated bishops, but we know nothing of them. Presumably Willibrord envisaged an ecclesiastical province based on Utrecht something along the lines of the province of Canterbury created by Augustine and Theodore. Whatever structure of ecclesiastical administration may have been set up, it did not long survive its founder: Utrecht was subsequently absorbed into the province of Cologne. However, the work of converting the Frisians did proceed, if slowly: much had been achieved, but much still remained to be done, by the time of Willibrord's death in 739.

It would seem that Willibrord had plans to extend his work beyond the mission field of Frisia. Echternach looks like a base for expansion into Thuringia and Hesse, the regions of central Germany south of Frisia where Boniface was to build on Willibrord's foundations in the 720s and 730s. Willibrord even tried to preach Christianity to the Danes, though with very little success.

The English missions to the Continent, which were to have such momentous consequences for the development of European civilization, began remarkably quickly after the conversion of the English themselves. The last pagan kingdom of Anglo-Saxon England, the Isle of Wight, was nominally converted only three years before Willibrord set off for Frisia. Why were the English so eager to undertake missionary work abroad? There are several possible answers to this question. The Christian culture into which the English were growing was influenced by the evangelizing concerns of Pope Gregory I and by the ideal of "pilgrimage for Christ" which, as in the case of Columba, merged imperceptibly into a missionary impulse. The two strands met in Wilfrid and Egbert, among others, and their pupil Willibrord. The Anglo-Saxons were conscious of the Germanic homeland from which they had once come and the more thoughtful churchmen among them felt a responsibility for the salvation of those who were, as Boniface put it in 738, "of one blood and bone with us." With Frisia in particular their connections were close. Frisians had settled in parts of eastern England. Anglo-Frisian trading connections of an intensity that we would not suspect from our few written references to them have been revealed by recent archaeological excavation. Above all, the Old English language of the seventh and eighth centuries was very close to the tongue of the Frisians: Anglo-Saxon missionaries were more intelligible to the Frisians than any others might have been.

The Frisians were gradually being conquered by the Franks. Frankish rulers such as Pippin II and his son Charles Martel perceived that missionaries who were not Franks would be more acceptable to the subjugated peoples than those that were. This circumstance could present the missionaries with painful moral dilemmas. Boniface certainly felt them, as we know from his letters, and it is fair to suppose that Willibrord did too. It has always been a source of anxiety for Christian missionaries associated with an expanding imperial power. Exactly how intimate were these links with the Franks it is hard to say. Pippin and Charles Martel may have looked on Willibrord as in some sense "their" man. But he may not have perceived the relationship in quite the same terms.

The problem thickens if we try to be aware of other missionaries, contemporaries of Willibrord's, in other regions of the Frankish eastern marches. A patriotic tendency in English historiography has focused attention too exclusively, if understandably, upon the Anglo-Saxon contribution to the conversion of Germany. There were other men at work, Irish, Aquitanian, Italian, Spanish, all of them to a greater or lesser degree dependent upon Frankish secular authority. Other men faced moral dilemmas, found different solutions to them. None of them, including Willibrord, was simply and cynically "used" by Frankish power. The German mission field was both active and diverse in the eighth century. To emphasize this is not to belittle Willibrord's achievement. He was a big man. So was Boniface. Between them they exerted a more far-reaching influence upon European culture than any other Englishmen who have ever lived.

W. Levison, *England and the Continent in the Eighth Century,* 1946, remains the best account in English of Willibrord.

ACCA (*d.* 740) was Bishop of Hexham from 709 to 731. A native of Northumbria, Acca spent much of his early life in the following of Wilfrid, whom he accompanied to Rome in 705. On his deathbed in 709 Wilfrid nominated Acca to the bishopric of Hexham, which he held until 731 when he was driven out in circumstances that remain obscure. Acca was an important patron of the arts. He embellished the church of Hexham, developed the skills of church music and singing, persuaded Eddius to compose his biography of Wilfrid, and encouraged Bede in his work of biblical commentary. Bede always referred to Acca in the warmest terms and dedicated nine of his commentaries to him. A writer of the eleventh century informs us that Acca's grave outside the church at Hexham was marked by "two stone crosses adorned with exquisite carvings." Considerable remains of these crosses survive and may be seen today in Hexham Abbey. They are important monuments to the art-historian because—unlike much Anglo-Saxon sculpture—they can be dated with reasonable accuracy. They are remarkably accomplished works of art in the school of Northumbrian stone sculpture, which has left us such masterpieces as the crosses of Ruthwell and Bewcastle.

D. P. Kirby (ed.), *Saint Wilfrid at Hexham,* 1974, contains material on Acca as well as Wilfrid.

CEOLWULF (*d.* 764) was king of Northumbria from 729 to 737. He is remembered chiefly as the ruler to whom Bede dedicated his most famous work, the *Ecclesiastical History,* on its completion in 731. Ceolwulf was a patron of learning, and it is just possible that like his predecessor King Aldfrith he had been educated in Ireland. His reign was a troubled one. In 731 he was deposed in circumstances of which we know nothing, but restored to power. In 737 he resigned his kingdom to become a monk at Lindisfarne, where he died in 764. He was a generous benefactor to the monks of Lindisfarne. It was later believed that their royal inmate brought about a relaxation of their monastic rule, permitting them to drink wine and beer in addition to the milk and water prescribed by their founder Aidan. If there is any truth in this story, it is all of a piece with other evidence for the gradual secularization of monastic life in eighth-century England.

ST. FRIDESWIDE (7th–8th century?) was a monastic foundress, later to be adopted as its patron saint by the University of Oxford. Frideswide is a very obscure figure indeed. Her name is recorded in only two documents of the Anglo-Saxon period. The first of these is a list known as "The resting-place of the saints," which tells us that Frideswide's remains rested at Oxford. The list in the form in which we have it dates from about 1030, but it probably derives from an original of some two centuries earlier. The second is a charter of King Ethelred II, dated 1004, which confirms the possessions of "a certain monastery, situated in the town which is called Oxford, where the body of the blessed Frideswide rests." There is plenty of later, post-Conquest legend, but its historical value is at best very slight. Most scholars would agree that Frideswide existed, and that she probably lived somewhere in the century between *c.* 650 and *c.* 750. The monastic house that she founded at Oxford was very probably a double house for men and women like Hilda's at Whitby and many others. Frideswide is further testimony to the importance of women in the monastic life of early Anglo-Saxon England. She may also serve to remind us of the fragility of our knowledge of early English monasticism. If our evidence relating to Frideswide and her monastery is so meager, late, and vague, we may be quite certain that there were very many founders of monasteries in England during this period of whom we shall never know anything at all.

DANIEL (*d.* 745) was bishop of Winchester from 705 to 744. What little we know of Daniel's long episcopate is typical of our patchy knowledge of early medieval bishops who found no contemporary biographer. We hear of his learning, attendance at church councils, journey to Rome in 721, contacts with the royal court, and so forth. Two features of Daniel's career render him a little clearer to us: his friendship with Boniface and his connections with Bede. To take the latter first, Bede tells us that Daniel was his principal informant on the history of the church in Wessex, and it is possible to trace in the *Ecclesiastical History* the information that must have come to Bede from him. Most surprisingly, Daniel seems never to have mentioned Boniface to Bede. (Bede was so interested in missions that it is inconceivable that he should not have at least referred to Boniface, had he known of him.) Daniel was Boniface's patron, perhaps one of his teachers. The two men corresponded during Boniface's prolonged absence as a missionary in Germany. In particular it was Daniel who in about 724 advised Boniface on the tactics he should adopt in presenting Christianity to the heathen: a letter of cardinal interest for the understanding of medieval missionary activity. Boniface's last surviving letter to Daniel (from 742–44) reveals that the elderly bishop had gone blind. It was doubtless for this reason that he resigned his see in 744 and retired, possibly to Malmesbury, about a year before his death.

ST. BONIFACE (*c.* 675–754) was a native of Wessex, a monk who became a missionary to Germany and ended up as archbishop of Mainz. Boniface's original name was Wynfrith. He adopted the name of an early Christian martyr, Boniface, on papal bidding in 719; rather as Biscop had adopted the name Benedict, or Willibrord the name Clement. His family came from the western part of Wessex; Crediton was later reputed to have been his birthplace. At an early age he entered a monastery at Exeter, and later moved to another at Nursling near Southampton. He led an exemplary life as a monk and achieved fame as a teacher of grammar and expounder of scripture. A short grammatical treatise composed by him has survived; this, and his letters, show stylistic affinities with the writings of Aldhelm. (Boniface is not known to have been taught by Aldhelm, but his abbot at Nursling, Winbert, was a correspondent and had perhaps been a pupil of Aldhelm.) At some point early in the eighth century Boniface was sent by King Ine of Wessex on an important diplomatic mission into Kent. A promising ecclesiastical career seemed to be opening before him. On the death of Winbert he was elected abbot of Nursling, but declined the office. We should not be surprised were we to learn that he was spoken of as a potential successor to, say, his friend Daniel in the bishopric of Winchester.

But this did not happen. Instead, at about the age of forty, Boniface embarked on a new career as a missionary. How the impulse arose we can only guess. It may have been implanted at an early age. It may have owed something to contacts and observations made while he was a monk. Nursling, at the head of Southampton Water, was close to the busy port of *Hamwih,* beneath the modern Southampton, and from the Frisian merchants who frequented it Boniface could have learned of Willibrord's missionary work in Frisia. Only a few hours' sailing distance from Nursling were the monasteries of Bosham and Selsey: Boniface could have been touched by the Irish ideal of "pilgrimage for Christ" through the influence of Dicuil, the Irish founder of Bosham; he could have learned from the monks of Selsey of the missionary exploits of their founder Wilfrid. For whatever reason, Boniface determined to work in Frisia. He crossed the Channel in 716. But the Frisians were rebelling at that time against Frankish dominion, the region was in turmoil, and no missionary work could be accomplished. So Boniface returned to England.

In 718 he tried again. On this occasion his tactics were different. Armed with a letter of introduction from Bishop Daniel, he left England once more—for the last time, though he could not have known this—and headed straight for Rome, as Willibrord had done in the 690s. In May 719 he received a commission from Pope Gregory II to preach to the heathen; it was on this occasion that he received the Christian name Boniface. He returned north and after a brief stay in Thuringia joined Willibrord with whom he worked closely over the next three years (719–22) in the reestablishment of the church in Frisia after the recent disturbances. Willibrord, now in his early sixties, wanted Boniface to succeed him at Utrecht. But Boniface had other ambitions. He left Frisia and travelled inland to Hesse. Then he revisited Rome, where he was consecrated a bishop in November 722 and given a papal commission, framed in extraordinarily wide terms, to preach "in the regions of Germany east of the river Rhine." On his return to the north Boniface paid a visit to the Frankish court and received the formal protection of the Frankish ruler Charles Martel in 723. Thus equipped, he set out across the Rhine to embark on work that would occupy him for nearly the next twenty years.

Hesse and later Thuringia were the regions of Boniface's mission; that is, roughly speaking, the area today enclosed within the triangle formed by Frankfurt and Kassel in West Germany and Erfurt in East Germany. At that time this was not a wholly pagan area, as, for example, was Saxony to the northeast. Christian communities existed here and there, as they did in Willibrord's Frisia and as they did farther south in Alemannia and Bavaria where other missionaries were active. Boniface's task was to extirpate the surviving pockets of paganism and to strengthen Christianity by providing leadership, teaching, organization, and routine. We know something, though not a great deal, of how he set about it. There were occasional spectacular—and courageous—acts of Christian assertion, such as felling of an oak sacred to the god Woden at Geismar. But for the most part it was more humdrum work. Boniface argued with the stubborn, perhaps along the lines suggested by Daniel of Winchester in a famous letter. He preached Christian faith and morals to the ignorant. He founded mission churches, as at Fritzlar (where the earliest chapel was built of the timber of the Geismar oak), Amöneburg, Ohrdruf, Kitzingen, and elsewhere. Whenever he could he staffed them with Benedictine monks and nuns, often of English origin; as, for instance, Wigbert, abbot of Fritzlar, or Leoba, a relative of Boniface, who became abbess of Tauberbischofsheim in Franconia. Again and again he turned to his friends in England for advice, prayers, recruits, and books. Can Archbishop Nothelm advise him on the canon law of marriage? Can Abbess Eadburga of Minster-in-Thanet have the Epistles of St. Peter written for him in letters of gold?—showy books impress the ignorant, and (he hastily adds) he will pay for the gold himself. Can Archbishop Egbert supply him with any of the works of Bede? Boniface also recruited locally. Gregory, a young Frankish aristocrat from near Trier, was one of his earliest recruits and later became bishop of Utrecht. Liudger, a Frisin, was another disciple, who later became the first bishop of Münster. Boniface referred difficult issues to the papacy. May Christians eat food previously offered to idols, even though it has been purified by the sign of the cross? No, replied Gregory II when this was put to him in 726. What should Boniface do about Christians who sell their slaves for ritual sacrifice by pagans? he asked in 732. Let the guilty do penance as for homicide, replied Gregory III.

Boniface's relations with Rome grew ever closer. In 732 he was raised to the rank of archbishop. In 738 he paid a third visit to Rome. In 739 it was as a papal representative that Boniface reorganized the Bavarian church, rather as Theodore had reorganized the English in the 670s, by setting up bishoprics at Passau, Regensburg, Salzburg, and Freising. Shortly after that, in 741–42, he founded new bishoprics in the Hesse-Thuringia-Franconia region, at Buraburg, Würzburg and Eichstätt. All of them went to his Anglo-Saxon disciples, the last-named to the much-travelled Willibald.

In certain quarters these actions were regarded as provocative. To the Frankish bishops of the Rhineland, Boniface was an interloper who was poaching on their territory and carving out a huge

ecclesiastical empire in which nearly all the top posts were re-
served for his countrymen. For his part, Boniface never troubled
to conceal his contempt for these bishops. They were ignorant and
slothful, living easy aristocratic lives in which boozing occupied the
time that was not given over to the pursuit of game or girls, un-
mindful of their responsibilities and unfitted to be bishops. (The
picture was overdrawn. A few were like this, there can be no doubt.
But the Frankish hierarchy as a whole was a good deal more respectable than Boniface wished to believe.) Tension between the
two sides was in evidence from the beginning of Boniface's mission
in 723. It came out into the open after the death of Charles Martel
in 741. Boniface, like Willibrord, was always uncomfortably aware
that his work depended for its success in large part upon the protection of Frankish secular power. The bishops may have hoped
that in the confused political circumstances following Charles's
death they might move against Boniface and his henchmen. If so,
they miscalculated badly.

The Frankish kingdom was divided between Charles Martel's
sons, to Carloman going the eastern half (Austrasia) and to Pippin
III the western half (Neustria). Carloman was more sympathetic to
Boniface's ecclesiastical ideals than his father had been. Boniface
was swift to take advantage of this. It was at his prompting, and
with papal encouragement, that Carloman convened councils in
742, 743, and 744 that issued comprehensive decrees of reforming
legislation designed to root out abuses in the Austrasian church.
Neustria followed suit: Pippin presided over similar councils in
744, 745, and 747. (And there were repercussions elsewhere. It was
partly at the instance of Boniface that Archbishop Cuthbert of
Canterbury and King Ethelbald of Mercia called a reforming council in England in 747.) The effects of these gatherings were far-
reaching. Boniface did not, as is sometimes said, "reform the
Frankish church": the task was beyond even him. But he did ensure that standards of disciplinary excellence were proclaimed,
with the sanction of the most formidable authorities to back them
up—the Frankish rulers and the pope. Boniface set in motion the
transformation of the church in Francia, which was to bear fruit in
the achievements of the succeeding age that we fittingly call the
era of "the Carolingian Renaissance."

The reforming councils of 742–47 drew Boniface still closer to
the ruling dynasty. In 744 he founded a monastery at Fulda on

land granted to him by Carloman. It was a community specially favored by Boniface who may from the first have envisaged it—and we should bear in mind that he was by now about seventy—as his final resting place. It was in about 746 that Carloman's influence settled him—for so long an archbishop without a seat—in the see of Mainz. After Carloman's resignation of power in 747 he was succeeded in Austrasia by his brother Pippin of Neustria. Four years later Pippin displaced the last representative of the long powerless Merovingian dynasty and was proclaimed king of the Franks. It was later believed that Boniface had anointed him to his new dignity. He may have done; the matter has been endlessly and inconclusively debated by historians, but it is unlikely that Boniface had no part in the debates that preceded the inauguration of the new dynasty.

In 753 Boniface resigned the see of Mainz into the hands of his disciple Lul and returned to the Frisian mission field. It was while working in the extreme northeast of Frisia, near the modern Dokkum in the north of Holland, that Boniface was attacked by pirates. He and fifty-three companions were killed there on 5 June 754. It is recorded that the elderly missionary held up a book to parry the blows of his assailant. That book, its margins scored by several violent sword-cuts, is still preserved at Fulda, whither the body of the martyr himself was borne and laid to rest by his disciples.

Boniface is accessible to us as no earlier Englishman is, above all through his correspondence, which was edited by Lul not long after his death. (As always it is sobering to reflect on the degree to which our assessment of him is conditioned by the nature of the evidence. A comparison with Wilfrid is not inapposite. Wilfrid might look very different had the letters that he must have written and received come down to us. By the same token Boniface might look very different had he found a biographer as robustly partisan as Wilfrid's biographer Eddius, rather than Willibald—not to be confused with the Bishop of Eichstätt—who composed a singularly discreet and unrevealing life of Boniface within fourteen years of his subject's death.) The letters shed light on many, though not all recesses of his complex personality: his energy, his imperiousness, his administrative talents; his urgent desire to save souls and his strong allegiance to Roman order in the church; his gift for friendship, particularly with women. What most strikes the reader accustomed to think of him, and rightly, as a man of titanic achievement, however, is the pervasive tone of anxiety in the letters. He longed to convert the Saxons, but hardly ever got near them and felt a sense of failure. He was uneasy about his relationship with Frankish secular authority, recognizing his dependence upon it but apprehensive of the dangers of too close a connection between missionary Christianity and Frankish political expansion. His dealings with the negligent Frankish bishops were marked by heart-searching as well as irritation and frustration. He was worried about what would happen to his fellow-workers after his death. He was anxious above all about whether he had discharged his responsibilities to God, burdens which, whatever *we* may think, he felt himself pathetically inadequate to shoulder. There he is, caught in the beam of his letters: human, anguished, and lonely; a very great man.

C. H. Talbot, *The Anglo-Saxon Missionaries in Germany*, 1954, contains translations of Willibald's biography and of generous selections from Boniface's letters. For an introduction to the Frankish background, E. James, *The Origins of France*, 1982, is excellent. T. Reuter (ed.), *The Greatest Englishman*, 1980, is an attractive collection of essays, and there is a fine chapter on Boniface in J. M. Wallace-Hadrill, *The Frankish Church*, 1983.

EGBERT (*d.* 766) was archbishop of York from 735 until 766. He was the brother of King Eadbert of Northumbria (737–58). Of his early life we know little: like Bede, he had been placed in a monastery (we do not know which one) as a child; at some stage he paid a visit to Rome where he was ordained deacon. In 732 he was promoted to the see of York on the resignation of Bishop Wilfrid II (who is not to be confused with his namesake St. Wilfrid, who died in 709).

In terms of ecclesiastical politics Egbert's most important achievement was to persuade the pope to raise the see of York to archiepiscopal status in 735. Paulinus had been an archbishop, but all the succeeding incumbents of York had been bishops and therefore in theory subject to the authority of Canterbury. Egbert's initiative was in line with the plans laid down for the organization of the English church by Pope Gregory I in 601. To the extent that his new dignity diminished Canterbury's power, we may surmise that it was not won without a struggle; but we know nothing of the negotiations that led up to it. Canterbury and York were to wrangle over issues of dignity, precedence, jurisdiction, and so forth for several centuries to come.

Egbert may have been prompted to take this step by several people. Among them was certainly Bede. In a famous letter addressed to Egbert in 734 Bede had reminded him of Pope Gregory's plan. But Bede's letter was occasioned by considerations much wider than the matter of the ecclesiastical rank of the pontiff of York. Bede looked to Egbert to reform a number of abuses in the church of Northumbria that had taken root in the thirty years following the death of King Aldfrith in 705. Bishops were too few, and too lax about performing their pastoral duties. Many pseudomonasteries had been founded by aristocratic families as a form of tax-evasion (because their landed endowments were exempted from rendering services to the king). There were not enough priests, and those that existed were ignorant. The laity, in consequence, were not receiving Christian instruction. Bede's letter was a comprehensive and perceptive indictment of the Northumbrian church's shortcomings, and there is some reason to suppose that it was an accurate diagnosis.

Did Egbert act on Bede's advice? It is very hard to tell. Certainly he was regarded by contemporaries such as Boniface as a churchman of high principles. The same impression emerges from his writings, which comprise a *Penitential* that owes something to Theodore's and the *Dialogue,* an exposition of certain points of ecclesiastical discipline in question-and-answer form. But of the degree to which Egbert succeeded in translating precept into practice it is hard to judge: we do not possess the evidence. If he tried to increase the number of bishoprics in Northumbria, he did not succeed; though we should remember that neither did any of his successors until the nineteenth century, barring only the twelfth-century creation of the see of Carlisle. Egbert may have attempted to extirpate the bogus monasteries to which Bede had directed his attention; but to argue this is to rest much on a single papal letter of 757–58, the correct interpretation of which is by no means clear. Egbert may have held synods on at least a semiregular basis, and these together with the *Penitential* might suggest an active concern for the discipline and activities of the lower clergy; but the priesthood of eighth-century Northumbria remains as elusive to the historian as does the priesthood of every part of Christendom in any century before the thirteenth.

The one achievement of Egbert's—and a very considerable one—that we *can* identify is his creative patronage of the school of York. During his archiepiscopate and owing to his encouragement it became under the direction of Albert, Egbert's kinsman and successor as archbishop, the most distinguished center of learning in western Europe. Alcuin, its most famous pupil, commemorated it in his poem on *The Bishops, Kings, and Saints of York* composed in about 792. Alcuin held Egbert in high regard. In his days the "happy times" that Northumbria enjoyed sprang from "the harmonious rule" of the two royal brothers, Eadbert and Egbert, king and archbishop. The Northumbrian coinage on which the names of both men sometimes appeared symbolized this concord and was perhaps intended to project precisely this image. For Alcuin, Egbert was all that a good archbishop should be: of princely rank and wealth; generous to the poor; an embellisher of churches; majestic, dignified, and just. Whether or not he lived up to Bede's exacting standards, he was what the best minds of the eighth century wanted their prelates to be.

P. Godman has edited and translated Alcuin's poem on *The Bishops, Kings, and Saints of York*, 1982.

EADBERT (*d.* 768) was king of Northumbria from 737 to 758. He was the first cousin of King Ceolwulf whom he succeeded in 737, and the brother of Archbishop Egbert of York. We know as little of the course of his reign in detail as we do of that of his contemporary, Ethelbald of Mercia, but enough to show that he was a powerful and effective ruler. He held his own against Mercians and Picts and, as Alcuin recorded, "extended the bounds of his kingdom, often subduing the enemy ranks with terror." Alcuin was probably thinking of Eadbert's wars against the British kingdom of Strathclyde, which brought the region of Kyle (roughly speaking, Ayrshire) under Northumbrian control in 750. "Those were happy times for the people of Northumbria," wrote Alcuin nostalgically in the conspicuously unhappy times of the 790s.

Although some earlier Northumbrian kings had issued coinage, Eadbert was the first one to do so on any scale. This is one indication of the prosperity of Eadbert's days. There were others.

Patrons who were wealthy as well as discriminating are implied by the dissemination of the works of Bede, the growth of the school of York, and the productions of the Hexham school of sculpture. The unknown Oshere, presumably a Northumbrian nobleman, whose magnificent helmet was excavated at York in 1982, was evidently a rich man who could command the services of skilled craftsmen. The unidentified monastery whose eighth-century abbots were celebrated in Latin verse by a certain Ethelwulf was clearly very well off: its Abbot Sigbald (*d.* 771) built a church there to which he gave a lead roof, a golden chalice set with precious stones, and an altar decorated with sculpture in relief. There may have been many other religious houses like it of which we know nothing. Northumbria in the eighth century was rich. It was this more than anything else that was to attract Viking raiders from the 790s onward.

Northumbria was also, by that time, vulnerable for political reasons. Eadbert himself, like all eighth-century rulers, had had to face opposition. A son of King Aldfrith, named Offa, had been dragged from sanctuary at the shrine of St. Cuthbert on Lindisfarne and butchered, presumably because he had contended for the throne. After Eadbert's retirement to a monastery in 758, where he died ten years later, Northumbrian politics became seriously unstable, with Eadbert's son and grandson both meeting violent ends, and successive members of two other leading aristocratic families contending for the kingship. Such dynastic feuds were not uncommon: Wessex seems also to have experienced them at much the same time. They were debilitating. The coinage collapsed in the last quarter of the century, Northumbrian culture began to lose its luster, and the Viking raids began. Alcuin was right: never again was the kingdom of Northumbria to enjoy the prestige that had been hers in the spacious days of King Eadbert.

CUTHBERT (*d.* 758) was archbishop of Canterbury from 740 to his death in 758. It is likely that he had been bishop of Hereford (736–40) before his promotion to Canterbury—probable therefore that he was of Mercian origin, his advancement to the headship of the English church reflecting the southern English overlordship of King Ethelbald of Mercia. (Cuthbert's two predecessors at Canterbury, Tatwine and Nothelm, had also been Mercians.) Cuthbert was a man of some learning. He composed Latin verse and a chance reference in a letter among the correspondence of Lul shows that he had borrowed a copy of the fourth-century Christian poet Optatianus Porfyrius from Bishop Milred of Worcester. At Canterbury he built a new church, dedicated to St. John the Baptist, immediately to the east of his cathedral: it served as baptistery, courtroom (ordeals were held there), library, archive, and most importantly, mausoleum for the archbishops; Cuthbert himself and nearly all subsequent Anglo-Saxon archbishops of Canterbury were buried there. The provision of a separate church as a baptistery, unique in Anglo-Saxon architectural history, may reflect continental models that Cuthbert had seen when he journeyed to Rome for his pallium in 741.

Cuthbert maintained the links between the church of Canterbury and the Anglo-Saxon missionaries in Germany. He corresponded with Boniface, and there survives a long letter of condolence upon Boniface's death, which Cuthbert wrote to his successor Lul. Cuthbert's most important achievement owed something to the prompting of Boniface. This was the holding of a church council at *Clovesho* (in line with the precepts of Archbishop Theodore) in 747, attended by all the bishops of the province of Canterbury. Shortly beforehand Boniface had written to Cuthbert informing him of decrees recently issued for the reform of the Frankish church and pointing to certain abuses in the English church. The message was plain. The decrees passed at *Clovesho* in 747 were intended to remedy the shortcomings identified by Boniface. But it would be unwary to assume that Boniface was the only begetter of Cuthbert's council. Reform was in the air. The letter of Bede to Archbishop Egbert of York in 734 had made the same sort of criticisms. To give but one example: clerical drunkenness, condemned by the council in its twenty-first decree, had been singled out as an abuse among the English clergy both by Bede and by Boniface.

The decrees passed in 747 laid down comprehensive guidelines for the pastoral organization of the English church. They testify to the high-minded seriousness with which Archbishop Cuthbert and his fellow-bishops approached their task. To what extent precept was translated into practice is difficult, for lack of evidence, to assess, save in one very important instance. King Ethelbald of Mercia attended the council. Some of its decrees were directed, though not explicitly, against his exploitation of the church. Two years later he made a number of concessions in response to ecclesiastical criticism. It is not fanciful to detect in this the influence of Archbishop Cuthbert.

N. Brooks, *The Early History of the Church of Canterbury,* 1984.

CUTHBERT (*fl. c.* 718–64) was abbot of Wearmouth and Jarrow in the middle years of the eighth century. Cuthbert entered the monastery in 718. He was a pupil of Bede, whose deathbed in 735 he movingly described in a letter to his friend Cuthwine. The dates of his abbacy are not known exactly: he may have become abbot between 747 and 753; he was still living in 764. Cuthbert was a correspondent of Lul, the successor to Boniface in the see of Mainz. Boniface's "discovery" of Bede's works seems to have occurred in the early 740s, and this was followed by repeated requests from the Anglo-Saxon missionaries in Germany for copies of them. This was to result in the rapid dissemination of Bede's works in the intellectual centers of the Frankish kingdom. It placed heavy demands on the scribal resources of Wearmouth and Jarrow. In one letter of 764 Cuthbert apologized to Lul for not sending more books over to Germany; the recent winter had been so cold that the scribes had not been able to get much writing done. It is a revealing glimpse of the physical discomforts that lie behind the masterpieces of calligraphic elegance that have come down to us from eighth-century England.

Cuthbert's letter on the death of Bede is translated in B. Colgrave and R. A. B. Mynors (eds.), *Bede's Ecclesiastical History of the English People,* 1969. E. A. Lowe, *English Uncial,* 1960, contains superb plates illustrating one particularly handsome type of script.

ETHELBALD (*d.* 757), the grandson of a brother of King Penda, ruled as king of Mercia from 716 until 757. Like many members of Anglo-Saxon princely families he spent much of his youth and early manhood in exile; it was during this period that he had some dealings with the hermit Guthlac. On the death of his rival King Ceolred in 716, Ethelbald managed to take power in Mercia.

   The Mercian kings of the seventh century, Penda (632–55) and his sons Wulfhere (657–74) and Ethelred (674–704), had been powerful rulers who had challenged the Northumbrian hegemony exercised by such kings as Oswald and Oswy. In the early eighth century the most prominent rulers of southern England were the kings of Wessex and Kent, respectively Ine and Wihtred. Ethelbald was able to profit from their deaths in 725–26 to establish Mercian overlordship over all the English kingdoms south of the Humber. We have the testimony of Bede that he had achieved this by the year 731. He maintained this Mercian ascendancy for the rest of his long reign. The signs of it may be read in diverse pieces of evidence. Ethelbald could dispose of land in the West Saxon shires of Somerset and Wiltshire. It is not coincidental that during his reign three successive archbishops of Canterbury were of Mercian origin—Tatwine, Nothelm, and Cuthbert. It was perhaps in his time that London and Middlesex passed definitively under Mercian control. In his charters Ethelbald could be styled "king not only of the Mercians but also of all the provinces which are called by the general name South English" and his name could be subscribed *Rex Britanniae*, "King of Britain."

The language of charters may not convey much about the political realities of the eighth century; or it may. The question has long been a focus for academic debate. What is certain is that Ethelbald succeeded in maintaining his overlordship for a longer period than any previous Southumbrian king. How did he do it? Partly, of course, by force: like any other early Anglo-Saxon ruler Ethelbald had to fight hard to maintain his superiority. There were rebellions against him by King Cuthred of Wessex (740–56). There were hostilities with King Eadbert of Northumbria and with the Britons of Wales.

Weight must also be given to the accumulating evidence for Mercia's wealth. The charters speak to us of tolls and toll-collectors, and allow us glimpses of a thriving salt industry at Droitwich in Worcestershire. Numismatists point to a large volume of coin in circulation, archaeologists to the evidence for urban growth. This economic superstructure—from which it would appear that the king could profit handsomely—must have been underpinned by a solid agrarian base, a thickly settled and efficiently exploited countryside. Wealthy kings were powerful kings: they could attract the best craftsmen and the best warriors into their retinues. We have here one explanation for Ethelbald's success. Another might lie, though this is a much more shadowy matter, in the development in

Mercia of what might grandiosely be called governmental institutions. It is not impossible that Ethelbald was responsible for some large-scale public works such as the fortification of Hereford and the building of the earthwork known as Wat's Dyke; the latter runs for nearly forty miles from the estuary of the river Dee in Flintshire south to the Severn near Shrewsbury. If this surmise is correct—and like much in early Anglo-Saxon history it remains speculative—then Ethelbald would have possessed the means of mobilizing a very large labor force under the direction of royal officers for the construction of these works. The means for estimating liability for service owed to the king lay to hand in the "hide." Originally, it seems, a rough-and-ready unit of a real measure, by this date the hide was a notional unit in terms of which subject peoples or individual landed estates were assessed for tribute or service to the king. Thus, for instance, the estate at Batsford in Gloucestershire that Ethelbald granted to the bishop of Worcester was assessed at eight hides. The most puzzling administrative document of the entire Anglo-Saxon period is that known as the Tribal Hidage. It is a list of peoples apparently subject to Mercian overlordship, each of them assessed in round numbers of hides, presumably for the payment of tribute or service; for instance, the South Saxons at 7,000 hides or the people of Elmet at 600. Although the document could belong to almost any period between c. 630 and c. 860 there is some likelihood that it was drawn up in the reign of either Ethelbald or his successor Offa. It may tell us something of the means by which Mercian overlords marshalled their resources.

We are on rather firmer ground when we turn to Ethelbald's dealings with the church. In 745–46 Boniface and seven other missionary bishops wrote a stern letter to Ethelbald reproaching him for the manner of his life and for certain aspects of the character of his rule. In particular they drew attention to Ethelbald's violation of the privileges of his churches, his usurpation of ecclesiastical revenues, and his exaction of forced labor from the clergy. Ethelbald did try to meet Boniface's criticisms. At a council held at Gumley in Leicestershire in 749 Ethelbald issued a charter that defined the services owed by the churchmen of Mercia to the king; these included the construction and defense of fortifications. The documents bearing on this issue are not easy to interpret, but it does look as though Ethelbald was trying to harness the enormous resources of the church to some secular purposes. This must materially have increased his power.

Boniface's letter, with its vigorous denunciation of Ethelbald's sexual sins (especially fornication with nuns) and his exploitation of the church, has colored the king's reputation. It is too easily overlooked that Boniface praised Ethelbald's faith and almsgiving, and the firm peace that his rule provided. Ethelbald granted endowments for the foundation of religious communities. He attended the important church council of *Clovesho* in 747, presided over by Archbishop Cuthbert of Canterbury; and it could hardly have been convened without the royal sanction. Ethelbald of Mercia may have fallen short of the highest ideal of Christian kingship; but in Boniface he was confronted by a churchman of exceptionally rigorous standards.

What is certain is that Ethelbald was a very strong king. As such, he had enemies. One contemporary described him as a tyrant. He met his end violently after reigning forty-one years, murdered by his own retainers in 757. We know the fact, but nothing of the feuds and resentments that may have brought it to pass. He was buried at Repton, in the crypt beneath the monastery church that had probably been constructed through his agency as a royal mausoleum for the kings of Mercia.

A. Dornier (ed.), *Mercian Studies,* 1977, is a recent collection of essays bearing largely upon the age of Ethelbald.

ST. LEOBA (*d. c.* 780) was a native of Wessex who went out to Germany to assist Boniface and ended her life as abbess of Tauberbischofsheim in Franconia. As a young girl she was placed in the monastery of Wimborne in Dorset, which had recently been founded by the sisters of King Ine of Wessex. When she grew up she spent some time pursuing her studies at the Kentish monastery of Minster-in-Thanet. It was from there that Leoba first wrote to Boniface, to whom she was related through her mother, in about 732, introducing herself, asking for his prayers, and proudly sending him some of her Latin verse. She seems to have returned to Wimborne shortly afterwards, for it was to her abbess there that Boniface addressed himself a few years later, probably about 738, to ask her to allow Leoba to come to join him in Germany. Boniface founded a nunnery at Tauberbischofsheim and placed Leoba in charge of it. She remained there as abbess for the rest of her life.

Leoba's career furnishes another example of the important role played by women in the early Anglo-Saxon and Anglo-German church. In addition to being a highly competent abbess, Leoba was remarkable for her learning. Her ninth-century biographer, who had access to the recollections of four of Leoba's pupils, tells us that to a good knowledge of the scriptures "she added by way of completion the writings of the church fathers, the decrees of councils and the whole of ecclesiastical law." Her personality was as formidable as her learning. Her pupils remembered reading to her at night when she was old. Even when she seemed to nod off to sleep she never relaxed her vigilance and would be quick to pounce on any mistakes made by the reader. Sometimes they made mistakes on purpose, to test her, but never did they go undetected. Leoba was one of the first in that long (and continuing) tradition of distinguished but sometimes alarming academic ladies who have contributed so largely to English intellectual life.

The ninth-century life of Leoba is translated by C. H. Talbot, *The Anglo-Saxon Missionaries in Germany,* 1954.

ST. WILLIBALD (*c.* 700–786) was an English monk who travelled widely in the Mediterranean region as a pilgrim and ended up as Bishop of Eichstätt in Germany. A native of Wessex and a relative of Boniface, Willibald was brought up as a monk at Bishops Waltham in Hampshire. Touched by the impulse to undertake a pilgrimage to Rome—as King Cadwalla of Wessex had done and as King Ine was shortly to do—he set off accompanied by his brother Winnibald and his father in 720. But Rome was not enough for Willibald. While staying there he formed the intention of extending his pilgrimage to the Holy Land. In 722 he set out by way of Sicily, Greece, Cyprus, and Syria and after various adventures, including imprisonment by the Muslim authorities in Homs, came safe to Jerusalem. After some considerable time spent in visiting the Holy Places of Palestine, Willibald travelled to Constantinople where he passed two years. In 729, after about seven years of travel, he returned to Italy and joined the monastic community at Monte Cassino. There he remained for about ten years. In about 739–40 he went to join his kinsman Boniface in Germany, and established a monastery at Eichstätt. In 741 Boniface consecrated him a bishop, probably intending him for the proposed new see at Erfurt. In the event, the establishment of Erfurt did not succeed, so a bishopric was created (by 745) for Willibald based on his own monastery at Eichstätt. He remained a missionary bishop in southern Germany for the rest of his life.

Willibald's brother Winnibald also gravitated to Germany. Together the brothers founded the monastery of Heidenheim. It was a double monastery for both monks and nuns on the Anglo-Saxon model. After Winnibald's death in 761 their sister Walburga became abbess: she has given her name, quite fortuitously, to the strange festivities of *Walpurgisnacht*. It was a nun of Heidenheim who took down from Willibald in his old age the story of his travels as a young man and recorded them in a work known as the *Hodoeporicon*.

Willibald was the earliest English traveller to the Middle East known to us. The *Hodoeporicon* reveals him as adventurous, inquisitive, observant, with a gift for vivid anecdote and a remarkable memory for detail. Many themes that have become familiar in English travel literature since his day were enunciated for the first time in Willibald's account. He was foolhardy and eccentric, climbing an active volcano in the Lipari Islands. He frequently fell ill. He did not always get on with foreign food: he refers to what seems to have been yogurt with suspicion and distaste. Like many later English travellers he was irked by foreign officialdom. One of his most enjoyable stories, recounted with pride, tells how he ingeniously smuggled some precious balsam past customs officials in the Muslim city of Tyre.

The *Hodoeporicon* is translated in C. H. Talbot, *The Anglo-Saxon Missionaries in Germany*, 1954.

ST. LULLUS or **LUL** (*d.* 786) was the successor of Boniface in the see of Mainz. Lul was a native of Wessex and had been brought up in the monastery of Malmesbury. It is possible that he was a distant kinsman of Boniface, and fairly certain that several of his relations worked alongside Boniface in the German mission-field where so many men and women of Anglo-Saxon stock achieved prominence. Lul probably joined Boniface in about 738–39. He rapidly distinguished himself as a man of outstanding talents and emerged as the favorite disciple of his master's old age. By 747 he had become Boniface's archdeacon (a bishop's most important subordinate). In 751 he represented Boniface on a mission to the pope. In 752 he was consecrated a bishop in order to act as an assistant-bishop to Boniface. In 753 when Boniface set out for Frisia on his last missionary journey he designated Lul his successor in the see of Mainz, although to do this was in breach of the law of the church governing episcopal elections. On Boniface's death in the following year Lul became bishop of Mainz, apparently with the support of the Frankish king Pippin III. He retained the see of Mainz for the remainder of his life.

Lul's personality and achievements have almost inevitably been overshadowed by those of his great predecessor. He has suffered neglect also because the sources bearing upon his career as a bishop are hard to interpret. For example, it was for long believed that Lul engaged in unseemly quarrels with Sturmi, the abbot of Boniface's monastery at Fulda; but it seems that this episode has been much exaggerated. It has been argued that the popes were distrustful of Lul because of the manner in which he had come to episcopal office, and it is indeed true that they did not grant him a *pallium* (the symbol of an archbishop's authority) until about 781; but we cannot be sure that this delay arose from suspicion. It has been suggested that Lul was inactive in the mission-field; on the contrary, however, it seems that he was urging upon Pippin's son Charles (that is, Charlemagne) more vigorous steps for the evangelization of Saxony and that Charles was responding eagerly to his teaching.

These matters remain uncertain. What we can be sure about is that Lul maintained contact with friends in England. The evidence comes from surviving letters to and from him, numbering about forty. To an even greater extent than the letters of Boniface, Lul's correspondence bears witness to the transmission of books from England to Germany. He asked for the works of Aldhelm. Abbot Cuthbert of Jarrow and Archbishop Albert of York were asked to send certain of the works of Bede. Lul did not confine himself to requests for recent works of Christian scholarship. To Bishop Cyneheard of Winchester he wrote asking for works of secular learning, instancing books on medicine. It is likely that it was through Lul's agency that certain works by classical authors reached medieval Germany. For example, the minor works of Tacitus (including his life of Agricola) have been transmitted to us by way of a ninth-century manuscript from the monastery of Hersfeld; and Hersfeld had been founded by Lul. The letters of Lul show him as an active patron of learning and serve as further reminder of the degree to which the scholarship of the Carolingian Renaissance rested on the intellectual resources of Anglo-Saxon England.

W. Levison, *England and the Continent in the Eighth Century*, 1946.

ST. WILLEHAD (*d.* 789) was the first bishop of Bremen in north Germany. He was educated in his native Northumbria, possibly at York with his contemporary Alcuin: the two men certainly knew one another in later life. Desiring to work as a missionary among the Frisians after the example of his fellow-countryman Willibrord, Willehad was dispatched across the North Sea with the blessing of a Northumbrian synod convoked by King Alchred (765–74), who was himself keenly interested in the progress of the Anglo-Saxon missions and a correspondent of Lul, the successor of Boniface in the see of Mainz: this would have been in about 770. He worked in Frisia for the next ten years.

In 780 he was sent by the Frankish king Charles (that is, Charles the Great or Charlemagne, 768–814) to work among the Saxons in the lower valleys of the rivers Elbe and Weser. Charles was at that time engaged in the gradual and ruthless conquest of Saxony and its incorporation into the Frankish kingdom. Two years later the Saxons rebelled under their leader Widukind against Frankish dominion. Willehad managed to escape from Saxony—several of his associates were killed—and after a pilgrimage to Rome settled at the monastery of Echternach, which had been founded by Willibrord and was at the time under the rule of an English abbot named Beornred, himself a relative of Willibrord and later to be archbishop of Sens. Willehad spent two years there (783–85), engaged in teaching and writing. In 785 he returned to Saxony, which Charles was engaged in pacifying, where he may have been responsible for the baptism of Widukind on his submission. In 787 he was consecrated bishop of Bremen, the first episcopal see to be established in Saxony. But he did not live long enough to supervise the setting-up of the new Christian establishment. He died in 789 only a few days after the consecration of his new cathedral.

ALBERT (*d.* 780) was archbishop of York from 767 until 778. He was a Northumbrian of noble family who was entered as a boy in the religious community attached to the cathedral church of York. His intellectual talents were rewarded by his kinsman Archbishop Egbert, who placed him in charge of the recently established York school: we do not know exactly when this was, perhaps about 745. Albert was evidently a teacher of genius. Under him York became the foremost center of learning in Western Europe. His most distinguished pupil was Alcuin, and nearly all that we know about Albert we owe to the affectionate memories of him recorded by Alcuin in his poem on *The Bishops, Kings, and Saints of York.* Alcuin tells us that the syllabus at York rested on the teaching of the seven liberal arts of grammar, rhetoric, and dialectic; arithmetic, astronomy, geometry, and music, after study of which pupils would proceed to more advanced biblical, computistical, and theological study. Like other Englishmen before him—Benedict Biscop for example—Albert travelled abroad in search of learning and books. Alcuin's poem contains a famous list of the authors whose works were available at York in Albert's day. Although the list presents difficult problems of interpretation, what is clear is that the library assembled by Albert was a very extensive one, perhaps bigger than that available to Bede at Wearmouth and Jarrow and less narrowly ecclesiastical in content. The correspondence of both Lul and Alcuin shows that York enjoyed a reputation on the Continent as a source of books, a reputation that continued down to the troubled middle years of the ninth century.

In Alcuin's eyes Albert was no less distinguished as an archbishop than as a teacher. A busy, devout, and decorous prelate, he was as splendidly generous as his predecessor Egbert. Albert was a considerable patron of the arts. Some at least of the books in the York library must have been purchased out of his personal fortune. He founded a chapel in York minster at the spot where it was believed that King Edwin had been baptized by Paulinus, and erected there an altar covered with gold, silver, and jewels surmounted by an enormous chandelier and accompanied by a cross of solid silver. He commissioned a jug of pure gold for holding sacramental wine before it was poured into the chalice. Most ambitious of all, he founded a new church in York dedicated to Sta. Sophia whose construction was supervised by his pupils Eanbald (later archbishop, *d.* 796) and Alcuin. It had no less than thirty altars and was evidently both big and lavishly decorated.

Albert retired from office in 778 and died two years later. The York school continued to enjoy great renown for long afterward. But it did not survive the Viking capture of York in 867 and the subsequent settlement of Danes there. Of the physical remains of Albert's work, nothing now survives. Not a single manuscript that can confidently be attributed to the scriptorium of York has been identified. We do not even know where in York the church of Sta. Sophia stood. As for the precious ornaments, they must long ago have disappeared—hacked to pieces or melted down, perhaps, as loot. It has been fashionable of recent years to underplay the disruptive effects of Viking attack. The case of York should give the lie to this. The Christian culture so painstakingly built up by Egbert, Albert, and Alcuin was destroyed in the second half of the ninth century. Not until the time of Archbishop Wulfstan early in the eleventh was York once more to be an intellectual center of any distinction; never again was she to enjoy the celebrity that had been hers in the eighth.

Alcuin's poem has been edited and translated by P. Godman, 1982.

ALCUIN (*d.* 804), scholar, teacher, poet, and intellectual luminary at the court of Charlemagne, was a native of Northumbria, a kinsman of Willibrord, born perhaps about 740. He received his education at York under Albert, for whose teaching he had the greatest respect. Albert had made the school of York the most distinguished center of learning of its day in Europe. In 767, when Albert became archbishop of York, Alcuin succeeded him as director of the school. Alcuin travelled to Francia and Italy with Albert on several occasions in the 760s and 770s, in the course of which journeys he made friends among the lay and ecclesiastical elite of the Frankish kingdom. The turning point in his career came in 781. On his way back from Rome Alcuin met Charles (Charlemagne), king of the Franks, at Parma. Charles invited Alcuin to his court to help in his educational plans and persuaded him to accept. In 782 Alcuin left England and settled in Francia. He spent the rest of his life there, apart from a brief trip back to England in 786 and another longer one between 790 and 793. Alcuin's services to Carolingian culture were very considerable; his rewards no less so. He collected the abbacies of Troyes and Ferrières, and to these in 796 he added the office of abbot of St. Martin's at Tours, one of the great plums of ecclesiastical preferment in the Frankish kingdom. His later years were largely spent at Tours, in retirement from the bustle of the court, and it was there that he died in May 804.

This early example of the brain drain presents us with the spectacle of a career that in crude material terms amounts to one of the greatest academic success-stories of all time; contemplation of which induces a mood of rueful envy in Alcuin's struggling twentieth-century successors. His rewards were well-merited. Charlemagne wanted to revive learning and to deepen Christian observance in the territories he ruled. To this end he gathered about him a small group of cosmopolitan intellectuals whose role was to act as a kind of "think-tank" in the articulation of the king's projects. Alcuin was one of the first of these men to be recruited and the most influential of them all. His influence can be detected behind the circular known as the *Admonitio Generalis* ("General Directive"), a comprehensive statement of the king's ideals drawn up in 789. He was responsible for the drafting of the *De litteris colendis* ("On the study of letters") a few years later, a memorandum to be circulated to all the higher clergy urging them to establish monastic and diocesan schools. He can be seen advising Charles about his role as a Christian ruler, and in the 790s nudging him toward the idea of the revival of empire, which would be realized in Charlemagne's coronation as Roman emperor in 800—the foundation of what was later to be known as the Holy Roman Empire.

Alcuin was a leading figure in the literary and artistic movement that we call the Carolingian Renaissance. He was a prodigious author: he wrote theology, scriptural commentary, sermons, saints' lives, textbooks for his pupils, reams of Latin verse, and over three hundred surviving letters. His most influential achievements were in the field of liturgy and textual studies. As a liturgist he edited a new lectionary and sacramentary that, in combination, were to form the Roman Missal, which became standard throughout medieval western Christendom and in the post-Reformation Roman church until the liturgical changes of the twentieth century. As a textual critic he supervised the production of an improved text of the Vulgate, i.e., the Latin Bible, which was to remain the standard version until the sixteenth century. In these two very significant ways, therefore, Alcuin can be said to have shaped the religious experience of millions of Catholic Christians.

Alcuin's most ambitious poem was devoted to the place that had done most to fashion his character and intellect—York. In it he celebrated the bishops, kings, and saints connected with the church of York from the days of Edwin and Paulinus down to his own time; particularly the men under whose care his youth had been passed—Archbishop Egbert, King Eadbert, and his master Albert. Alcuin wrote an enormous amount of other poetry: verse-letters to a large circle of friends; hymns, prayers, and lyrics; a moving lament on the Viking sack of Lindisfarne in 793. His surviving letters are greater in number than those of any other Englishman before the fifteenth century. Together the letters and poems enable us to know more about Alcuin than we can know about any earlier Englishman, even Boniface. They reveal a personality of great charm—cheerful, companionable, loyal, humane, with a marked talent for making and keeping friends.

Selections from the letters are translated by S. Allott, *Alcuin of York*, 1974. Helen Waddell memorably translated some of Alcuin's verse in *Medieval Latin Lyrics*, 1929, and many reprints, and *More Latin Lyrics*, 1976. There is as yet no really good modern study of Alcuin. Professor D. A. Bullough (who has one in preparation) has written the best recent account of *The Age of Charlemagne* (2nd ed., 1973).

OFFA (*d.* 796) was king of Mercia from 757 until 796, the builder of the biggest earthwork in early medieval Europe—Offa's Dyke—and by common consent the most imposing Anglo-Saxon ruler before Alfred. Like Ethelbald, his predecessor as king of Mercia, Offa claimed descent from a brother of King Penda. He fought his way to the kingship of Mercia against a rival named Beornred in 757. Mercian hegemony over southern England had crumbled after Ethelbald's murder. Offa gradually put it together again. He seems to have established lordship over Kent by 764 and over Sussex by 771. Beorhtric of Wessex (786–802) was a client-king who married one of Offa's daughters—often a token of political subjection—in 789. Offa had power over East Anglia, and even Northumbria may have submitted to him, for its king, Ethelred, married another of Offa's daughters in 792. From 774 onward he was frequently styled *rex Anglorum,* "king of the English," in his charters. Like any other ruler of his age, Offa had to fight hard to achieve and maintain his supremacy. Kent caused him a great deal of trouble: Offa's army was defeated at Otford in 776 and from then for perhaps as much as nine years Mercian ascendancy over Kent was suspended. Offa exiled Egbert, an anti-Mercian claimant to the kingdom of Wessex. He executed a king of East Anglia, Ethelbert, later to be venerated as a saint, in 794. He extinguished local dynasties in small kingdoms such as Sussex and Lindsey.

Thus far, Offa looks like any successful warlord. But there was more to him than this. Consider first the Dyke. Offa's Dyke is an earthwork defining the frontier between Mercians and Welsh, consisting of a ditch to the west and a bank that originally rose up to twenty-five feet high to the east, the whole being about sixty feet wide. The bank may have been surmounted by a wooden palisade, possibly even in some places by a stone wall. The frontier it defined or defended was about 150 miles long: twice as long as the frontier guarded by the Wall of Hadrian. It was an astonishing achievement, not simply in physical but also in organizational terms. Its administrative implications are thought-provoking: speculation continues. It was no ordinary king who could plan and execute a work of engineering on this scale. (For comparison: Charlemagne planned and began the digging of a canal to link the rivers Danube and Main in 793; the project was abandoned before a thousand meters had been dug.)

The same impression of order and efficiency, of a government that could make plans and then carry them through, is suggested by Offa's coinage. In the third quarter of the eighth century the kings of Kent began to issue a new coinage of silver pennies (or *denarii*), partly modelled on new Frankish coins and differing in weight, fineness, and design from previous Anglo-Saxon issues. When Offa reestablished his control of Kent in about 785 he took over the mint at Canterbury and had its moneyers start striking coin in his name. There were several other mints that struck for him, in Mercia, East Anglia, and Wessex. When early in the 790s Charlemagne slightly increased the weight of the Frankish penny, Offa followed suit in England. These developments are evidenced by the surviving coins themselves. They constitute unimpeachable testimony to firm royal control over the coinage.

The existence of the mint at Canterbury was one reason why Offa was so eager to maintain control of Kent. Another was the presence of the archbishopric. Archbishop Jaenberht (765–92) was probably among the leaders of Kentish opposition to Offa in the 770s and 780s. Offa's riposte was drastic. A papal legation visited England in 786 and was brought to sanction a revolution in English ecclesiastical organization. In the following year, at a church council described as "contentious," Offa forced through a decision to raise the bishopric of Lichfield to archiepiscopal rank. This created a new metropolitan province in the Mercian territory of midland England—at the expense of Canterbury. The archbishopric of Lichfield did not last long—it was wound up shortly after Offa's death, in the years 801–3—but while it did it materially increased Offa's power over the church. One of its firstfruits was the anointing of his son Ecgfrith as king in 787. This was the first time, as far as we know, that a king's son had been anointed in England. Offa was probably copying the example of Charlemagne who had had his sons anointed in 781. The purpose was clear: Offa was trying to establish his dynasty as a hereditary monarchy hedged about with the sanction of the most solemn Christian ritual. (It is of some interest that the genealogy of the Mercian royal family seems to have been recorded in writing for the first time, at Lichfield, at about this date.)

Offa's desire to secure a Mercian archbishopric was not simply political. The multiplication of metropolitan or archiepiscopal provinces in the interests of pastoral efficiency was a concern of contemporary reformers in Charlemagne's realm, among whom, we should remember, there were Englishmen known to Offa, such as Alcuin—who had accompanied the papal legates to Offa's court in 786. Offa was a responsible Christian ruler. The council that he held with the legates enacted reforming legislation. He founded monasteries, for example, at St. Albans. He embellished the tomb of St. Oswald—and his interest in the cult of a saint who was a soldier-king is noteworthy. Offa is known to have possessed a copy of the *Ecclesiastical History* of Bede, and that work may have influenced his thinking about kingship. Stray references and survivals indicate a flourishing Christian culture in eighth- and ninth-century Mercia. It is sobering to consider how different Offa's Mercia might look to us had one of the great midland monasteries—Repton, say, or

Breedon—produced a continuator of Bede to tell us about it. If any such work were produced, it must have perished in the wreckage of Mercian culture inflicted by the Vikings.

We can sense, then, a certain statesmanlike quality about Offa, coexisting—not necessarily uneasily—with the warlord roistering with his thanes about him in his mead-hall. This impression of shrewdness and sophistication is borne out by what we know of his dealings with Charlemagne. Anglo-Frankish contacts were undoubtedly more intense than the surviving sources show. Cross-Channel trade was even more important in Offa's day than it had been in the time of Ine or Ethelbald. If, as seems likely, there was something in the order of five million silver pennies of Offa in circulation in England about the year 790, we must ask ourselves where the bullion came from, for English native deposits of silver are negligible. Commodities must have been exported to cause an influx of silver in return. Fortunately we know from a letter of Charlemagne to Offa in 796 that English textiles were exported to Francia. It is our first certain evidence of what was to become one of the great staples of English commercial life—the export of wool or woollen cloth yielded by English sheep. That Charlemagne and Offa could correspond about trade is another indication of its importance. They were in contact with each other about other matters: the possibility of a marriage alliance, the harboring of English political exiles in Francia, the exchange of diplomatic gifts, the passage of pilgrims to Rome through Frankish territory, and so forth. Frankish churchmen attended the English church council of 786; English churchmen attended Charlemagne's council of Frankfurt in 794. Of course, the Francia of Charlemagne was a vastly bigger affair than the Mercia of Offa; but not necessarily a more complex one. As kings, Offa and Charlemagne were cast in similar molds.

Although there is a large periodical literature devoted to Offa there is as yet no modern book on him: in its absence, the reader may turn to the fine chapter in J. M. Wallace-Hadrill, *Early Germanic Kingship*, 1971.

NENNIUS (early 9th century?) was the name of a Welsh ecclesiastic to whom is ascribed authorship of the work known as the *Historia Brittonum* ("History of the Britons"). The *Historia* was put together in the form in which we have it in the first quarter of the ninth century. The attribution to Nennius is not attested in all surviving manuscripts, so it is not clear whether Nennius, whoever he may have been, was the original compiler or a later editor. The *Historia* is an assortment of texts—genealogical, annalistic, hagiographical, geographical—assembled on no very clear principle. It preserves early chronicle material, some apparently from the seventh century and some conceivably from the fifth, which has historical value. It also contains a good deal of legendary matter about Julius Caesar, Magnus Maximus, St. Germanus, Ambrosius Aurelianus, Arthur, St. Patrick, and others. The *Historia Brittonum* is of interest as presenting a distinctively British perspective on the events of the fourth to the seventh centuries and as indicating what materials were available early in the ninth to a Welsh antiquarian looking at the British past.

The most recent translation of "Nennius" is by John Morris, *Nennius: British History and the Welsh Annals,* 1980.

ST. CYNEHELM or **KENELM** (*d. c.* 812) was a Mercian prince, the son of King Cenwulf (796–821), who died by violence and was later venerated as a saint. Kenelm's existence is attested by his subscription of a number of charters dated between 803 and 811. Of the circumstances of his death we know nothing for certain. He was apparently buried at Winchcombe in Gloucestershire, a monastic house founded by King Offa and patronized by Cenwulf. Monastic life at Winchcombe decayed in the later ninth and tenth centuries but was revived in about 970 by Bishop Oswald of Worcester. A sacramentary composed at Winchcombe in about 980 features Kenelm's name prominently among the martyrs, and this forms the first certain evidence of his cult. The cult of Kenelm flourished in the eleventh century: an account of his death—largely legendary—was composed in about 1050 and the splendid Winchcombe Psalter, now in Cambridge, written and decorated in the second quarter of the eleventh century, furnishes further evidence of the cult. Kenelm's relics continued to be venerated at Winchcombe for the rest of the Middle Ages.

CYNEWULF (9th century?) is the name, spelled in runes, woven into the texts of four Old English poems to indicate their author.

These poems are all on religious themes. They are those known as *The Fates of the Apostles*; *Elene*, on the discovery of the True Cross by Helena the mother of Constantine; *Christ*, also known as *The Ascension*, to which theme it is devoted; and *Juliana*, on the life and martyrdom of that saint. Together these poems amount to about 2,600 lines of verse. Apart from the fragments attributed to Caedmon and Bede they constitute the only Old English verse attributable to a named author. Of Cynewulf himself we know nothing. It is likely that he was a native of Mercia and that he lived in the first half of the ninth century. He had had a good education and had probably learned Latin, which makes it likely though not certain that he was an ecclesiastic. There is some probability that his poetry was committed to writing from the start, rather than transmitted orally. This, little as it is, is all that may reasonably be inferred about the author and his work.

That work is of high quality. Like Caedmon, Cynewulf adapted the metrics and vocabulary of traditional secular verse to Christian ends. Much of the surviving anonymous Old English religious poetry may have been composed in the eighth and ninth centuries, even though practically the entire corpus is preserved in only three manuscripts of the late tenth. The practice of composing Christian verse in the vernacular—a cultural fashion that the Anglo-Saxons may have owed to the Irish—was exported by the English missionaries to Germany. Surviving religious poetry in Old High German of the ninth and tenth centuries may well derive directly or indirectly from the monastery of Fulda founded by Boniface. In England and Germany alike the use of the vernacular for religious teaching did much to further the gradual Christianization of society.

The poetry of Cynewulf (assuming that he *was* a Mercian) is one testimony to the cultural vitality of Mercia in the age of Offa and his successors. Others exist in different media—the book of Cerne; the sculpture of Breedon or Wirksworth; the ivory carving of the Gandersheim casket, which came originally from Ely; and the architecture of such churches as Repton and Brixworth. Little as we know of the age of Mercian greatness, it is becoming evident that its literary and artistic achievements were notable. This makes it a little easier to understand the role of Mercians such as Werferth and Plegmund in the cultural revival sponsored by King Alfred.

The most recent translation (into prose) of all Cynewulf's verse, with useful introductory material, is to be found in S. A. J. Bradley, *Anglo-Saxon Poetry*, 1982.

EGBERT (*d.* 839) was king of Wessex from 802 until 839. He claimed descent from Ingild, a brother of King Ine of Wessex. His father was a certain Ealhmund who ruled briefly in Kent *c.* 784 in opposition to Offa of Mercia. When King Cynewulf of Wessex died in 786, Egbert disputed with Beorhtric for possession of the kingdom. Beorhtric, Offa's *protégé*, came out on top and Egbert departed into exile at the Frankish court. On Beorhtric's death in 802 Egbert returned and established himself as king of Wessex in a successful revolt against Mercian ascendancy.

Egbert ruled an independent Wessex for the next twenty-three years, of which we have little record. This was succeeded by a period of frenzied activity. In 825 he defeated King Beornwulf of Mercia at the battle of *Ellendun* (probably Wroughton in Wiltshire) and immediately afterward sent his son Ethelwulf eastward to wrest Kent, Surrey, Sussex, and Essex from Mercian overlordship. He also received an appeal for protection from the East Anglians who had rebelled against the Mercians. The Mercian empire seemed to be falling apart as rival claimants contended for kingship over the next few years. In 829 Egbert conquered Mercia and went on to lay waste part of Northumbria and exact submission and tribute from its king Eanred. For a short period he was overlord of all the English kingdoms. But in 830 Mercia threw off West Saxon lordship and for the rest of his reign Egbert's direct authority was restricted to Wessex and the southeast.

It has sometimes been claimed that Egbert was the first "King of all England." But this is absurd. The notion is based upon the treatment of Egbert in the *Anglo-Saxon Chronicle*, put together in the form in which we have it at the court of Egbert's grandson Alfred and concerned above all else to magnify the exploits of the West Saxon royal dynasty. Mercian supremacy did not end with Offa. Ninth-century Mercia may have been subject to dynastic instability—as which Anglo-Saxon kingdom was not?—but it could still produce some imposing rulers such as Cenwulf (796–821), Wiglaf (827–40), and Beorhtwulf (840–52). Farther to the north the Northumbrian King Eanred (808–40) continued to rule a kingdom stretching from the Humber to the Firth of Forth: the submission to Egbert in 829 had no lasting effect.

Nevertheless, Egbert's reign is an important one. In the first place, he consolidated West Saxon domination over the remaining British princes of the southwest in a series of campaigns in 815, 825, 830, and 838. Secondly, his annexation of southeastern England in 825 was to be permanent. Kent became a dependency where West Saxon princes could learn the business of kingship; just as Egbert entrusted Kent to his son Ethelwulf, so after his accession in 839 Ethelwulf placed his son Athelstan in authority there. Egbert and Ethelwulf were at pains to cultivate good relations with the archbishops of Canterbury; they had learned the lessons of Offa's failure in this respect. In particular, they tried to ensure that the see of Canterbury should be well-disposed not just to individual kings of Wessex but to the dynasty as a whole; in their own words, in a charter of 838, "that we and our heirs for ever afterwards may have firm and unbroken friendship from the archbishop and all his successors." They wanted to break free from the snares of dynastic instability and discontinuity that plagued Mercia, Northumbria, and their Frankish neighbors over the Channel. That they succeeded in doing so no doubt owed much to luck, but also something to shrewd management. Finally, Egbert showed that he could cope with new enemies, the Vikings. They ravaged the Island of Sheppey in 835, and defeated him at Carhampton in 836. But when in 838 they made common cause with the Britons of the southwest Egbert defeated them at Hingston Down in Cornwall. In the last battle of his life Egbert showed that the Danes were vulnerable.

ST. WIGSTAN or **WYSTAN** (*d.* 849) was a prince of the royal family of Mercia who was murdered by a remote kinsman in a dynastic conflict in 849. After his death he was regarded as a saint and a local cult of him grew up at Repton where he was buried. Recent excavations at Repton have produced archaeological evidence of a flourishing cult in the pre-Conquest period, notably the construction of a system of passages giving access to the crypt where Wigstan's relics rested, apparently for the use of pilgrims coming to venerate them. Wigstan's relics were moved to the monastery of Evesham during the reign of Canute and the cult continued lively there during the remainder of the Middle Ages.

ST. SWITHUN (*d.* 862) was bishop of Winchester from 852 to 862. Very little is known for certain of Swithun beyond the dates of his episcopate. His holding the important see of Winchester would indicate close connections with the royal family of Wessex. Later tradition held that he had been the tutor of King Ethelwulf, which is not impossible, and that he was prominent among that king's counsellors. In a poem composed within a century of his death he was credited with the construction of a stone bridge over the river Itchen just outside Winchester. The only other event of local importance during his episcopate of which we know was a Danish attack on Winchester in 860. All that may reasonably be said of Swithun is that he conducted himself with credit in difficult times.

A small-scale and local cult of Swithun as a saint may have flourished at Winchester from soon after his death. But the man really responsible for Swithun's posthumous fame was his tenth-century successor, Bishop Ethelwold of Winchester. In 971 Ethelwold removed Swithun's remains to a new and splendid shrine, apparently commissioned by King Edgar, in Winchester Cathedral. Miracles were worked there, pilgrims came not only from distant parts of England but also from northern France. In the 990s Swithun's sanctity and miracles were celebrated by two Winchester writers, Wulfstan and Lantfrid, in Latin verse and prose; also by Aelfric in his Old English *Lives of the Saints*. This vigorous promotion of the cult of Swithun was part of the process by which Edgar and Ethelwold sought to enhance the glory and dignity of Winchester as the main seat of English royal power and an important focus of English piety.

Swithun's cult continued to flourish throughout the Middle Ages. He is mainly remembered today in a jingle about the weather, "Rain on St. Swithun's day (15 July), rain for forty days" (and variants), first attested in the sixteenth century. Like other proverbial attempts to impose order on that elusive element, the English climate, it is more often than not inaccurate.

RAGNAR LOTHBROK (*d.* 852–56?) was a Viking freebooter who was active in the second quarter of the ninth century. Most historians of the Viking age would agree that Ragnar existed and that he lived about this period; but his origins and doings remain almost impenetrably obscure. It is not that we lack information about him. On the contrary, there survives a superabundance of materials relating to his career. The trouble is that nearly all the sources are late and legendary. The few that are early are laconic and resist easy interpretation. Plausibility is all that may be claimed for what follows.

Ragnar was a leading member of the Danish-Norse warrior aristocracy. His zone of influence may have centered upon Zealand and other islands of the Kattegat, the water which separates Denmark from southern Sweden. His power depended therefore on the possession of ships and command of the sea. The young warriors who manned his ships and fought for him expected adventure and profit: these rewards were the condition of their loyalty. (One is reminded of Anglo-Saxon war bands of an earlier age, such as that led by Guthlac before his conversion.) That meant piracy. The Vikings were parasitical upon the rich lands beyond the North Sea, to which their ships gave them access. Ragnar can be traced in the Orkneys and Hebrides. It is possible that he is to be identified with the Viking leader named *Reginherus* in contemporary Frankish sources who led a fleet up the Seine to plunder Paris in 845. It is reasonably certain that he was active in Ireland in 851–52 where he seems to have been fighting against the Norwegians who had founded Dublin in 841. Ragnar met his end shortly afterward, possibly while campaigning in Anglesey or north Wales.

Ragnar's byname Lothbrok means "shaggy breeches" and refers to his clothing of leather boiled in pitch, which had the magic property of making him invulnerable. According to legend he met his death at the hands of King Aelle of Northumbria, who discovered the secret of his magic clothes, stripped him of them, and flung him into a snake pit where he was killed. The story is a fiction, probably invented at a later date to provide a retrospective justification—revenge for their father's murder—for the invasion of Northumbria by Ragnar's sons in 866. However, it is not impossible that Ragnar campaigned in Northumbria at some stage of his career.

The first accurately datable Scandinavian attack on England occurred in 793 when the monastery of Lindisfarne was sacked, though it is likely that sporadic raids of which we know nothing had been taking place for half a century or so before that. There exists no simple explanation of the Viking movement overseas. The diffusion of the use of iron in Scandinavia gradually made possible more intense agricultural exploitation. This in turn permitted demographic growth that would in time press upon the limited resources of the Scandinavian environment. Technical advances in shipbuilding, which would produce such masterpieces of strength and elegance as the Gokstad ship (c. 880), opened the seaways of the North Sea and the Atlantic to Viking enterprise. The influx of silver bullion from the Islamic Middle East, well-attested archaeologically and attracted by trade in slaves, furs, and timber with the distant lands of the caliphate in Iran, may have had far-reaching consequences for Scandinavian society. It provided capital for shipbuilding, weaponry, and trading ventures. It drove a wedge between those who were its beneficiaries and the rest. An elite of wealth and status emerged, competitive and acquisitive, whose members attracted retinues of unruly young warriors on the make; and these men in their turn, as we have seen, had to be rewarded. The emergence of stronger kings in Denmark and Norway, for reasons not unconnected with this new wealth, could make life at home difficult for these turbulent nobilities. It is to some such cluster of factors as these that we should attribute the beginnings of Viking activity in western Europe.

There is, finally, the consideration that the English, Frankish, and Irish kingdoms were rich and vulnerable, attractive to predators. Who would settle in Orkney or Iceland when Lincolnshire, Leinster, or Normandy lay open? who plunder the humble churches of the Hebrides when Jarrow or Kells or Noirmoutier were there for the picking? The appearance in western waters from the 830s onward of large Viking fleets, carrying well-equipped armies several thousand strong under the leadership of high-ranking aristocrats, bent on systematic plunder, was the response to these opportunities. Ragnar was one of these men. In the next generation they would go a step further and carve out territorial principalities for themselves.

A. P. Smyth, *Scandinavian Kings in the British Isles, 850–880,* 1977.

ETHELWULF (*d.* 858) was the son of King Egbert of Wessex and reigned as subking in Kent from 825 and then over Wessex from 839 until 858. During his reign the Danish raids on England increased in size and frequency. There were attacks on Southampton and the coast of Dorset in 840; on Kent in 841; on London,

Rochester, and Southampton in 842; on Somerset in 843 and again in 845; on Devon in 850. In that year a Danish army wintered in England for the first time, on Thanet. In 851 they stormed Canterbury and London before being defeated by Ethelwulf in Surrey. Kent was attacked again in 853. In 854–55 the Danish host once more wintered in England, on Sheppey. This is to list only the known descents upon the territory of Wessex and its dependencies. Other parts of England suffered too. Lindsey and East Anglia were attacked in 841, King Redwulf of Northumbria was killed in 844, King Beorhtwulf of Mercia was defeated in 851, and we hear of a Danish army active in the inland parts of Mercia, in Shropshire, in 855.

Ethelwulf and his subjects put up a stout resistance to the Danes. But it was exceedingly difficult to make effective provision for resisting an enemy whose forces were big, well-equipped, and above all, mobile. Other rulers in western Europe faced the same dilemma. It is instructive, as ever, to set the English experience in a continental context. The Viking bases on Thanet and Sheppey were mirrored in those of Dublin and Noirmoutier; attacks on trading communities like Southampton and London were matched in raids on Dorestadt, Quentovic, and Rouen; and after wintering in England in 850–51 the Danes crossed to Francia and wintered there in 851–52. The West Saxon kings of the ninth century had much in common with their Frankish neighbors. Not surprisingly, Ethelwulf had dealings with them. Two letters of the Frankish abbot, Lupus of Ferrières—himself a pupil of a pupil of Alcuin— reveal that Ethelwulf had a Frankish secretary named Felix. When Ethelwulf married for the second time in 856 his queen was Judith, daughter of the West Frankish king Charles the Bald.

Ethelwulf's second marriage took place while he was on his way back from a pilgrimage to Rome in 855, accompanied by his youngest son Alfred. The contemporary biography of Pope Benedict III (855–58) lists the treasures that Ethelwulf offered at the shrine of St. Peter: they included among much else a golden crown, a sword chased with gold, precious vestments, and hangings decorated with gold embroidery. We are also told, by Asser in his *Life of Alfred,* that Ethelwulf undertook to make an annual payment of three hundred gold pieces to the see of Rome; as Asser pointed out, this was "a great sum of money." The pilgrimage and the offerings demonstrate Ethelwulf's piety and generosity. They also show that he was very wealthy. The same impression is given by other sources. The correspondence that Lupus of Ferrières had with Ethelwulf was occasioned by his desire to secure a present of lead for roofing the monastery church at Ferrières: and Ferrières was an important monastic house, not beneath Alcuin's notice, its church probably an ample one with a roof that would require no small quantity of lead.

Ethelwulf's most lavish act of piety at home in England consisted in a series of grants of lands and privileges to the churches of Wessex in 854. The documents that purport to record these grants are peculiarly difficult to interpret—they are the most baffling of all Anglo-Saxon royal charters—and there is no agreement among scholars about what was going on. But what is plain is that Ethelwulf was a king who could afford to be generous where the royal lands were concerned. We can just make out a little of why this should have been so. Asser tells us that Ethelwulf took steps to ensure "that his sons should not quarrel unnecessarily among themselves." He does not tell us exactly what these provisions were, but the will of his son Alfred, drawn up in the 880s, casts a little light on the matter. Ethelwulf planned that his sons should succeed one another as kings of Wessex. Each reigning king was to be permitted by his younger brothers a life-interest in their share of the dynasty's landed wealth. In this way the union between the family property of the royal house and the office of king would be preserved. The reigning monarch would be assured of a substantial royal demesne—that is, of the material resources for effective rule. The constitutional implications of the scheme may not have presented themselves clearly to Ethelwulf. He was perhaps simply seeking a harmonious solution to a new set of circumstances—for while he and his father had been only children, or only survivors, he had fathered five sons—at a time of national danger when the preservation of a strong kingship was essential. Ethelwulf had only to look at his Frankish neighbors to see what might happen if some such steps as these were not taken. What the scheme presupposed was patient restraint on the part both of the temporarily disinherited younger sons and of the children of elder sons.

Harmony within the dynasty was probably a good deal more frail than our very discreet sources choose to reveal. While Ethelwulf was absent from England in 855–56 his eldest son Ethelbald plotted against him with the bishop of Sherborne and the Alaerman of Somerset. Whether Ethelbald disapproved of his father's dynastic schemes or feared the possibility of offspring of his father's recent second marriage is not clear; but the results were serious. When Ethelwulf returned, his direct authority was confined to Kent and the southeast, while Ethelbald ruled in Wessex. As it so happened, Ethelwulf's plans did in the event work out well. On his death in 858 Ethelbald succeeded him and his younger brother Ethelbert ruled as a subking in Kent. On Ethelbald's death, childless, in 860, Ethelbert succeeded to the whole kingdom. On his death, childless, in 866, his brother Ethelred similarly. On Ethelred's death in 871 the youngest of the brothers, Alfred, succeeded. But Ethelred had not died childless, and his son Ethelwold was to try to supplant his cousin Edward, Alfred's son, a generation later.

Doubtless the success of Ethelwulf's plan owed much to biological accident. Of his five sons one predeceased him, three others died fairly young, and two of these three were childless. Yet that Ethelwulf could diagnose the sources of dynastic insecurity and take effective measures to neutralize them showed intelligence and political courage. Ethelwulf has been dismissed by an eminent historian of the Anglo-Saxon period as "a religious and unambitious man for whom engagement in war and politics was an unwelcome consequence of rank." This judgment seriously underestimates him. He was a forceful and capable ruler whose achievement was the essential precondition for the doings of his more famous son Alfred.

HALFDAN (*d.* 877) was a Viking leader who carved out an English principality for himself and ended his days as the first ruler of the Scandinavian kingdom of York. Halfdan was among the leaders of the large Danish force, referred to by contemporaries as "the great army," which landed in East Anglia in the autumn of 865. His antecedents, despite ingenious scholarly attempts to make bricks with very little straw, remain mysterious. He may have been a son of Ragnar Lothbrok. He had two brothers who also campaigned with him in Britain, one of them known to legend, though not to history, as Ivar the Boneless.

Three of the four existing Anglo-Saxon kingdoms were conquered by the great army in the nine years after its arrival in England. Northumbria went first: in 866 York was occupied, and in

867 a Northumbrian attempt to recapture the city was decisively defeated. After a foray into Mercia in 868 the army transferred its attention to East Anglia: in 869–70 the army of the East Angles was defeated—its king Edmund slain and the kingdom overrun. Then the Danes moved on Wessex. After wintering at Reading in 870–71 they engaged King Ethelred I in five hard-fought battles in the early months of 871 of which the general outcome was indecisive. Shortly afterward Halfdan's army was reinforced by the arrival of another Danish army, perhaps under the command of Guthrum. The combined Danish forces defeated King Alfred, who had recently succeeded his brother as king of Wessex, at Wilton, and compelled him to buy a humiliating peace. They wintered once more at Reading and in 872 moved to London where they bullied the Mercians into buying peace likewise.

The year 873 brought a change. When they had conquered Northumbria in 867 the Danes had set up a puppet ruler there named Egbert. In 872 the Northumbrians had rebelled against Danish control and expelled Egbert. In 873 the combined Danish forces moved up to York to reassert their authority, and appointed another puppet king, Ricsige. They spent the winter of 873–74 at Torksey in Lincolnshire. In 874 they overran Mercia, dethroned its king, and there too set up a puppet ruler of their choice. They wintered that year at the ancient center of Mercian royal power at Repton in Derbyshire. Thus by the end of 874 Northumbria, East Anglia, and Mercia had all been conquered by the Danes.

The Danish forces divided in 875. Halfdan led his army back to Northumbria, Guthrum his to East Anglia. For Halfdan the year 875 was one of frenzied activity. He ravaged Bernicia, the northern half of Northumbria: it was as a result of this that the monks of Lindisfarne began their seven years of wandering exile with the body of their patron saint, Cuthbert. Halfdan attacked the Britons of Strathclyde, and harried the Picts to secure his northeastern flank. He put in a brief appearance at Dublin where he killed a Norwegian rival, before returning to winter in the valley of the Tyne. It was perhaps at this point that Ricsige was jettisoned. At any rate it was under Halfdan's authority that in 876 he settled his followers on the land of Northumbria. But he could not rest there. In 877 he went back to Dublin in a bid to restore his authority over his Norse rivals. He was defeated and killed in a sea-battle fought at Strangford Lough in County Down.

In a famous passage the contemporary *Anglo-Saxon Chronicle* recorded that in 876 Halfdan "shared out the land of the Northumbrians, and they [i.e., his Danish followers] proceeded to plough and to support themselves." The question of Scandinavian settlement in England—and in Normandy—as a result of the Viking invasions and conquests has given rise to much debate. Owing to the nature of the sources this has been for the most part inconclusive. The place-names, language, archaeology, and art of Anglo-Scandinavian England cannot furnish satisfactory answers to the questions historians pose about the chronology, extent, and intensity of Scandinavian settlement and its longer-term effects upon the structure of English society. Obsessive preoccupation with agrarian settlement, urban growth, and legal niceties may have led to neglect of larger questions about the integration of the immigrants into the culture of the Anglo-Saxon world. For example, the questions "How quickly, in what circumstances, through whose agency, and with what results did the Scandinavian settlers become Christian?" have not yet been as thoroughly investigated as they deserve. The fact that the son, named Oda, of one of Halfdan's presumably pagan warriors could become archbishop of Canterbury in 941 is very remarkable indeed. It may have much to hint about the readiness of the immigrants to acclimatize themselves to what they found in England and about the willingness of the English to make the new arrivals welcome.

A. P. Smyth, *Scandinavian Kings in the British Isles, 850–880,* 1977, may be used, with caution, for the careers of Halfdan and his brothers. P. H. Sawyer, *Kings and Vikings,* 1982, contains an up-to-date introduction to the problems of settlement.

ST. EDMUND (*d.* 870) was king of East Anglia from *c.* 855 until his death at the hands of the Danes in 870 (or possibly 869). Nothing at all is known about his life and reign except its end. After being defeated by the Danish army under Halfdan, he was killed. We cannot be sure how he met his death. He may simply have been killed in battle. But it is rather more likely that he was killed while a prisoner in Danish hands, in such a way that people could regard him as a martyr for the Christian faith. (It has even been suggested, though on slender evidence, that he was killed as a ritual sacrifice to the Scandinavian god Odin.) It is certain that within a generation of his death coinage was being issued bearing the legend "O holy king Edmund": he was already regarded as a saint. This series of coins, the so-called "Saint Edmund memorial coinage," was probably struck in East Anglia, the earliest issues quite possibly by the Danish king Guthrum. Minting of these coins was on a fairly large scale; 1,800 of them were discovered in a hoard at Cuerdale in Lancashire excavated in 1840, which had been deposited in about 903. The use of this legend on the coins is best interpreted as an attempt to advertise a saint's cult. Coins were a form of propaganda as well as a medium of exchange.

How Edmund's cult developed over the next three generations or so we do not know. The next stage was marked by the composition of an account of his death and posthumous miracles by the distinguished French monk and later Abbot of Fleury, Abbo, in the years 985–87 when he was staying at the monastery of Ramsey in the Fenland. Ramsey had been founded not long before by Oswald, archbishop of York. It may be that he wanted to promote a saint's cult in East Anglia in rather the same way that his contemporary Ethelwold promoted the cult of St. Swithun at Winchester. Abbo's work was dedicated to Dunstan, archbishop of Canterbury; in his youth at the court of King Athelstan Dunstan had met a very old man, Edmund's armor-bearer, who had been with the king on that fateful day in 870.

By Abbo's day St. Edmund's body reposed at a place that he calls *Beodricsworth*, where a small religious community acted as guardian of the relics. In the 1020s King Canute and Queen Emma took an interest in the house. They lavished lands and privileges upon it and built it up into one of the most renowned of all English medieval monastic houses. The town which grew up nearby still bears its name: Bury St. Edmund's.

ALFRED THE GREAT (849–99), the most justly celebrated of all Anglo-Saxon rulers, was king of Wessex from 871 until 899. Alfred was born at Wantage in 849, the youngest son of King Ethelwulf of Wessex. The short reigns and early deaths of his elder brothers Ethelbald (858–60), Ethelbert (860–65), and Ethelred I (865–71) brought Alfred to the throne of Wessex at the age of about twenty-two in 871.

Alfred's lifetime was overshadowed by the Danish invasions of England. Between 865 and 870 the Danes had conquered the kingdoms of East Anglia and Northumbria and had forced Mercia into submission. In 870 they decided to move against Wessex and established themselves in winter quarters at Reading. Five battles were fought in the winter and early spring of 870–71, at Englefield, Reading, Ashdown, Basing, and the unidentified *Meretun.* Of these only Ashdown was a West Saxon victory. Shortly after the last battle the Danes were reinforced by another Viking army. At the time of Alfred's accession in April 871 the advantage lay firmly with the invaders. For the new king the outlook was bleak, and it was to remain so for some time. In May Alfred was defeated again, at Wilton, after which he decided to capitulate as the Mercians had done. A contemporary put the best interpretation on it that he could: "The Saxons made peace with the Vikings on condition that they would leave them; and this they did." What this almost certainly means is that Alfred paid them to go away; what later generations were to call paying Danegeld.

The Danes kept their word. Between 871 and 875 they busied themselves with Mercia and Northumbria. A second invasion of Wessex occurred in 876–77. Under their leader Guthrum the Danes struck deeper than ever before into Wessex, and established themselves first at Wareham in Dorset and then at Exeter. Once more Alfred was forced to buy peace from them and they withdrew across the Mercian border in the summer of 877 to a new base at Gloucester. A third invasion followed soon. In January 878 the Danes entered Wessex, settled at Chippenham, and subjected large areas of the kingdom to their authority. Alfred was taken completely unawares and could offer no resistance. With only a small following he fled to the west and found refuge at Athelney in Somerset, in the marshy country of the Parrett valley. (The episode of Alfred and the cakes, first committed to writing about a century after his death, was located during the retreat at Athelney.) Had the king died at this point he would be remembered, if at all, only as a failure.

But Alfred survived and prospered. During the spring of 878 he quietly mustered troops and from the fortress that he had constructed at Athelney he waged guerrilla war upon the Danes. By May he was ready to challenge them openly. He advanced eastward, gathering support from the county levies of Somerset, Wiltshire, and Hampshire as he went. They encountered Guthrum's army at Edington in Wiltshire and decisively defeated it, pursuing the survivors as far as their stronghold at Chippenham. After a fortnight the Danes surrendered. Their leader Guthrum was baptized a Christian in June and they swore to leave Wessex in peace, a promise that they carried out later in the year. Alfred had won the struggle for survival.

Toward the end of 884 part of a Viking army, which had been campaigning in Francia, crossed the Channel to Kent and laid siege to Rochester. Alfred relieved the town and eventually managed to chase the intruders back to the Continent. Guthrum's followers, settled in East Anglia since 880, had assisted the Vikings from the Continent, and it was in an attempt to neutralize them that Alfred sent a naval force against East Anglia in the summer of 885, which had mixed success, and in 886 occupied London. Shortly afterward he made a peace-treaty with Guthrum. Apart from these events, during the fourteen years between 878 and 892 Wessex was unmolested. These were the creative years in which Alfred initiated his program of military reform and cultural revival, which will be examined presently.

In 892 the Danes returned in force and Alfred's defensive measures were put to the test. The war of 892–96 is reported at considerable length in the contemporary record of the *Anglo-Saxon Chronicle*. Without following the campaigns in detail we may say that once more the Danish strategy rested upon the occupation of bases from which raids could be launched. However, there were contrasts with the earlier crises of 870–71 and 875–78. Whereas the earlier invaders had repeatedly penetrated into the heart of Alfred's kingdom (e.g., Wilton 871, Wareham 876), those of 892–96 got into Wessex only once, in 893. Whereas the earlier invaders had won victory after victory, particularly in the years 870–71, the Danes who broke into Wessex in 893 were defeated by the king's son Edward at Fareham before they had got very far. Furthermore, although the Danes were difficult to pin down and bring to battle, the English forces could on occasion do this. They matched the mobility of the Danes, pursuing them right up the valley of the Severn in 893. They could dislodge them from their bases, as at Chester in 894 and in the valley of the river Lea near London in 895. They could sometimes corner and defeat them, as Alderman Ethelred of Mercia, Alfred's son-in-law, did at Buttington in 893. They could also by now engage the Danes by sea as well as on land, as in 896, with at least fair success. By the summer of 896 the

Danish leaders had realized that Wessex was too well-defended for them. Their army dispersed, some to East Anglia or Northumbria, some to further campaigning across the Channel in Francia. The remaining three years of Alfred's reign are ill-documented but were apparently peaceful. He died on 26 October 899, aged about fifty, and was buried at Winchester.

Even from so brief a sketch as this it will be apparent that we know far more about Alfred than we do about even the greatest of earlier Anglo-Saxon rulers such as Edwin or Offa. The sources that bear upon his life and reign are abundant (by early medieval standards), diverse, absorbing, and problematical. The best introduction to Alfred is to *read the sources* relating to him: nearly all of them are available in translations. In the first place there is the biography of Alfred by his friend, teacher, and bishop, the Welshman Asser, composed in 893: see the entry under Asser for some discussion of it. Then there is the set of vernacular annals known as the *Anglo-Saxon Chronicle*. The *Chronicle*'s account of the reign of Alfred is full if not always completely frank and was probably put together in the 890s. In other words, the *Chronicle*, like Asser, is a contemporary authority. There has been much debate about the origins and authorship of the *Anglo-Saxon Chronicle*. To my mind there can be little doubt that the work is in some sense an official production, the composition of men who had close connections with the royal court and worked under the patronage of the king—though this is a view that not all scholars would accept. Thirdly, the code of laws issued by the king perhaps about 890 sheds light not only on the institutions and social life of Alfred's Wessex but also on his interpretation of his role as a Christian ruler. Further revelations of Alfred's thought and aspirations are furnished, in the fourth place, by the king's own writings, which will be discussed below. Finally, some official documents survive from his reign. These include such texts as the treaty with Guthrum, King Alfred's will, records relating to the building of fortresses, a small amount of diplomatic correspondence, and a handful of charters recording grants of land. Finally there remains a certain amount of physical, archaeological evidence that includes such diverse items as specimens of Alfred's coins, the famous "Alfred Jewel," treasure-hoards such as those of Croydon or Trewhiddle, the recently recovered evidence of the replanning of

Winchester, the ramparts of some fortresses, and a small number of manuscripts. All in all, it is a fairly impressive array.

These sources can be used to shed light on Alfred's major achievement, the transformation of the military capacities of Wessex in the years of relative peace between 878 and 892. We have already seen that there are several points of contrast between the fighting of 870–78 and that of 892–96. The main reason why the Danes found it so much harder to break into Wessex in the 890s was that the kingdom was by then protected by a ring of fortresses known as *burhs*. A document known as the Burghal Hidage, which in its original form probably dated from Alfred's reign, lists thirty such fortresses round the frontiers and in the interior of Wessex, and furnishes statistics that make it possible to calculate both the length of the ramparts and the size of the garrison that defended them. Excavation has shown in several instances that there was an almost exact correspondence between the size of the fortress as built and the size stipulated in the Burghal Hidage, the government's blueprint. This is a very important point, for it establishes that Alfred's government could achieve on the ground what it planned in the council-chamber. Not all governments can. If we can take the figures for measurement seriously it follows that we are empowered to take the manpower figures seriously too. They show that some 27,000 men were assigned to the maintenance and defense of the *burhs*. Of course, these men were not all serving at once and they were scattered from east Sussex to north Devon. Yet it remains an astonishing number of troops in the light of what we know, or think we know, of ninth-century warfare.

The *burhs* were of various types. Some were former Roman towns or forts (Chichester, Portchester), some were fortified royal estates (Wilton, Eashing), some involved the strengthening of positions of natural defensive potential (Lydford), some were new fortified settlements on open and vulnerable sites (Cricklade, Wallingford). It is difficult to date their construction at all closely. Shaftesbury was fortified in 880. Asser makes it plain that several had been completed by 893 (e.g., Lyng, Wareham), while a famous entry in the *Chronicle* shows that at least one was "only half-made" in 892. The program of fortification was certainly incomplete at the end of the reign: the crown did not acquire the Roman fort at Portchester until 904.

Slow though it may have been, the process of fortification remains a remarkable achievement. But it was only one of Alfred's military reforms. A system of fortresses geared to static defense can only operate effectively in conjunction with a mobile army in the field. Alfred needed a striking force, not necessarily very big, but well-equipped and above all well-mounted. Early Anglo-Saxon military organization remains fairly mysterious, but it is accepted that by the ninth century at the latest military service was exacted from landholders in respect of assessments reckoned in numbers of "hides" of land (see the entry devoted to King Ethelbald of Mercia). Levies were mustered by counties under the command of the alderman of the shire. The army raised in this fashion was called the *fyrd*. In a much-discussed passage the *Anglo-Saxon Chronicle* tells us that by 893 "the king had divided his army into two, so that always half its men were at home, half out on service." Exactly what is meant is not clear. One possible interpretation of these words is that Alfred had pooled the resources due from the assessments in order to levy a smaller but more effective fighting force. An example will make the point clearer. In 892 Alfred granted an estate assessed at ten hides at North Newnton in Wiltshire to Ethelhelm the alderman of Wiltshire. Let us suppose—and there are some grounds for the supposition—that every unit of five hides was required to send one warrior to the king's army. Under the prereform system North Newnton would have been liable for the service of two men. After Alfred's reform only one man would have been due, but he would have been supported by the resources of the whole estate. In this fashion the king could raise an army of half the traditional size, but better equipped in weapons, armor, horse, saddlery, and provisions—an army of specialist soldiers.

Alfred also challenged the Danes on the element where they had long enjoyed mastery—the sea. The *Chronicle* tells us in its annal for 896 that the king

> ordered long-ships to be built with which to oppose the Viking warships. They were almost twice as long as the others. Some had sixty oars, some more. They were both swifter and more stable and also higher than the others.

Earlier Anglo-Saxon rulers had disposed of ships, for example, Ecgfrith of Northumbria, so Alfred was not, as long-cherished national mythology maintains, "the founder of the English navy." Furthermore, his fleet was less effective than he might have hoped. Nevertheless, sea power was an important element in the armory of his tenth-century successors such as Edgar, and it is the case that a royal navy has had a *continuous* history in England from Alfred's day until our own.

Frisian seamen distinguished enough to rate an obituary notice in the *Anglo-Saxon Chronicle* were in Alfred's service in 896 and their presence in England is confirmed by Asser. The king's debt to them as shipwrights and captains may have been considerable. It is likely that this was only one of several debts that Alfred owed to his neighbors across the Channel. The military reforms outlined above are paralleled in ninth-century Francia. Of course, rulers confronted by similar problems are apt to try to solve them in similar ways without necessarily borrowing ideas or techniques one from another. Nevertheless, one may usefully speculate on the nature of Alfred's overseas relations and the repercussions on West Saxon institutions and practices that they might have had.

Alfred was probably a good deal more aware of the continent of Europe than have been at least some among nineteenth- and twentieth-century historians who have devoted their attentions to him. He had visited Rome as a boy in the company of his father. He regularly sent alms to Rome and received at least one letter from Pope John VIII. His sister Aethelswith, the wife of King Burgred of Mercia who was deposed by the Danes in 874, spent her later years in Italy until her death in 888. Alfred's father Ethelwulf, we should recall, had had a Frankish secretary and had married as his second wife a Frankish princess. Alfred's wife Ealhswith—they were married in 868—was English, a noblewoman descended from the Mercian royal dynasty. Of the five children of their marriage who lived to maturity, one of the daughters, Aelfthryth, married Baldwin II, count of Flanders, between 893 and 899. Alfred corresponded with Archbishop Fulk of Rheims, and attracted scholars from Francia to his court such as Grimbald and John. The compiler of the *Anglo-Saxon Chronicle* was knowledgeable about Frankish affairs. We can sense a web of contact between Alfred's Wessex and the western European continent that may have been a good deal more dense than the surviving evidence allows us to see.

It was not only in the military field that Alfred may have been indebted to his Frankish neighbors. Consider these other and diverse pieces of evidence. First, there is the code of laws, which was probably drawn up about 890. We cannot be certain that any English ruler had issued laws since King Ine of Wessex nearly two centuries earlier. (The theory that Offa of Mercia had issued laws is now regarded as ill-founded.) Frankish rulers of the ninth century, especially Charles the Bald (d. 877) whose court Alfred had visited, had been tireless, one might almost say frenzied, legislators. If we were to seek immediate precedents for Alfred's role as a legislator we should find them in western Francia. It is of interest that some of the individual clauses in Alfred's laws betray the influence of Frankish practice, for example, the requirement that his subjects should swear an oath of loyalty to him. Secondly, there is the exquisite Alfred Jewel, now preserved in the Ashmolean Museum in Oxford. It was found in 1693 at North Petherton in Somerset, not far from the Alfredian burh at Lyng and the Alfredian monastery at Athelney. It bears an inscription reading "Alfred ordered me to be made." Whatever the function of the jewel, about which there has been much debate, there can be no doubt that the patron referred to was the king. Some of the decorative techniques it displays are not Anglo-Saxon but Frankish. Asser indeed tells us that the king "assembled craftsmen in almost countless quantity from many races." In the third place there is the remodelling of Winchester. During the 880s, in all probability, the town of Winchester was comprehensively replanned inside its refurbished Roman defenses. A new grid-pattern of streets was laid down, bounded by a road that ran round the inside of the walls. This operation involved the laying of at least five miles of road and their surfacing with nearly 8,000 tons of flint cobbles. Only a king could have mobilized the resources for such a task: the initiative must have been Alfred's. The purpose was not simply defensive. Winchester included a royal palace, a cathedral and its community, a new monastery probably planned by Alfred though not completed until after his death, and a nunnery founded by Queen Ealhswith. It also housed a royal mint, merchants on whose services the court depended, and residences for the counsellors in attendance on the king. Alfred's Winchester was not exactly a capital city in our sense of the term, but it was the closest thing to one in Wessex—a favored royal residence, a place of ceremonial, prayer and liturgy, a fit setting for solemn acts of state, and a mausoleum where kings would rest and be remembered after their deaths. Surely its inspiration, at least in part, was

Frankish. Alfred's Winchester was to Wessex what Charlemagne's Aachen was to the kingdom of the Franks.

Like Frankish rulers such as Charlemagne or Charles the Bald, though on a more modest scale, Alfred was a patron of learning. Unlike them he personally contributed to the intellectual revival that he sponsored and it is this activity that is his most enduring claim to fame. Alfred regarded his attempts to rehabilitate English learning as part and parcel of his kingly responsibilities. The connection may not be obvious to us but it was clear to Alfred. The Danish invasions were a sign of divine displeasure. In the last resort it would be only with the help of God that the English could resist them. God would extend his help only to a devout people. Learning was one path to godliness. Alfred himself put the matter thus:

> Remember what punishment befell us in this world when we did not cherish learning nor transmit it to others.

It was, then, a central part of a Christian ruler's duties to encourage learning. To this end Alfred recruited a number of learned men. They included Plegmund, a native of Mercia who became archbishop of Canterbury in 890; the Welshman Asser, who became bishop of Sherborne; another Mercian, Bishop Werferth of Worcester; a Flemish monk, Grimbald of St. Bertin's; and a monk from continental Saxony named John who was made abbot of Alfred's monastic foundation at Athelney. One is reminded of the circle of scholars headed by Alcuin whom Charlemagne had gathered about him at Aachen. Through the efforts of these five men, and doubtless of others whose names we do not know, the ground was prepared for the intellectual achievements of the tenth century.

Alfred's own contribution to the revival of learning was to translate from Latin into Old English "certain books," in his own words, "which are the most necessary for all men to know." He had learned to read the vernacular as a child and went on to learn Latin as a grown man: he seems to have become proficient in Latin in 887. Alfred personally translated three works. The earliest, perhaps done about 890, was the *Liber Regulae Pastoralis* ("Book of Pastoral Rule") of Pope Gregory I. The work had been intended by its author as a guide to good conduct for bishops but by Alfred's day, largely under the influence of Frankish scholarship, its precepts were being applied to the office of a king. Alfred composed an important preface to his translation in which he outlined his intellectual and educational ideals. The other two works were the *Soliloquies* of St. Augustine of Hippo and the *Consolation of Philosophy* by Boethius. The latter work was for the early Middle Ages the classic account of endurance in the face of adversity and the pursuit of wisdom as a means of rising above earthly misfortune. Augustine's *Soliloquies* dwelt on the immortality of the soul. Alfred's very free rendering of this text enabled him in the course of reflecting on this topic to produce a kind of spiritual self-portrait. In addition to these three works the king began but did not live to complete a translation of the psalter into Old English. Alfred was helped in his translations by members of his team of scholars. They in their turn translated other works, the most important of which was the *Ecclesiastical History* of Bede.

These works were not chosen at random. Together they formed a coherent body of literature designed to expound righteousness to a troubled society: the understanding of God's actions in history, the responsibilities of authority, and the Christian aspirations of mankind. The Alfredian translations, together with the *Anglo-Saxon Chronicle* and the king's code of law, constituted an intellectual "survival-kit" for an embattled nation. They were intended for his people's comfort and instruction, and the king did his best to ensure that they were widely disseminated.

Alfred was first called "the Great" by the thirteenth-century chronicler Matthew Paris. It has been acutely observed that "we hold that Alfred was a great and glorious king in part because he rightly implies this." In other words the sources on which our knowledge of his doings is based were for the most part put together directly or indirectly at his instigation. Asser's biography and the *Chronicle* have provided as it were a frame in which we have unavoidably to see their portrait or image of the king. It was the chronicler who contrived to obscure the extreme fragility of Alfred's position in the years 871–77. It was Asser who rendered unforgettably those aspects of Alfred's character that so appealed to the Victorians: his moral uprightness, his warm family life, his struggles against ill-health, his earnest self-improvement. It is not easy to step outside this frame and try to see the king from a different angle. The few hints that we do have are enough to suggest, unsurprisingly, that the reality was more complicated than the image. Alfred was not above laying hands on ecclesiastical endowments to supplement his revenues: so much is suggested by a surviving letter from Pope John VIII to Archbishop Ethelred of Canterbury and by Alfred's posthumous reputation as a seizer of church property with the monks of Abingdon. The king who in 885 sent his ships to East Anglia "full of warriors in search of plunder" was behaving more like his Viking enemies than like the temperate statesman of later mythology. The ruler who incurred unpopularity by imposing a vast program of forced labor on his subjects thought it prudent to lay down Draconian penalties for plotting against the king's life. Alfred was a man of robustly traditional tastes—a warrior, a hunter, a ring-giver—as well as the scholar and seeker after knowledge revealed in his writings.

"Alfred is the most perfect character in history." This breathtaking claim was made about a hundred and twenty years ago by the distinguished historian E. A. Freeman. It shows to what lengths the adulation of Alfred could be taken in the nineteenth century. (And not just in the nineteenth century. Visitors to the gardens at Stourhead should climb two-and-a-half miles to the northwest and read the inscription on Alfred's Tower, built in 1772. George III as well as Queen Victoria christened a son Alfred.) To react against this adulation is not to "debunk" but to try to attain a juster appreciation of the historical Alfred. He was a man of his time, like everyone else. His achievements rested in some degree on foundations laid by his father Ethelwulf and on lessons learned from his Frankish neighbors. He was uniquely fortunate, among English monarchs, in his propagandists. His insular countrymen have too readily forgotten that there were ninth-century kings in France, Germany, Spain, and Italy who likewise successfully defended their kingdoms from invasion.

All this may be said, and it is not—and certainly not intended—to detract from his achievement. Our abiding impression of Alfred is of a man who was quite singularly *interesting*. He had an orderly mind (see Asser on his organization of his revenues) and he was fertile in practical expedient (whether in the construction of ships or of lantern-clocks). Unlike many practical people he was also endowed with a speculative mind, charged with intellectual vitality. How many kings have taught themselves Latin at the age of thirty-eight? In his writings we can eavesdrop on his thoughts: observe his intellectual curiosity and his capacity for wonder (for example, his fascination with Ottarr's account of his voyage round the North Cape); witness his anxious self-examination and reflections on his responsibilities as a Christian king. And all this, we should remember, from a man who suffered from bodily infirmity and all the tribulations of the cares of state. "He stood, I believe, head and shoulders above all the kings of England who came before and after him." This was the verdict of an Anglo-Norman historian writing in about 1120. I see no reason why a historian writing in the 1980s should dissent from that judgment.

M. Lapidge and S. Keynes, *Alfred the Great*, 1983, contains translations of the more important texts with elaborate commentary upon them.

GUTHRUM (*d.* 890) was a Viking leader who became king of the Danish kingdom of East Anglia. Guthrum may have been the leader of what the *Anglo-Saxon Chronicle* referred to as "the great summer army" that arrived in England in 871 and joined forces with Halfdan to campaign against Wessex. Guthrum and Halfdan campaigned together successively against Wessex, Northumbria, and Mercia. In 875 the Danish forces divided: Halfdan and his followers returned to Northumbria, while Guthrum led his men into East Anglia where they based themselves at Cambridge for a year.

In 876 Guthrum struck against Wessex. In a move of great daring he slipped past the West Saxon forces and penetrated to Wareham in the heart of the kingdom. Alfred, helpless and outmaneuvered, was forced to buy peace. But Guthrum was not to be pinned down by treaties. He penetrated yet deeper into Wessex, as far as Exeter, vainly pursued by Alfred, and seems to have wintered there. In August of the following year, 877, Guthrum withdrew his troops from Devon, apparently spontaneously, and retired to Mercia. The army settled at Gloucester for the winter of 877–78. Early in January 878 Guthrum's army stole into Wessex and occupied Chippenham. It was a bold move, executed in the depths of winter when campaigning was usually suspended, and it took the West Saxons by surprise. Alfred fled westward and sought refuge at Athelney in what was then the trackless fenland of north Somerset. Wessex seemed to lie at Guthrum's feet. However, Alfred made a surprising recovery. From his base at Athelney he mustered support and began to undertake guerrilla warfare against the Danes. Early in May he moved eastward, gathering an army about him. The decisive battle was fought at Edington in Wiltshire about the middle of May: Guthrum was defeated and his army chased back to Chippenham. Two weeks later the Danes agreed to terms. These included the baptism of Guthrum as a Christian, with Alfred as godfather, in token of submission. The ceremony took place near Athelney in June, and Guthrum adopted the Christian and Anglo-Saxon name Athelstan.

Guthrum and his army remained peacefully in Mercia until 880 when they returned to East Anglia. In the words of Alfred's biographer Asser they then "divided up the province and began to settle there," as Halfdan's followers had done in Northumbria in 876. Guthrum reigned over them as their king until his death in 890. We know very little about his reign. His men remained a potential menace to King Alfred: in 884, for example, they joined a party of Vikings who descended on Kent. But Guthrum himself seems to have taken seriously his new role as a Christian king. He issued coinage modelled on Alfred's and bearing his baptismal name Athelstan; his coinage may have included the pieces struck in memory of King Edmund of East Anglia who had been killed by the Danes in 870. He collaborated with Alfred in drawing up a treaty between 886 and 890, which defined their common frontier and was intended to facilitate peaceful relations between English and Danes.

Not the least interesting feature of Alfred and Guthrum's treaty is its revelation that trading links between English and Danes were already in existence. Written and archaeological evidence shows that East Anglian towns such as Norwich, Thetford, and Stamford experienced a surge of economic growth and prosperity from the late ninth century through to the end of the Anglo-Saxon period and beyond. So did other towns where Vikings settled, such as York, Lincoln, Dublin, and Rouen. Trading existed alongside raiding. It was the creative contribution of the Scandinavians to early medieval economic and social life.

A. P. Smyth, *Scandinavian Kings in the British Isles, 850–880*, 1977. The text of the treaty is to be found in S. Keynes and M. Lapidge (trans.), *Alfred the Great*, 1983.

ASSER (*d.* 909 or 910) was a native of Wales who became bishop of Sherborne and composed, during its subject's lifetime, a remarkable biography of King Alfred. Asser was brought up at St. David's where he became a monk and priest. A kinsman of his named Nobis was bishop of St. David's from 840 to 874, and it is just possible that Asser too was bishop of St. David's before his translation to the English see of Sherborne. It was probably in 885 that Asser travelled to Wessex, apparently on a diplomatic mission, and met Alfred for the first time at Dean in Sussex. Alfred invited him to become a member of the royal household. We may presume that the king had been impressed by Asser's learning: it was at this period that Alfred was gathering learned men at his court to assist in his educational plans, as for example, Plegmund and Grimbald, and Asser fits neatly into this context. Asser's obligations to the community at St. David's did not permit him to take up Alfred's invitation unreservedly. A compromise was reached by which Asser agreed to divide his time equally between Wales and Wessex. We sometimes catch a glimpse of him on his journeys to Wessex over the next few years. In 886, for example, Asser recorded that "I read aloud to him whatever books he wished and which we had to hand," and in 887 he was in the king's company when Alfred learned to read Latin.

Asser did eventually settle permanently in Wessex. His rewards were very considerable, in lands, churches, rights, and goods. They included foreign luxuries of great rarity and value, such as a silk cloak and—in Asser's words—the weight "of a strong man's load" in incense. The most important of all was the bishopric of Sherborne, granted to him at some point that cannot be precisely determined in the course of the 890s, perhaps about 894. Sherborne was no longer the exposed frontier diocese that it had been in the time of Aldhelm. It was the largest diocese in Wessex, embracing Dorset, Somerset, Devon, and Cornwall; the reliability of its bishop therefore a matter of concern to the royal house. It is Asser himself who makes this clear when he tells in his *Life of Alfred* of a conspiracy in the 850s against King Ethelwulf in which the then bishop of Sherborne was implicated. Asser's promotion to Sherborne marked him out as a man in whom Alfred placed special trust. One might suspect that the services performed by Asser were not confined to guiding the king along the pathway to learning. Like Plegmund, Asser was an important prop of the Alfredian regime.

In particular he may have played a significant role in Alfred's negotiations with the Welsh, whose princes were not above making
common cause with the king's Viking enemies.

Asser's biography of Alfred may fruitfully be considered in the
same light, as a work in some sense moved by purposes not unconnected with Alfred's rule. Such circumlocutory cautions as these
are necessary because Asser's work is extremely odd: so odd that
some scholars have, misguidedly, argued that it is an eleventh-century forgery. Its oddness consists partly in its clumsy arrangement,
partly in its turgid style, but most of all in its uniqueness; there is
no other English source from the pre-Conquest period that is anything like it. Its closest literary counterparts are not English but
Frankish. Asser had read Einhard's *Life of Charlemagne*, and there
are analogies between the *Life of Alfred* and other Carolingian royal
biographies composed in the ninth century.

Asser completed the biography in 893. In considering its functions it is important to bear in mind that it was devoted to a living
king, not to the commemoration of a dead one. Asser's principal
theme was that Alfred was the perfect ruler: victorious, merciful,
pious, generous, just, wise, temperate, and earnest; a perfect man
as well as a perfect king. Asser never permitted himself a hint of
criticism of his hero. His discretion was as rigid as that of Bede—
an author cultivated and indeed translated at Alfred's court. In
considering Asser, as in considering Bede, it is worth asking some
such questions as these. What does he *not* tell us about? For whom
was the work intended? How was this primary audience meant to
react to it?

Questions like these are easier to ask than to answer. Asser
never tells us anything at all about the internal politics of Alfred's
reign. But he does go out of his way to furnish information dis-
creditable to the memory of two of Alfred's royal brothers, Ethelbald and Ethelred I. The latter's son Ethelwold rebelled against
Alfred's son Edward in the years 900–902. It would be most surprising had there been no stresses within the West Saxon dynasty during Alfred's lifetime. But if there were, Asser drops never a hint of
their presence. Or again, Asser devotes a chapter to the dire fate of
those who were reluctant to undertake the work of fortress-build-
ing ordered by the king. The passage incidentally reveals that the
vast program of public works built by forced labor had roused re-
sentment that had been harshly punished by the king. Evidently

not all of Alfred's subjects shared Asser's image of a ruler activated by wise forethought and mild benevolence.

These are two instances of ways in which Asser was concerned to project an image of the king that may not have corresponded in every particular with reality. Such an image was presumably directed at the ruling elite of Alfred's kingdom, with the aim of eliciting loyalty to this paragon of rulership; or even perhaps at the king himself, so that he and his immediate family could warm themselves at the fireside of Asser's devotion.

Whatever Asser's immediate aims and audience, about which we can never be certain, one thing is for sure: with posterity his work has been a resounding success. We have to see Alfred the way Asser wants us to.

PLEGMUND (*d.* 923) was archbishop of Canterbury from 890 until his death. He was a native of Mercia. Later tradition asserted that he had lived as a hermit at Plemstall, near Chester. There is no means of testing this tradition, but it should be noted that the earliest recorded form of the place-name is *Plegmundes stow*, "the holy place of Plegmund." At some time unknown, but before 887, he was attracted to the court of King Alfred, by whose agency he was promoted to the archbishopric of Canterbury in 890.

Plegmund's archiepiscopate was long and important. It is unfortunate that we know so little about it. What we do know suggests that Plegmund was an active and creative figure in the life of the English church. His most enduring contribution to that life was an administrative one. Between 910 and 918 he subdivided the two enormous dioceses of Wessex, Winchester, and Sherborne, and created three additional ones. Seats for bishops were established at Crediton (with a diocese embracing Devon and Cornwall), Wells (Somerset), and Ramsbury (Wiltshire and Berkshire); Sherborne was thenceforward left with Dorset alone, and Winchester with Hampshire and Surrey. In its main lines the administrative reorganization lasted for nearly a thousand years. Whether or not it owed something to Plegmund's reading of what Bede had had to say about Archbishop Theodore—and it may well have done— Bede would have approved of it. He would also have approved of the fact that Plegmund undertook it after consultation with the pope, whom he had visited in 908.

There are some other indications that Plegmund was a churchman of reforming temper. Archbishop Fulk of Rheims (883–922) wrote to Plegmund at some point, apparently—for we know of the letter only through a tenth-century chronicler's précis—congratulating him on his attempts to extirpate clerical marriage among the English. It is likely that this refers to legislation issued by Plegmund, presumably in an ecclesiastical council. We also possess the text of a letter from Pope Formosus (891–96), whom Plegmund may have visited in 896, which seems to suggest that the English bishops were taking steps under their archbishop's guidance to convert the Scandinavian settlers in the Danelaw to Christianity—a tantalizing allusion to an important but obscure activity.

Plegmund's reforming initiatives, administrative and otherwise, could only have been undertaken with the active support of the two kings he served, Alfred and Edward the Elder. Of his relations with Edward we know practically nothing: the civil government of that king is very ill-documented. But we are better informed about his association with Alfred. In the preface to the translation of Pope Gregory's *Pastoral Care* into Old English, attributed to Alfred, the king thanked four men for their assistance: Plegmund, Asser, Grimbald, and John. We may take it that Plegmund was closely involved with Alfred's educational plans. This is confirmed by the evidence of surviving documents written at Canterbury. The charters of the period between about 850 and 890 were drafted by men who were barely literate: knowledge of Latin was shaky, calligraphic standards abysmal. And this at the oldest seat of English Christianity—one is put in mind of Alfred's observation that at the time of his accession in 871 there were very few people left in England who could understand the services of the church or translate a document from Latin into English. But under Plegmund there came a change for the better, which it is surely correct to attribute to his initiative. Basic literacy returned; Latinity and script improved; the modest yet firm foundation for the tenth-century intellectual revival was laid down.

Plegmund was associated with Alfred's other projects. In 898 he attended a meeting called by the king, along with Alderman Ethelred, his wife Ethelflaed, and Bishop Werferth of Worcester, to discuss what was described as the *instauratio* of the city of London; by which was probably meant such matters as planning and fortification in the wake of Alfred's takeover of London from the Danes in 886. Plegmund acquired property in the city, including a river-frontage, for his church of Canterbury. He had therefore close connections with the Alfredian program of urban renewal and defense.

Legislation was another area of activity where Plegmund might have been of service to Alfred. The king's code of law, issued probably in the 890s, was more intellectually elaborate than any of the codes promulgated by previous Anglo-Saxon rulers and more deeply impregnated with Christian values. It is difficult to believe that churchmen of high rank did not have some say in drafting it. (Wihtred and Ine had legislated with the advice of their bishops, and Archbishop Wulfstan was to draft a whole series of codes for Ethelred II and Canute. Again, Alfred's Carolingian contemporaries across the Channel were accustomed to receiving episcopal guidance and admonition.) The case is strengthened by the circumstance that some of the linguistic usages of Alfred's law-code display Mercian rather than West Saxon forms of Old English. The mind turns irresistibly to Alfred's Mercian archbishop of Canterbury.

This is as much as we can know, and reasonably infer, about Archbishop Plegmund. The sketch is necessarily indistinct. But we can sense the outlines of a statesman who was a sturdy prop of the Alfredian and Edwardian regime.

WERFERTH (*d.* 915) was bishop of Worcester from about 872 until his death, and one of the collaborators with King Alfred in the revival of English learning. Like Plegmund he was a native of Mercia and was appointed to his bishopric toward the end of the reign of King Burgred (852–74). In 874 he received an important grant of privileges from the succeeding king, Ceolwulf, the puppet ruler set up by the Danes. Perhaps he had to be enticed from Mercian loyalties by more than intellectual interests. He was later to refer to Alfred as "his ring-giver . . . the greatest treasure-giver of all the kings he has ever heard tell of," and to be left a large sum of gold in Alfred's will. One suspects that Werferth may have found the service of Alfred as materially rewarding as did Asser.

We cannot be sure when he entered Alfred's entourage, though it was probably in the first half of the 880s. He had translated the *Dialogues* of Pope Gregory into English before 893, probably with a collaborator, at the king's command. We know that he received a copy of Alfred's translation of Gregory's *Pastoral Care,* for his own manuscript of it has survived: it is now in the Bodleian Library in Oxford. Like other associates of the king, Werferth was prominent in public affairs as well as in intellectual endeavor. He was instrumental in having the town of Worcester fortified by Alderman Ethelred and his wife Ethelflaed in the 890s. He received a grant of land and privileges in London in 889 and a further grant in 898 when the replanning and fortification of the city were under discussion.

Over forty years a bishop, Werferth, like his fellow-Mercian Plegmund, was a force for stability and continuity in anxious times and probably an important agent in the drawing together of Mercia and Wessex, which preceded their more effective integration in the tenth century.

GRIMBALD (*d.* 901) was a monk of St. Bertin's in Flanders who was recruited by King Alfred to help him in his plans to revive religious and intellectual life in England. He was born probably in the 820s, entered the monastery of St. Bertin's between 834 and 844, and is last traceable in Flanders in the year 885. He seems then to have entered the service of Archbishop Fulk of Rheims, who had previously been abbot of St. Bertin's. Alfred apparently wrote to Fulk asking that Grimbald be allowed to come to England; how Alfred knew of Grimbald we do not know. Fulk's reply to this request has survived. He was prepared to let Grimbald go, but anxious to ensure that he be suitably rewarded. The implication was that Grimbald might expect to be offered a bishopric in England. Grimbald crossed the Channel to attach himself to Alfred's court probably in 886 or 887.

Fulk had praised Grimbald's skill as a teacher. Asser tells us that Grimbald was "extremely learned." Alfred acknowledged the help of Grimbald, along with Asser, Plegmund, and John, in his preface to the translation of Pope Gregory's *Pastoral Care.* Presumably Grimbald assisted with other Alfredian translations. It is likely that he brought books to England; a manuscript now in Cambridge has been tentatively identified as one of them. It is very likely that it was owing to Grimbald that the *Anglo-Saxon Chronicle* sponsored by Alfred included so much information about Frankish affairs in the 880s and 890s. He was the most important link between England and the Carolingian world in the late ninth century.

Grimbald never got the promised bishopric. Later tradition held that he had been offered Canterbury in 889 but had turned it down in favor of Plegmund: the story may be true. Grimbald was given what was described as "a little monastery" at Winchester where he seems to have spent his latter years. He was apparently involved in the planning that preceded the foundation of the monastery known as the New Minster at Winchester by Alfred's son, King Edward the Elder. Grimbald died in 901 and was buried at Winchester where he was revered after his death as a saint.

JOHN THE OLD SAXON (*fl.* 887–904) was a German monk and scholar who entered the service of King Alfred and became abbot of Athelney. Asser tells us that Alfred summoned from abroad a certain John, "a priest and monk, a man of most acute intelligence, immensely learned in all fields of literary endeavour and ingenious in many other skills." Elsewhere he informs us that John was "of Old Saxon stock," that is, a native of Saxony in the East Frankish or German kingdom. John was one of several scholars recruited by Alfred from outside Wessex to assist in his plans for the revival of English culture: others were Plegmund, Grimbald, and Asser himself. The help these four men rendered the king was acknowledged by him in his preface to his translation of Pope Gregory's *Pastoral Care*. The only other surviving evidence of John's learning consists of three short Latin poems conjecturally attributed to him. However, he may have played a more important part in the Alfredian intellectual revival than this meager evidence suggests. For example, he may have brought manuscripts with him from East Francia. There is a sense in which John brought back to Wessex elements of the culture, now lost in the home country, which had been exported to Germany by such as Boniface and Lul a century and a half earlier.

Alfred appointed John abbot of Athelney, in Somerset, probably round about 890, as part of his plan to revive monastic life in Wessex. The experiment was not a success. Because the English were unenthusiastic about monasticism Alfred had to fill the monastery with foreigners recruited by rather dubious means. The monks of Athelney sound like a job lot. Two of the Frankish inmates tried to murder their abbot, but he survived. Whether or not John persisted as abbot of Athelney after this fracas, we do not know. All we do know about his later life is that he outlived his patron Alfred: his name last features among the witnesses of a royal charter of the year 904.

ETHELRED (*d*. 911) was the alderman of western Mercia from about 883 until his death, and the son-in-law of King Alfred. Nothing certain is known of his ancestry, earlier career, or relations (if any) with previous kings of Mercia. He emerges into the light of history in 883 as the alderman of Mercia—that is, western or non-Danish Mercia—exercising quasi-regal powers there but in some sense the deputy of King Alfred of Wessex. Three years later in 886 Alfred entrusted London to his administration and shortly afterward, probably in 887, gave him his daughter Ethelflaed in marriage.

The heartland of Ethelred's rule was in the valley of the river Severn. We can trace him holding court at Droitwich in 888, at Gloucester in 896, and at Shrewsbury in 901. It was at Gloucester that he and his wife founded a church dedicated to St. Oswald, whose relics were moved there from Bardney in Lincolnshire in 909: recent excavations have shown what a splendid building this was. Other religious communities of the Severn valley also experienced Ethelred's generosity, for example, at Berkeley, Worcester, and Much Wenlock.

Ethelred played an important part in consolidating the English position in western Mercia and in beginning to extend English rule at the expense of the Danes to the east and the Welsh to the west in collaboration with the rulers of Wessex. Asser, the biographer of Alfred and himself a Welshman, tells us that "the might and tyrannical behavior" of Alderman Ethelred and the Mercians drove the petty kings of southeast Wales into submission to the kings of Wessex. Attempts to establish their supremacy over the Welsh princes were to form one of the steady preoccupations of West Saxon rulers—and their Norman and Angevin successors—for several centuries to come.

Ethelred stoutly defended his territories from the Danes. He was one of the leaders of the English army that defeated the Danes at Buttington, near Welshpool in Montgomeryshire, in 893. It was a famous victory; still talked of a century later, as the chronicler Ethelweard tells us. Like his father-in-law in Wessex Ethelred consolidated his hold on Mercia by the building of fortifications. At Worcester he and Ethelflaed "ordered a fortress to be built for the protection of the people" in the 890s. Other forts were constructed "north of the Thames and west of the Severn" at the same period. Unfortunately our source does not tell us where they were, though one of them was very probably at Hereford. Chester was fortified in 907. Ethelflaed was to continue this policy of establishing strong-points after her husband's death. Other and more peaceful means of extending English influence at the expense of the Danes can be traced. A reference in a charter of King Athelstan dated 926 reveals that between 900 and 910 a certain Uhtred had bought from the Danes a large tract of land in north Derbyshire—well outside those parts of Mercia under direct English control—"on the orders of King Edward and Ealdorman [Alderman] Ethelred." There may have been many more such transactions.

There is some reason to suppose that Ethelred was a sick man for the last few years of his life. In 909 a Mercian army ravaged the territory of the northern Danelaw, but we are not told that Ethelred commanded it; and in 910 it was to his wife, not to him, that the building of a fortress at the unidentified place *Bremesburh* was attributed. He died in 911. Ethelred's long rule over western Mercia and his harmonious cooperation with Alfred and Edward were significant factors in the extension of West Saxon authority over regions outside Wessex. Ethelred may not have known it, but he contributed in important ways to the formation of a unified kingdom of England.

INGIMUND (*fl.* 902–7) was the leader of a Viking invasion and settlement of the northwestern regions of England. He was a member of the Norwegian colony in Dublin. Expelled from Ireland in 902, Ingimund attempted to settle in north Wales but was driven off. Pushing farther east he managed to settle his followers in the Wirral peninsula of north Cheshire. It is not impossible that this was a peaceful settlement made under treaty with the English authorities, Alderman Ethelred of Mercia and his wife Ethelflaed— akin to the settlement of Scandinavians in Normandy in 911, though on a smaller scale. Whether or not the initial settlement was peaceful, hostilities soon broke out between the new arrivals and the indigenous population. At some point the Norse attempted to seize Chester: this incident may lie behind the reference in the *Anglo-Saxon Chronicle* to the "restoration" of Chester in 907. The slightly later construction of English fortresses in northwest Mercia—Eddisbury (914), Runcorn (915), Thelwall (919), and *Cledemutha* (probably Rhuddlan, 921)—is best interpreted as a successful attempt to contain Norse expansion from the Wirral.

Ingimund is a very shadowy figure, but he serves to symbolize the Norwegian contribution to the Scandinavian settlement of England. West of the Pennines from the Wirral to the Solway and in much of southwestern Scotland there is plentiful evidence for a Norse presence in the tenth and eleventh centuries. This evidence consists principally of place-names formed from Old Norse, such as Thingwall, Amounderness, Wasdale, or Beckermet. There is a little archaeological evidence as well. To call these settlers "Norse" is to oversimplify. They probably came for the most part from Viking settlements, themselves not exclusively Norse in origin, of quite long standing in Ireland, the Isle of Man, and the Western Isles of Scotland, where mixture with the indigenous Gaelic-speaking populations had taken place. Not surprisingly, therefore, there is evidence of Hibernian, Manx, or Scottish elements among the new settlers. In Cumberland, for instance, the place-name Ireby is marked by the suffix -*by* as a name of Scandinavian type, but the first element *Ire*- points elsewhere: the name means "settlement of the Irish." Or again, Irish as well as Scandinavian and Old English names occur among the moneyers who operated the mint at Chester in the later tenth century. This mingling of cultures in the regions washed by the Irish Sea could give rise to some spectacular works of art: the Gosforth cross is one of the grandest monuments of the Viking age.

F. T. Wainwright, *Scandinavian England*, 1975, contains much material on the Norse settlements. R. N. Bailey, *Viking Age Sculpture in Northern England*, 1980, is a fine treatment of the surviving stone monuments.

ETHELFLAED (*d.* 918), the "Lady of the Mercians," was the wife of Alderman Ethelred of Mercia. She was the eldest child of King Alfred and his queen Ealhswith, born about 869 and married to her much older husband probably in 887. The ill-health of Ethelred's later years brought his wife ever more firmly into the forefront of public affairs and on his death in 911 Ethelflaed stepped into his position as governor of Mercia. Contemporary documents styled her "Lady of the Mercians" and it is under this title that she is still remembered.

Ethelflaed was half-Mercian by birth and was obviously acceptable to the Mercians as their ruler. She was clearly a woman of formidable character, endowed with remarkable talents as politician, diplomat, and general. Her deployment of these skills and her loyal cooperation with her brother King Edward of Wessex during the years 911–18 did much toward the conquest of the Danelaw and the emergence of a unified English kingdom.

Ethelflaed's achievement was fourfold. First, she continued her husband's policy of establishing fortresses to be used both for offense and defense in the joint West Saxon and Mercian advance against the Southumbrian Danes. These included Tamworth, an ancient center of Mercian royal power, and Stafford, fortified in 913, and Warwick, fortified in 914. Secondly, she actively collaborated with her brother Edward in his military campaigns: in 917, for example, she captured the important Danish stronghold of Derby. Thirdly, she kept up Mercian pressure on the Welsh. We hear of a campaign in Wales in 916—and of course there may have been others of which we hear nothing—and some of her fortresses may have been directed as much against the Welsh as against the Danes, for instance, Bridgnorth (912) or Chirbury (915). After her death the Welsh princes submitted to Edward, and it is likely that this was simply a transfer of allegiance from one late Mercian ruler to a new one. Finally, Ethelflaed took initiatives against the Scandinavian settlers of the northern Danelaw. The fortresses of northwestern Mercia, for example, Eddisbury (914) and Runcorn (915), seem to have been directed against Norwegian settlers in Cheshire and Lancashire. She may have sent Mercian troops to join a coalition of northern English and Scottish forces, which fought against Ragnall, the Danish ruler of York, at Corbridge in 918. She was certainly negotiating with the Danes of York—presumably a faction hostile to Ragnall—who promised her their submission shortly before her death in June 918.

These were no mean achievements for a rule of only seven years. It has been suggested that the Old English poem *Judith* was composed in Ethelflaed's honor. Though this can be neither proved nor disproved it may at least be said that the poet's exuberant celebration of Judith's courage, shrewdness, and beauty would have been a fitting and tactful tribute to the "Lady of the Mercians."

The public role of royal women in early medieval Europe has been interestingly explored by P. Stafford, *Queens, Concubines, and Dowagers,* 1983.

EDWARD THE ELDER (*c.* 872–924) was the second child and eldest son of King Alfred whom he succeeded as king of Wessex from 899 until 924. He was born about 872 and given a good education. There are indications that by the late 880s he was regarded as his father's heir-apparent. (This was by no means a foregone conclusion: succession was governed by no hard-and-fast rules, and there were other potential claimants.) He first emerges clearly into the light of history in 893 when he defeated a large army of Danish raiders at Farnham. His succession to the throne in 899 did not go uncontested. His cousin Ethelwold, the son of Alfred's elder brother Ethelred I, rose in rebellion against him, entered into alliance with the Danes of Northumbria and East Anglia, and invaded English Mercia and northern Wessex in 902. In an indecisive battle Ethelwold was killed and his bid for the kingship was over. While he lasted he had been extremely dangerous. Ethelwold's revolt hints at the strains inside the West Saxon dynasty, about which our sources usually maintain a discreet silence.

Edward's most striking achievement as king was his conquest of the Danelaw up as far as the river Humber in a series of campaigns between 909 and 920. In these operations he was assisted by his sister Ethelflaed, the "Lady of the Mercians." His strategy focused upon the building of fortresses, or *burhs*, at key points on the fringes of his territories. Their function was at once defensive and offensive: they served both to discourage Danish raids into English land and to provide bases from which further English advances could be launched. Between 910 and 921 no less than twenty-eight *burhs* were constructed by Edward and Ethelflaed—a very considerable investment of resources.

Edward perceived that the Danes of Northumbria had to be neutralized before he could concentrate his efforts against the southern Danes. A combined Mercian and West Saxon campaign in Northumbria in 909 brought retaliation in 910. A Northumbrian army struck into Mercia and was decisively defeated at Tettenhall in Staffordshire. Danish Northumbria gave Edward no more trouble for the next few years. In 911 he built a *burh* at Hertford and in 912 moved against the Danes of Essex, receiving many submissions and constructing a *burh* at Witham. The eastern advance was suspended in 913 and 914 as Edward beat off raiding-parties from the midlands and a much more serious attack from Danes based in Brittany who penetrated up the Bristol Channel into the lands bordering the lower Severn. After this the king resumed activities in the east. His advance was marked by the building of fortresses at Buckingham (914), Bedford (915), and Maldon (916). The year 917 was one of intense military activity, unusually well-documented in the contemporary record of the *Anglo-Saxon Chronicle*. By the end of the year Edward was in control of the whole of East Anglia together with Cambridgeshire, Huntingdon-shire, and Northamptonshire; fortresses had been built or restored at Towcester, Huntingdon, Colchester, and the unidentified *Wigingamere* (probably in Cambridgeshire). Ethelflaed, meanwhile, had conquered Derby from the Danes. In 918 she went on to occupy Leicester, while Edward moved up the eastern side of the country, absorbing Lincolnshire and Nottinghamshire (*burhs* at Stamford and Nottingham). His northern frontiers were made more secure by fortresses at Thelwall, Manchester, and Bakewell in 919–20. West Saxon power had been carried as far as the river Humber. In a famous passage the *Anglo-Saxon Chronicle* recorded that in 920 the rulers of mainland Britain beyond the Humber— the Danish king of York, the Anglian lord of Bamburgh, the king of the Britons of Strathclyde, and the king of Scots—submitted to King Edward and "chose him as father and lord." At the very least this constituted an undertaking to live at peace with Edward, perhaps to pay tribute too, and it would appear that the promises were honored for the remainder of his reign.

Edward had absorbed not merely the southern Danelaw but also English, i.e., western, Mercia. On the death of Alderman Ethelred of Mercia in 911 Edward annexed London and Oxford "and all the lands which belonged to them" in the valley of the Thames. Immediately after the death of his sister Ethelflaed in 918 he occupied Tamworth "and all the nation in the land of the Mercians which had been subject to Ethelflaed submitted to him." Shortly afterward Ethelflaed's daughter Elfwyn was removed from Mercia to Wessex: nothing more is heard of her. The West Saxon takeover of English Mercia may have been a less peaceable affair than our sources—exclusively West Saxon—permit us to see. Of one thing we can be certain: it was followed up by a thoroughgoing reorganization of the administrative structure of Mercia. The system of local government based on shires administered by royal officials, whose origins we can dimly discern in the Wessex of King Ine two centuries before Edward's day, was extended to Mercia in the tenth century. The shires of English Mercia from Cheshire in the north to Bedfordshire in the south were artificial creations whose boundaries cut across ancient tribal units. It was an assertion of ordered power by an imperialistic West Saxon government riding roughshod over local sentiment and tradition. Exactly when the reorganization was carried through we cannot be certain, but it is likely that that it should be attributed to Edward's initiative. Bedfordshire and Buckinghamshire may have been in existence in 906; perhaps Oxfordshire originated in 911; the west midlands might have been carved up into shires between 918 and 924. In the southern Danelaw, by contrast, Edward was more respectful of earlier arrangements. Essex is the ancient kingdom of the East Saxons, and the "North-folk" and "South-folk" of the East Anglian kingdom were perpetuated as the shires of Norfolk and Suffolk. In the east midlands it seems that the Danes had themselves established administrative units that cut across earlier divisions, and Edward preserved these. Thus, for example, the territories of the Danish "army of Northampton" became the English Northamptonshire.

Edward "the Elder" was the ablest strategist ever produced by the Anglo-Saxons. His campaigns displayed qualities of tenacity and imagination; their follow-up testified to a remarkable ability to organize. Our sources concentrate attention upon his military achievements. But there were others too. The fortresses of Edward's reign were not just military in function. They were intended from the first to be civilian settlements as well as military strongpoints; in a word, towns. Like the *burhs* of Alfred's reign they were in some cases quite big: Stamford was about twenty-eight acres, Stafford about thirty-eight, Warwick about fifty-six. Archaeologists have shown that several of them had planned street-systems. As towns they would have had to be sustained at least to some degree by trade and industry. That this hope was realized is suggested by the history of the coinage. During the reign of Edward's son Athelstan Anglo-Saxon coins started to bear the names of the towns where they were struck. Of the Edwardian *burhs* Chester, Derby, Gloucester, Hereford, Maldon, Nottingham, Oxford, Shrewsbury, Stafford, and Tamworth possessed mints in Athelstan's reign. It is likely that several towns in this list were striking coin in Edward's day. Further evidence, which suggests a lively, developing economy, is furnished by Edward's legislation. Of his two legal ordinances the first addressed itself particularly to issues connected with the buying and selling of livestock; and it is significant that the king wished to channel such transactions into the towns.

Edward continued his parents' development and embellishment of Winchester. Early in his reign he founded a religious community there, the New Minster, so-called to distinguish it from the cathedral or Old Minster next door to it: its church was dedicated in 903. He was probably responsible for completing his mother's foundation for women at Winchester, the so-called Nunnaminster, after her death in 902. His daughter Eadburga (*d. c.* 951) became a nun there and was later regarded as a saint. Edward's religious patronage brought him into contact with foreign churchmen. New Minster was provided with relics of St. Judoc, a Breton saint of the seventh century. We hear casually, in a letter from the prior of Dol in Brittany to King Athelstan written in about 926, that Edward had been linked by confraternity to the canons of Dol. Since Athelstan acquired relics from this source it is possible that Edward got Judoc's relics from Dol. There may have been more contacts of this type and it is extremely likely that books and works of art also passed to England by such means.

There were in addition diplomatic contacts with foreign rulers. His sister Elfthryth had been married to the count of Flanders between 893 and 899: Anglo-Flemish contacts remained close throughout the tenth century. Between 917 and 919 Edward married his daughter Eadgifu to Charles, king of the West Frankish kingdom (i.e., France). When Charles was deposed in 922 Eadgifu came back to England as a refugee with her young son Louis. The boy was brought up in England until he was recalled to the throne of France in 936. Louis was not the only political exile in England. There were members of the Breton aristocracy, driven out by Viking invasions of Brittany in 919. Edward's court also attracted foreign churchmen. Theodred, bishop of London from *c.* 926 to *c.* 951, was probably a German: he was promoted to an important bishopric so soon after Edward's death that it is likely that his rise to prominence occurred during the king's reign. Oda, later to be archbishop of Canterbury, was another foreigner who made his mark under Edward.

Our knowledge of these doings and persons is fragmentary, inferences to be drawn from them hazardous. Such as it is, the evidence suggests that Edward was more than just an exceptionally talented soldier. In historical reputation he has always been somewhat overshadowed by his father and his son. It was his misfortune to have had no Asser to transmit an image of him to posterity. If any such work were composed, which is possible, it has not survived. Yet his achievements were on a par with those of Alfred and Athelstan.

In 924 the people of Chester rebelled. Edward went north and suppressed the revolt, and died shortly afterwards at Farndon, a little to the south of Chester, on 17 July. He was buried in the New Minster at Winchester.

ATHELSTAN (*c.* 894–939) was the eldest child of King Edward "the Elder" whom he succeeded as king of Wessex from 924 until 939. He was brought up in the household of his aunt Ethelflaed, the "Lady of the Mercians," and was given a good education. He was the first prince of the West Saxon dynasty to have been brought up in and therefore to have had an intimate knowledge of Mercia. This undoubtedly helped him in the government of the recently enlarged dominion—Wessex *and* Mercia—which his father left to him. His succession to the throne, like that of his father and of several others in the tenth century, did not go uncontested. A certain Alfred who may possibly have been a member of the royal family challenged Athelstan's succession. That Alfred may have been more dangerous than our sources let on is suggested by the fact that Athelstan's coronation did not take place until September 925, fourteen months after his accession.

Early in 926 Athelstan married one of his sisters to Sihtric, the ruler of the Viking kingdom of York. Perhaps he wanted to maintain the peaceful relations that his father had established in 920. However, Sihtric died in the following year and Athelstan moved against his brother and successor Guthfrith. In the summer of 927 he overran the Viking kingdom; went on to receive near Penrith an acknowledgment of his overlordship from three other northern princes—the rulers of Scotland, Strathclyde, and Bamburgh; destroyed the fortifications of York and distributed to his followers the booty that he found there. For the first time a West Saxon king ruled directly over York. Athelstan's authority there has its tangible memorial in the coin struck in his name at the York mint. Several moneyers worked for him at York and the die that one of them used for striking coin was found recently in the Coppergate excavations in York. However, his hold on the north of England was not secure. It was apparently challenged in or shortly before 934 by the king of Scots, for in the summer of that year Athelstan led a punitive raid against Scotland. A much more serious challenge occurred in 937. Olaf Guthfrithson, the claimant to the kingdom of York, Constantine king of Scots, and Owen king of Strathclyde came together and invaded England. They were met and defeated by Athelstan and his brother Edmund in a hard-fought battle at *Brunanburh*. (The site of the battle has never been satisfactorily identified. It was probably somewhere in the east midlands.) It was a famous and decisive victory, celebrated in verse in the *Anglo-Saxon Chronicle*, which told how the king and his brother "won by the sword's edge undying glory in battle." The north gave no further trouble during Athelstan's reign.

The king was also busy protecting his frontiers with the Britons to the west. At some point in the late 920s he compelled the princes of Wales to submit to him at Hereford. The river Wye was fixed as their common frontier and the Welsh agreed to pay an enormous annual tribute in gold, silver, oxen, hawks, and hounds. Shortly afterward Athelstan chased the Britons of the southwest back across the river Tamar into Cornwall, fortified Exeter in anticipation of possible future raids, and established (by 931) a separate bishopric for Cornwall at St. Germans, west of the Tamar, which was to be subject to Canterbury.

Athelstan maintained and extended the contacts with European rulers that had distinguished the West Saxon dynasty since at least the age of King Ethelwulf. We know more about his foreign relations than we do about those of any earlier English ruler. At the time of his accession his half-sister Eadgifu, wife of the deposed king Charles of West Francia (i.e., France), was a refugee at home in England with her son Louis. In 926 the leading magnate opposed to Charles, Hugh Duke of the Franks, approached Athelstan to seek a similar marriage alliance and was rewarded with the king's half-sister Eadhild. Ten years later Louis was peaceably restored to the kingdom of France over which he ruled until 954. Meanwhile in 928 Henry I of East Francia (i.e., Germany) requested an English bride for his son Otto (later to become the emperor Otto I, *d.* 973), who married another of Athelstan's half-sisters, Edith. It was for the grandchild of this marriage, Matilda, that Ethelweard later composed his chronicle. Yet another half-sister, Aelfgifu, married King Conrad of Burgundy. Athelstan was thus connected by marriage to all the leading rulers of western Europe. He also had friendly dealings with the counts of Brittany. Further to the north, he was on good terms with Harald Fairhair, king of Norway, whose son Haakon was brought up at his court. A ring of protective alliances from which only—and significantly—the Danes and their kinsmen in Normandy were excluded thus ran from the Atlantic coasts of Brittany to the fiords of Norway to guard England's eastern and southern flanks.

Athelstan's foreign policy brought him more than security. It brought him renown as a great king, "surpassing in fame and praise all earthly kings of this age," as a Frankish abbot addressed him in about 925. Of course, in assessing such compliments we must make some allowance for what might be termed the Disraeli factor. "Everyone likes flattery; and when you come to Royalty you should lay it on with a trowel." However, the evidence that Athelstan was regarded by contemporaries as a kind of superking is too widespread and consistent to be discounted. In 926 the ambassadors of Hugh duke of the Franks presented Athelstan, among much else, with the sword of Constantine and Charlemagne's lance (believed to be the Holy Lance with which Christ's side had been pierced on the cross): presents heavy with imperial overtones.

Athelstan's far-flung diplomacy also assisted him to attract men of learning to his court. We know less about his team of scholars than we do about his grandfather's, but recent and subtle investigation of the manuscripts that survive from Athelstan's reign has placed it beyond doubt that such a group existed. There were important contributions that these men could make to Athelstan's regime. They could project an image of the king to his subjects—in the most literal sense. In 934 Athelstan presented a lavish manuscript of Bede's *Life of St. Cuthbert* to the community of St. Cuthbert at Chester-le-Street. The book—which is now in Cambridge—had been prepared at the king's orders, probably in Winchester, and it bore a frontispiece depicting him humbly offering it to the saint. There was more than piety in this gesture. If Athelstan were going to secure his shaky hold over the north of England he needed to attract the loyalty of those who kept alive the memory of the most cherished of the northern saints. Scholars and artists as well as soldiers were the pillars of his authority.

Like any other early medieval king Athelstan was constantly on the move. Take the year 931 for example. On 23 March he was at Colchester in Essex, in late May or early June he was in or near Winchester, and then he moved gradually westward until we find him at Lifton in the west of Devon on 12 November—no doubt to hunt on Dartmoor with his Welsh hawks and hounds and to see to the establishment of the nearby bishopric of St. Germans. The entourage that gathered about the king was big. A charter issued at Lifton was witnessed by a hundred important persons. One should multiply this figure several times (to allow for families, retainers, grooms, servants) to arrive at an idea of the size of the royal court on that occasion. (One should note in passing that among these witnesses were two Welsh princes. To butter them up with some first-rate hunting while impressing them with the magnificence of the English court was one way of keeping such men docile.) The logistics of itinerant kingship must have been of some complexity. How were advance preparations made for the board and lodging of six or seven hundred persons and their mounts? We do not know the answers, for the subject is one about which we are ill-informed, but we may be certain that the administrative skills of literate and numerate royal servants would have been employed.

These skills were also utilised in the drawing up of official documents. Some fifty charters have survived, most of them in copies of a later date, which have reasonable claims to be regarded as authentic records of grants of land or privilege made by Athelstan. Who wrote them? This simple question has generated and still sustains an enormous amount of academic debate, for behind it lurk larger issues. Did Athelstan have a "chancery," in the sense of an organized body of clerks in regular attendance upon him to handle his secretarial needs? Or did the king, when writing was to be done, simply turn to the local scribal skills that happened to be available at, let us say, Colchester, Winchester, or Lifton? In a word, how *organized* was his central government? The question is exceedingly difficult to answer for a number of technical reasons arising from the nature of the evidence. The likelihood is that the answer lies somewhere between the alternatives posed above. It is probable that there was a small group of clerks, not always in attendance on the king and certainly not organized into a chancery, on whose services Athelstan could draw as needed: the tiny nucleus of a civil service.

The same men were presumably responsible for drafting the legal ordinances of which several survive from Athelstan's reign. For example, at some date unknown the king and his counsellors met at Grately in Hampshire and legislated on a wide range of issues that included the treatment of thieves, the regulation of trade, the administration of ordeals, the organization of the coinage, the responsibilities of kinsmen for their members and of lords for their dependents, the punishment of witchcraft—and more besides. This document and others like it are generally referred to as law-codes. It is a somewhat misleading term. They are really administrative ordinances. Their closest parallels are with the similar ordinances, known as capitularies, issued in large quantities by Frankish kings of the eighth and ninth centuries. One is reminded yet again of the debt owed by English rulers of this period to their continental neighbors.

Athelstan died on 27 October 939 and was buried at Malmesbury. He had never married, and was succeeded by his half-brother Edmund. A contemporary has left us a description of him. Athelstan was of middling height, slim and fair-haired. "He was much beloved by his subjects out of admiration for his courage and humility, but like a thunderbolt to rebels by his invincible steadfastness." In both war and peace he was a great king, who built firmly and deliberately upon the foundations laid by his father and grandfather. It was singularly fortunate for England that she experienced, at that juncture in her history, the guidance over seventy years of three such outstandingly gifted rulers.

EDMUND (921–46) was the son of King Edward "the Elder" who succeeded his brother Athelstan as king of Wessex over which he ruled from 939 to 946. The politics of his reign were dominated by his struggle to preserve the conquests of his father and brother. Olaf Guthfrithson, determined to make a comeback after his defeat at *Brunanburh* in 937, returned to England and before the end of 939 had occupied York. In 940 he led his army south across the midlands. He was repulsed at Northampton, then stormed Tamworth and awaited Edmund's retaliation at Leicester. Peace was negotiated between the two armies by Archbishop Oda of Canterbury and his colleague of York, Wulfstan I. It was highly disadvantageous to Edmund. He had to cede to Olaf the lands of northeast Mercia between Watling Street and the Humber (Leicestershire, Derbyshire, Nottinghamshire, Lincolnshire), i.e., the region conquered by his father in the years 918–20. Olaf Guthfrithson died in 941 and was succeeded by his cousin Olaf Sihtricson. Edmund moved against this second Olaf in 942 and recovered the territories lost in 940. The event was celebrated in rousing verse preserved in the *Anglo-Saxon Chronicle*. In 943 Olaf made peace with Edmund and was baptized a Christian. In the following year fighting broke out between Olaf and a rival claimant to the Scandinavian kingdom of York. Edmund took advantage of this to invade Northumbria and bring it under his control. He consolidated his hold on the north in 945 by ravaging the British kingdom of Strathclyde and making a treaty with the king of Scots.

Edmund maintained the traditions of government that had characterized his brother's rule. He issued two law-codes and maintained firm control of the coinage. He cooperated harmoniously with Archbishop Oda in the government of the church. He was a patron of nuns and in an initiative that was to have far-reaching consequences he promoted Dunstan to the abbacy of Glastonbury. He conducted an active foreign policy, sustaining his nephew Louis IV as king of France and receiving at least one embassy from his brother-in-law Otto I of Germany.

Edmund married twice. By his first wife Elfgifu (*d.* 944) he had two sons, Edwy and Edgar. His second wife Ethelflaed survived him by at least thirty years.

Edmund died by violence at the age of only twenty-five. On 26 May 946 he was murdered at Pucklechurch in Gloucestershire while attempting to defend his steward from an attack by an outlaw named Leofa.

EADRED (*c.* 924–55) was the son of King Edward "the Elder" who succeeded his brother Edmund as king of Wessex over which he ruled from 946 until 955. His reign started peaceably enough, with Northumbria accepting his authority. But the appearance on the northern scene of Eric Bloodaxe in 947 changed the situation entirely. His acceptance as king at York brought Eadred to Northumbria with an army in 948. A campaign of ravaging and an indecisive battle at Castleford enabled Eadred to dictate terms. Eric was expelled and Northumbria returned to its allegiance. But in 949 Olaf

Sihtricson—king of York in the years 941–43—came back to Northumbria and apparently managed to maintain himself there for nearly three years. In 952 Olaf was driven out and Eric returned as king of York. Two years later, in 954, Eric was once more expelled and Eadred brought Northumbria back under his lordship. The details of these confused events are lost to us. It is likely that the person mainly responsible for Eric's downfall was Oswulf, who had been governing Bernicia from Bamburgh from at least 949 and who was rewarded with the earldom of all Northumbria after Eric's death, which he held until about 965.

It is customary to regard the year 954 as marking a stage in the unification of England: the king of Wessex became king of all England. It is easier for posterity to see this than it was for contemporaries. The year was marked by no change in the king's title as recorded in Eadred's charters or on his coins. In his will the king left a very substantial sum of money "so that his people may redeem themselves from a heathen army if they need." Evidently he envisaged the possibility of further Viking attacks. West Saxon rulers, and indeed their Norman successors, found it hard to exercise effective authority over their remote and restive northern province.

Eadred continued his brother Edmund's ecclesiastical policies. Dunstan was one of his leading counsellors, and it was during Eadred's reign, probably about 953 or 954, that Ethelwold was granted the abbacy of Abingdon.

The males of the West Saxon dynasty were on the whole not a long-lived lot. Edmund was no exception. He died on 23 November 955, aged about thirty. He had never married.

ERIC BLOODAXE (*d.* 954) was the last of the Viking kings of York. He was the son of Harald Fairhair, king of Norway, whom he succeeded at some point in the early 940s. His rule in Norway was short and bloody. It was probably to acts of savagery, which certainly included fratricide, committed during it that Eric owed his nickname. In 946 he was deposed in favor of his surviving brother Haakon, a milder man who had been brought up a Christian in England at the court of King Athelstan. Eric went into exile and supported himself by a life of pillage in the Orkneys and Western Isles of Scotland. In 947 he was invited to take up the kingship of Scandinavian York. His reign lasted only about a year. In 948 King Eadred of Wessex invaded the north, the Northumbrians threw Eric over and he returned to his base in the Isles. In 952 he came back to York and ruled there once more for two years. In 954 he was again expelled and again retreated northwestward. He was betrayed into the hands of his enemies and killed in the bleak moorland country of Stainmore on the Pennine heights between Yorkshire and Cumberland.

The poet Egil Skalla-grimsson memorably evoked Eric in his hall at York,

> where the king kept his people cowed
> under the helmet of his terror.
> From his seat at York he ruled unflinchingly
> over a dank land.

The waterlogged soil of York, which underlies Eric's dank kingdom, has the property of preserving organic materials such as wood, leather, and cloth. This has assisted archaeologists to reconstruct the economic and social life of York in some detail. A very different scene is revealed from what the violent career of Eric Bloodaxe might lead us to expect. York in the Viking age was a thriving industrial and commercial city. Excavations, particularly those conducted on the Coppergate site between 1976 and 1981, have revealed plentiful evidence of textile production and of working in wood, leather, bone, metal, and glass. York had an active mint—at least six moneyers worked for Eric Bloodaxe—and coin circulated freely. Eric and his henchmen could drink wine imported from Germany and eat bread made from the fine flour ground by the lava millstones brought from the Rhineland; they could draw on Scandinavian amber for their jewelry. York's overseas contacts were even wider than this. Silk was imported from the Byzantine empire or further afield. The coin minted in early tenth-century Samarkand had travelled over three thousand miles before coming to rest in York; a cowrie shell from the Red Sea or the Gulf of Aden, almost as far. Byrhtferth of Ramsey, author of the biography of Archbishop Oswald in about the year 1000, informs us that merchants came to York "from all over the place." He claimed that York had a population of 30,000: we cannot prove him wrong. This would have included native as well as visiting businessmen and entrepreneurs; the sort of people, perhaps, who were buried beneath the finely carved tombstones discovered under York Minster in recent excavations.

The urban bourgeoisie of England has a continuous history from the tenth century onward. There is a hoary old chestnut still to be found lurking in history books, called "the rise of the middle class," located for preference in the sixteenth or seventeenth century. It did indeed occur, but at a much earlier epoch: in the late Anglo-Saxon period; and it owed a great deal, directly or indirectly, to the Vikings.

R. Hall, *The Excavations at York: The Viking Dig*, 1984.

ODA (*d.* 958) was archbishop of Canterbury from 941 until his death. He was of Anglo-Scandinavian origin. The biography of his nephew Oswald by Byrhtferth of Ramsey tells us that Oda's father had come to England with the Danish army led by Halfdan in the third quarter of the ninth century. It is of great interest that a second-generation immigrant, son of a father who had presumably been born a pagan, could rise to the highest ecclesiastical office in the land; and it may have something to suggest to us about the nature of English society in the tenth century. As a young man Oda attached himself to the household of a certain Athelhelm, presumably the man of that name who was successively bishop of Wells (909–23) and archbishop of Canterbury (923–26). Oda's rapid rise in the English church must have owed much to the interest of so distinguished a patron. Oda accompanied Athelhelm to Rome in 923 and shortly after his return was promoted by King Athelstan to the bishopric of Ramsbury. As tenth-century bishops were expected to be, Oda was a diligent servant of his king. The witness-lists of charters show that he was a regular attender at the royal court. In 936 he was entrusted with a delicate diplomatic mission to France. He may have accompanied the English army to the battle of *Brunanburh* in 937. Athelstan's successor King Edmund continued to favor Oda. In 940 he negotiated a treaty with the Danish kingdom of York. In the following year Edmund promoted him to Canterbury.

Not a great deal is known of Oda's archiepiscopate, but enough evidence survives to indicate its importance. He resumed the practice of holding church councils and issuing ecclesiastical legislation, thus providing leadership and direction for the English church. He reestablished a bishopric in East Anglia. Since the destruction of Christian institutions there by the Danes in the 860s— some of them, perhaps, Oda's kinsmen—the church life of the region had been supervised by the bishop of London. However, such a situation was obviously unsatisfactory and Oda set about remedying it by reestablishing the bishopric of Elmham (which later moved to Thetford and finally to Norwich). At Canterbury Oda carried out major alterations to his cathedral church, heightening its walls by twenty feet, presumably for the insertion of a clerestory. He made important additions to Canterbury's relic collection. The body of St. Wilfrid was brought from Ripon probably in 948, and at some date unknown the relics of St. Ouen (or Audoin) were brought from Rouen in Normandy. Oda was a patron of learning. The deacon Frithegodus, who wrote poems in honor of these two saints in astonishingly complicated Latin, was remembered at Canterbury as a famous teacher. His name was not Old English but German, so it looks as though Oda—like King Alfred before him—looked to the Continent for scholars to revive English learning.

Oda also concerned himself with monasticism. He had himself taken the monastic habit—in an act of personal piety, not as a formally professed monk—at the famous monastery of Fleury (now St. Benoît-sur-Loire), possibly at the time of his embassy to France in 936. It was to Fleury that he sent his nephew Oswald for training in the monastic life. It was not by chance that it was during Oda's archiepiscopate that his friend King Edmund initiated the monastic revival by appointing Dunstan abbot of Glastonbury; and that Edmund's successor Eadred followed this up by appointing Ethelwold abbot of Abingdon. It is possible that Oda intended to refound the monastery of Ely. He received a generous grant of land there, enough to endow a monastic house, from King Eadwig in 957. But whatever plans he may have had for Ely were cut short by his death in 958.

The great trio of reforming churchmen in the second half of the tenth century, Dunstan, Ethelwold, and Oswald, did not start from scratch. They built upon foundations laid by the prelates of the generation preceding their own, among whom Oda was the most distinguished.

Oda deserves more attention than he has yet received from historians. For the present, see the few pages devoted to him in N. Brooks, *The Early History of the Church of Canterbury*, 1984.

ATHELSTAN HALF-KING (*d.* after 956) was a leading member of one of the great magnate families of tenth-century England. The family was probably of West Saxon origin. Athelstan's father Ethelfrith achieved prominence in the service of Alderman Ethelred of Mercia and his wife Ethelflaed, "the Lady of the Mercians." Athelstan became alderman of East Anglia in 932 and held the office until 956. Two of his brothers held aldermanries respectively in Kent and the southeastern counties (940–46) and in central Wessex (942–49). Thus the family was responsible for the administration of about half the English kingdom during the reigns of Edmund and Eadred. A still more significant token of Athelstan's closeness to the royal family lies in the fact that King Edmund entrusted his young son Edgar to him after the death of his first queen in 944. Edgar therefore grew up with Athelstan's sons. It is not surprising to find that two of these sons continued to hold the East Anglian aldermanry during Edgar's reign and beyond, until 992. Athelstan was a friend of Dunstan. After he resigned his aldermanry in 956 it was to Dunstan's monastery of Glastonbury that he retired to end his days as a monk. (He was, incidentally, a very good "catch" for Glastonbury because he made over to the abbey a proportion of his vast landed wealth.) Athelstan was among the early benefactors of the monastery refounded by Ethelwold at Abingdon. His son Ethelwine, alderman of East Anglia from 962 to 992, was associated with Oswald in the foundation of Ramsay Abbey in the Fens. The circle of those who *mattered* in tenth-century England was a small one.

Athelstan's nickname "Half-King," recorded by Byrhtferth in his biography of Oswald, was indicative of his enormous power and prestige. His career and connections form an interesting case-study of the sort of opportunities which the West Saxon kings could make available to reliable followers as their kingdom expanded in the tenth century. As well as being bold generals and skilled manipulators of institutions these rulers had to be masters of the art of patronage. Owing to the accident of documentary survival we happen to know a fair amount about Athelstan. His success and renown were probably remarkable in degree rather than in kind. We know a little of some other aristocratic families such as those of Byrhtnoth and Wulfric. We know practically nothing at all about the families of somewhat less exalted rank, the gentry, or squirearchy, but we know just enough to be reasonably sure that they too were prospering, and for the same sort of reasons. This can be put in a different and perhaps provocative way. In the tenth century English landed society took on the shape that it was to keep for many centuries to come.

EADWIG or **EDWY** (*c.* 940–959) was king of England from 955 to 957, after which his rule was restricted to Wessex from 957 until his early death in 959. Eadwig was the eldest son of King Edmund. He succeeded his uncle Eadred in 955 at the age of about fifteen. In 957 his younger brother Edgar rebelled against him and succeeded in establishing his authority over Mercia and Northumbria: the line dividing the brothers' zones of authority was marked by the river Thames. Eadwig ruled over Wessex to the south of the river until his death at the age of only about nineteen on 1 October 959.

Eadwig's short reign is one that historians have found hard to interpret. It is pretty clear that there was a dispute about the succession to the throne on Eadred's death in 955. Given the lack of clear rules governing royal succession, this is not surprising. Comparable succession-disputes had occurred earlier in the century, for instance on the death of Edward "the Elder" in 924, and were to happen again, notably after Edgar's death in 975. In view of the tender age of the two contenders in 955, about fifteen and twelve, respectively, we may plausibly seek to identify factions among the Anglo-Saxon elite, which were divided on the issue. The pro-Edgar party may be cautiously identified from Eadwig's actions. He despoiled his grandmother Queen Eadgifu, the widow of Edward the Elder, of her property and he sent Dunstan, abbot of Glastonbury, into exile in Flanders. These two seem to have been the leaders of the opposition to Eadwig. Other members of their party are more difficult to identify, but may have included Cynesige, bishop of Lichfield, a kinsman of Dunstan apparently absent, possibly banished, from the royal court in 956, and Athelstan Half-King, alderman of East Anglia, who retired from politics, perhaps not altogether voluntarily, in the same year.

Eadwig's supporters are more difficult to identify. They must have included the family of his wife Elfgifu, whom he married shortly after his accession. She was said to have been responsible for Dunstan's banishment. It is likely that she was a sister of Ethelweard the chronicler. Ethelweard was descended from King Ethelred I of Wessex, the elder brother of King Alfred. It follows that Eadwig and his wife were distantly related. They were separated on the grounds of consanguinity by Archbishop Oda of Canterbury, probably in 957. The affair must have shaken the fabric of the higher reaches of English society. Unfortunately we can only speculate as to whether Oda was acting in the interests of the pro-Edgar faction or simply in obedience to the norms of ecclesiastical law. Whatever the reason, the separation may have struck a blow at the integrity of Eadwig's party. Another man prominent among his supporters seems to have been Ethelwold, abbot of Abingdon, who may have been the king's tutor. Shortly after Eadwig's death Ethelwold was to rise to great heights in the service of King Edgar, a point that should serve to remind us how fluid and shifting the aristocratic factions of this period were.

Eadwig can be observed bidding for support in the phenomenal number of surviving charters, about sixty in all, which he issued in his first twelve months as king. These documents record grants of land made in many instances, one may suspect, to purchase the loyalty of potential supporters. These lavish handouts of the royal demesne lands are important evidence of just how wealthy the house of Wessex had become by the extension of its authority over Mercia and the Danelaw during the previous fifty years. They also hint at the existence of tensions among the aristocratic elite. Some people had done very well for themselves out of West Saxon expansion; others had not. Eadwig may have been trying to enlist the support of the latter.

He did not succeed. Edgar managed to detach Mercia and Northumbria, and Eadwig's opportune death in 959 permitted the younger brother to reunite the English kingdom. Eadwig's posthumous reputation is a good example of the dictum that history is written by and for the winning side. The memory of Eadwig was systematically vilified in the earliest biography of Dunstan, which portrayed the king as foolish, headstrong, vindictive, and lecherous. Most historians have concurred in this verdict. But not all. The chronicler Ethelweard, who may as we have seen have been his brother-in-law, tells us that Eadwig was "deserving of affection." Eadwig's reign was unhappy, but the king may not have been a bad man.

EDGAR (943–75), often known as Edgar the Peaceable, was the second son of King Edmund. He, or at any rate the faction of notables that acted in his name, rebelled against his brother Eadwig in 957 and established his authority over Mercia and Northumbria. On Eadwig's early death in 959 Edgar succeeded him as ruler of the entire kingdom of England, which he governed until his death at the age of only thirty-two on 8 July 975. It is commonly reckoned that during his reign the Anglo-Saxon monarchy attained a pinnacle of power and prestige that was never to be surpassed.

Edgar was brought up in the household of Athelstan "Half-King," the most powerful landed magnate in England about the middle years of the century. Athelstan was close to Dunstan, and Edgar's first exercise of ecclesiastical patronage was the appointment of Dunstan to the bishopric of Worcester in 957. Dunstan's promotion in quick succession to London (959) and Canterbury (960), and the advancement of Oswald to Worcester (961) and of Ethelwold to Winchester (963) set the scene for the most striking achievement of Edgar's reign, the revival of Benedictine monasticism and the reform of the English church. The character of the so-called tenth-century reformation is examined in the entries that deal with the careers of these three leading churchmen. What needs emphasis here is that at every point the reformers depended on the support of the king. Edgar threw all the very considerable weight of royal patronage behind them. It was the king who advanced them to bishoprics; who provided endowments on a colossal scale for the new monasteries; who sanctioned assertions of power such as Ethelwold's expulsion of the unreformed clergy from Winchester in 964; and who issued legislation in support of reforming ideals, such as making the payment of tithe compulsory.

What did Edgar get in return? In the first (and for the people of that age the most important) place he got the services of experts in prayer. Their intercession with God harnessed the most potent forces in their universe to the prosperity of His servant, the king. Here is the witness of Bishop Ethelwold:

Truly the Almighty God, who is cognizant of all things,
who knows beforehand all that is to come, and who
knew how beneficial he (Edgar) would be, was ever
very gracious to him, and ever had in store for him all
good things in his profit; as if the righteous and faithful
Rewarder preached not with words but with deeds, and
said thus: "Now that you zealously protect and advance
my name and dominion—that is, my Church which I
rightly have in my special dominion—as a recompense
to you I will glorify your name and increase and
advance in prosperity your kingdom which you hold
under my dominion."

In the second and more mundane place the king by his patronage acquired the loyalties of a cadre of devoted royal servants. The bishops and abbots of tenth-century England commanded ample resources in land and men and were charged with important administrative responsibilities. Kinsmen they may have had, but they were themselves celibate; that is, they could not found local dynasties. Their ecclesiastical offices were in the king's gift. To put the matter crudely: Oswald, as the king's nominee to the bishopric of Worcester and the archbishopric of York, was a prop of royal authority in the western and northern marches of the kingdom where that authority was weaker than it was in Wessex.

Edgar "carried out his office like the Good Shepherd." This astonishing and to our eyes almost blasphemous statement was made by Ethelwold in the introduction to the document known as the *Regularis Concordia* composed in about 970. This was how the king's propagandists wanted his subjects to think of him. They used their skills in an attempt to exalt the monarch far above his people. Edgar's father had died by violence and his eldest son was to meet the same fate. In an uncertain world the divinity that might help to hedge a king was not to be despised. Specialists in liturgy and ceremonial, Edgar's churchmen provided him with a spectacular coronation at Bath in 973.

The ceremony at Bath is the most puzzling as well as the most famous event of his reign. Its significance has stimulated much discussion. It is likely that Edgar had been inaugurated as king by coronation and anointing early in his reign, like other tenth-century English kings. The coronation of 973 must have been an inauguration into something else. The question is, what? In trying to answer this we need to examine what little is known of Edgar's foreign relations. Near-contemporaries such as Wulfstan and Aelfric recorded Edgar's supremacy over other rulers in the British Isles and laid stress on its peaceful nature.

> And God also supported him so that kings and earls willingly submitted to him and were subjected to whatever he wished. And without battle he brought under his sway all that he wished.

Edgar's reign may not have been quite as peaceful as this passage suggests. He was remembered as "bold in battle" and as "a dispenser of treasure to warriors." We know that in 969 he ordered the devastation of Thanet to punish its inhabitants for their maltreatment of merchants from York. There may have been more such incidents that went unrecorded. Edgar had a fleet, like Alfred and Athelstan before him, and we are told that it circumnavigated Britain annually: a demonstration of Edgar's might and a reminder of its ultimate sanction of force.

The account of Edgar's coronation in contemporary sources links it to a subsequent event:

> And immediately after that the king took his whole naval force to Chester, and six kings came to meet him, and all gave him pledges that they would be his allies on sea and on land.

Another tradition has it that there were eight kings and that they rowed the king—who acted as cox—upon the river Dee in token of subjection. There is some dispute about who the six or eight kings were, but they certainly included Kenneth of Scotland; Malcolm of Strathclyde and Cumbria; Maccus, king of Man and the Western Isles; and Iago of Gwynedd; they may have included one or more of the Norse princes established in Ireland. The idea that "empire" consisted in the hegemony of a great king over subject kings was one that was familiar to tenth-century people, among them Edgar's uncle Otto I of Germany, acclaimed an emperor in 962. The dual ceremonies of 973 occurred at cities that were heavy with memories of a Roman and imperial past. Was Edgar inaugurated at Bath and Chester into some sort of "empire of Britain?" Quite possibly.

Another very important event took place in 973. This was a thoroughgoing reform of the English coinage. The coins in circulation were called in and recoined to a new design. Arrangements were set in train for the royal management of the coinage, which were to persist for nearly two centuries. The key feature of the system was regular change of coin-type under government supervision. At fixed intervals, usually six years, all coin in the land was demonetized. That is to say, every possessor of coins had to take them to the local mint-town and have them melted down and recoined by the king's moneyers. There were about forty mint-towns under Edgar, about seventy in the time of his grandson Edward the Confessor. The moneyers used dies that were issued by the central government in return for a fee; they could recoup themselves by taking a cut from the public at the moment of recoinage. The government was thus enabled to control the design, weight, and fineness of the coins in circulation, while simultaneously profiting handsomely from the operation. It was a remarkable administrative achievement without parallel in the western Europe of the day. With very rare exceptions the only denomination minted between 973 and 1066 was the silver penny. On its obverse it bore the king's bust and title, on its reverse the name of the mint-town and moneyer and a design that changed at each successive recoinage. It was a good coinage, and unhesitatingly accepted as such. The government never irresponsibly meddled with the bullion content; the die-cutters were artists with a consistently elegant sense of design; and the moneyers—or those craftsmen whom they employed, for the moneyers themselves were big capitalists—struck clean, crisp impressions. A large amount of coin circulated, in Edgar's reign probably at least ten million pennies at any one time, and the volume was much greater in the eleventh century. Since England has few native deposits of silver, bullion must have entered the country from without, presumably in payment for English exports. Among these, wool or woollen textiles—already prominent as commodities of trade in the time of King Offa—may have been the staple items. The volume of the coinage is witness to this favorable trade balance.

Our understanding of the monetary system of later Anglo-Saxon England has been enlarged by some brilliant work on the part of numismatists over the last thirty years or so. The coinage has several lessons for the historian. It is testimony to the sophistication of the royal administration in the century before the Norman conquest. It demonstrates that the economy of late Saxon England, so far from being "primitive" or "under-developed" as earlier historians thought, was strong, diverse, and buoyant. We should also try to remember what the coins might have conveyed to their primary users, the ordinary men and women of England. There in their hands when they bought and sold, paid taxes, went to law, or gave presents was the image and superscription of the king. The coinage was not simply a medium of exchange: it showed who was in charge; it was a potent instrument of royal propaganda.

The men who present Edgar to us as a great and good king were for the most part looking back to a golden age of peace and prosperity from the dark days of his son's reign. Little though we know of Edgar personally, we can sense a rightness in their vision, though perhaps for different reasons. There is a sense in which his reign saw the harvest of the seeds sown by the kings of the previous hundred years. Institutions that were to endure for a long time become clearly visible in the third quarter of the tenth century, beside which the monetary system, which lasted nearly two centuries, or even the monasteries, which lasted nearly six, have an ephemeral look. The shires of England scarcely altered their shape from Edgar's day until their wanton destruction in 1974. The administrative subdivisions of the shire, the hundreds and wapentakes, are clearly visible for the first time in Edgar's reign. Compulsory payment of tithe gave impetus to the definition of parish boundaries, which still continue to influence local administration and local society in this country. The incorporation of the northern Danelaw into the English kingdom, achieved by Edgar's uncles, was steadily working into men's consciousness as an accepted fact of national life. Edgar legislated, in his own words, for "all the nation, whether Englishmen, Danes or Britons." His cession of Lothian to the king of Scots in 973 defined the Anglo-Scottish border in the northeast in essentials where it still runs today. Something big was taking shape: a kingdom of England.

Edward was twice married. By his first wife Ethelflaed, the daughter of Alderman Ordmaer, he was the father of King Edward the Martyr. His second wife was Aelfthryth, daughter of Alderman

Ordgar of Devon and widow of Ethelwold, alderman of East Anglia and one of the sons of Athelstan "Half-King." She gave birth to two sons: Edmund, who died in early childhood, and Ethelred, later to be remembered as Ethelred the Unready. By a mistress named Wulfthryth Edgar had a daughter named Eadgifu. Wulfthryth became abbess of Wilton and Eadgifu abbess of the two nunneries of Barking and Winchester. Both ladies were later regarded as saints.

Edgar's reign has not received the full-scale study that it deserves. R. H. M. Dolley, *Anglo-Saxon Pennies*, 1964, is the best introduction to the coinage.

ST. DUNSTAN (*c.* 910–88) was abbot of Glastonbury, archbishop of Canterbury from 960 to 988, the guiding spirit behind the monastic revival of the tenth century, and the leading counsellor of successive English kings. Dunstan was born into an aristocratic family settled in Somerset about the year 910. He seems to have received his education at Glastonbury. As a young man he gravitated toward the royal court during the reign of King Athelstan. Under the influence of his kinsman Bishop Elfheah of Winchester (934–51) he decided to become a monk. In 940 King Edmund made him abbot of Glastonbury. However, Dunstan remained an important figure at court during the reigns of Edmund and his brother Eadred. On the death of the latter in 955 Dunstan supported the claims to the throne of Edgar against his brother Eadwig. The temporary victory of Eadwig and his supporters sent Dunstan for a short time into exile in Flanders. But Edgar recalled him in 957 and gave him the bishopric of Worcester. On Eadwig's death in 959 and Edgar's succession to the undivided kingdom of England, Dunstan was promoted in rapid succession to the bishopric of London (959) and the archbishopric of Canterbury (960).

Dunstan's appointment to Glastonbury is rightly regarded as a turning point in English ecclesiastical history. From 940 until the Dissolution in the reign of Henry VIII—almost exactly six hundred years—monastic life had a continuous history in England and left a deep impression on English life. We have to be careful to define our terms. To what extent had monastic life died out in England in the late ninth and early tenth centuries? The answer must be that it depends on what is understood by "monastic life." Religious communities did exist. Glastonbury was one such, Crediton another. There were communities grouped at the resting-places of the earlier Anglo-Saxon saints, for example, the clergy of St. Cuthbert at Chester-le-Street (until their final move to Durham in 995). There were bodies of clergy who served the churches known as "old minsters," who also were often the guardians of local shrines, as, for instance, the clergy of St. Frideswide at Oxford. But in the eyes of reformers such as Dunstan these were not genuinely monastic. The monastic life for them meant following the monastic rule of St. Benedict. It was on this aspect of Dunstan's abbacy at Glastonbury that his earliest biographer, writing in about 1000, laid most emphasis. The impulse to restore a correct monasticism came partly from abroad. We should remember Alfred's attempt to found a monastery at Athelney under John the Old Saxon, or the interest taken by Archbishop Oda in the renowned French monastery of Fleury. It also perhaps came from a sharpened awareness of the monastic past of the Anglo-Saxons, which we might attribute to the Alfredian intellectual revival. Desire to refound the godly communities of the age of Aldhelm and Bede went hand in hand with West Saxon expansion into Mercia and the Danelaw: the rugged piety of imperialism. Glastonbury evidently had a good library in Dunstan's youth, for we are told that he studied hard there. We should very much like to know what books he read. Was Bede among them? There is some reason for supposing that Glastonbury possessed a copy of Bede's *Ecclesiastical History* and we know that the work formed part of the court library of King Athelstan.

Dunstan's advancement depended at every point upon royal patronage. The tradition of historiography that presents him as dreamy and unworldly is misleading. His responsibilities at court under Edmund and Eadred were thoroughly secular in character. He was a principal adviser of these two martial kings and under the second of them he had important financial duties. He had been accustomed to the turbulent life of the royal court from the reign of Athelstan onward. Court life was physically exhausting because it was constantly on the move, and because it was so faction-ridden it was taxing in other ways too. Dunstan's background obviously gave him entry, but to get where he did he must have been ambitious, tough, ready to risk enmity and to face danger in a game where the stakes were high and the potential rewards great. Dunstan's ecclesiastical career was a hard-won success in much the same way and for much the same reasons as was the secular career of his slightly older contemporary Athelstan Half-King. One can feel sure that Dunstan's kinsmen were important too in assisting his rise to the summit of the English hierarchy. Unfortunately, owing to the nature of our sources, they remain tantalizingly elusive. He had "relatives"—unspecified—at the court of King Athelstan. Among his traceable kinsmen were Athelhelm, successively bishop of Wells (909–23) and archbishop of Canterbury (923–26), Bishop Elfheah of Winchester, and Bishop Cynesige of Lichfield (949–63): a powerful team of ecclesiastics. He was related in some way to a lady named Ethelflaed who was herself related to the royal family: she lived near Glastonbury and often entertained the royal court there. He had a brother named Wulfric who was evidently close to the royal family, for he received many grants of land in Somerset from Edmund and Eadred, which he later donated to the abbey of Glastonbury. This is not a great deal to go on, but it strongly suggests that Dunstan was well-connected in the small circle of people who really counted for something in mid-tenth-century Wessex.

The movement of monastic revival was vigorously supported by Edgar. King and archbishop acted in harmonious concert. It was at Dunstan's request that Oswald was appointed to the bishopric of Worcester in 961, and it was presumably after consultation with Dunstan that Ethelwold was advanced to the see of Winchester in 963. This trio of prelates dominated English ecclesiastical life over the next generation. While it is not easy to distinguish individual contributions, Dunstan's influence can be detected in the following fields. First, several monastic houses were founded, refounded, or reformed from Glastonbury directly or indirectly through his agency. These included Muchelney, Westminster, Athelney, Bath, Milton, and Malmesbury, all between 959 and 965. Tavistock, founded by Alderman Ordwulf, the brother-in-law of King Edgar, in about 975, was probably colonized from Glastonbury. Secondly, Dunstan initiated a connection between the abbey of Glastonbury and the see of Canterbury that was long to outlast his lifetime. Every archbishop of Canterbury between 960 and 1038 had previously been a monk at Glastonbury. It was all part of a sustained attempt by the reforming clique to monasticize the episcopate. Monks trained in the reformed houses constituted a majority of the English episcopate until the middle of the eleventh century. It was an "old boy network" on the grandest scale. Thirdly, Dunstan's connection with the king bore fruit in areas other than that of ecclesiastical patronage. He was an assiduous attender at the royal court and may be envisaged—with all the cautions attendant upon using an anachronistic term—as a sort of "prime minister" not only to Edgar but also to his son Edward. Only in the last phase of his life, during the early years of King Ethelred II, did his authority suffer some diminution. It is hard to pin down the specific contributions of a counsellor in frequent attendance upon his monarch. This conceded, it seems likely that Dunstan had a hand in drafting some of Edgar's legislation and in organizing his coronation in 973. Given Dunstan's financial expertise, it is tempting to associate him with the great reform of the coinage in the same year, but there is no evidence for this.

This does not exhaust the achievements of this remarkable man. His earliest biographer tells us that Dunstan was a skilled musician and painter. A drawing plausibly attributed to him survives in a Glastonbury manuscript now in the Bodleian Library in Oxford. He was a scholar who would rise at dawn to correct manuscripts and who could compose Latin verse in the elaborate style then fashionable. He was a gifted teacher and a patron of learning both at Glastonbury and at Canterbury. He was a traveller of aristocratic largesse whose liberality to the poor in Rome shocked his thrifty steward: a cosmopolitan man of the world who corresponded with a circle of friends in France and the Low Countries.

Dunstan was not just a great ecclesiastical statesman, though he certainly was that. He was a man of diverse talent, and he was also regarded as a man of special holiness. As his biographer put it, he spoke "face to face" with God. Dunstan died on 19 May 988.

The standard history of English monasticism during this period is D. Knoles, *The Monastic Order in England*, 2nd ed., 1963. J. A. Robinson, *The Times of Saint Dunstan*, 1923, is an excellent book containing much that is still of great value. For modern research on the tenth-century revival see D. Parsons (ed.), *Tenth-Century Studies*, 1975.

ST. ETHELWOLD (*c.* 910–84), abbot of Abingdon and from 963 until his death bishop of Winchester, was perhaps the most forceful of the triumvirate of reforming churchmen, alongside Dunstan and Oswald, who transformed English ecclesiastical life in the second half of the tenth century. His parents were natives of Winchester, evidently well-connected for they were able to place Ethelwold as a youth at the court of King Athelstan. Like other promising young men he gravitated to the circle of Bishop Elfheah of Winchester (934–51): he and Dunstan were ordained priests by Elfheah on the same day. After Dunstan had become abbot of Glastonbury in 940 Ethelwold became a monk there. A few years later he contemplated going abroad to continue his studies and learn about continental monastic observance but he was prevented by Queen Eadgifu, the very long-lived widow of Edward "the Elder" and mother of King Eadred. Eadgifu persuaded Eadred to give Ethelwold the monastic site at Abingdon in the early 950s. A monastery had been founded there in the seventh century but had long ago been abandoned. Ethelwold was made abbot at the king's command and set about reviving monastic life there with a team of monks from Glastonbury. One of these, Osgar, later to be Ethelwold's successor as abbot of Abingdon, was sent to Fleury to study the monastic customs followed there—just as Oswald was doing at the same time.

The accession of King Edgar in 959 gave a great boost to the monastic revival. In 963 Ethelwold was promoted to the bishopric of Winchester. In the following year he expelled the secular clergy who constituted the cathedral chapter and replaced them with monks from Abingdon. Winchester thus became the first English "monastic cathedral," an example that was to be followed at several other English bishoprics in the course of time, notably Canterbury, Worcester, Durham, and Norwich. Like Dunstan and Oswald, Ethelwold founded or refounded or reformed a string of monastic houses, which included Chertsey, Peterborough, St. Alban's, Ely, Thorney, and St. Neot's. Ely's abundant surviving documents reveal Ethelwold as a canny businessman, rapidly building up the endowments of the community; by 1066 Ely's landed wealth was second only to Glastonbury's among English monasteries. Like the other reformed houses of the tenth century Ethelwold's foundations were a nursery for the men who were to staff the English episcopate in the next generation. Peterborough's first abbot, for example, went on to become bishop of Worcester and archbishop of York, and his successor ended up as bishop of Winchester. Such men were powers in the state as well as in the church.

Ethelwold's organizing abilities are also evident in the document known as the *Regularis Concordia* (Agreement about the Rule). This was drawn up under his direction in about 970 as a supplement to the Rule of St. Benedict, designed to standardize the observance of the English monastic communities. It is an elaborate document that embodies many of the central characteristics of the tenth-century reform movement. Ethelwold drew freely upon the customs of reformed continental houses, notably Fleury, Ghent, Trier, Verdun, and Einsiedeln, in this reflecting the strong foreign influences upon the English movement. The unusually close connections between the house of Wessex and the monastic revival are exemplified in other features of the *Regularis Concordia*. Ethelwold required English monks to pray for the royal family no less than seven times each day and laid special emphasis on the need to utter these prayers slowly and distinctly. An illustration in an early manuscript of the *Concordia* depicts King Edgar flanked by Dunstan and Ethelwold.

In its style and decoration the *Regularis Concordia* may also serve to remind us that Ethelwold was a patron of learning and art. In this he was like Dunstan and Oswald, but we know far more of his activities than we do of theirs. Ethelwold's first biographer laid stress on his learning and his gifts as a teacher. Its author was Aelfric, himself a pupil of Ethelwold and one of the leading figures in the English intellectual renaissance that grew out of the monastic revival. Another leading figure, Archbishop Wulfstan of York, was probably a pupil of Ethelwold's at one remove—if we are correct in supposing that he had been trained as a monk at Ely under its first abbot Brihtnoth who had been taught by Ethelwold. Aelfric tells us that Ethelwold delighted in expounding books to his pupils in English. Doubtless it was in large part owing to Ethelwold's influence that an emphasis on the use of the vernacular for literary purposes was so marked a feature of late Anglo-Saxon intellectual life. Ethelwold himself translated the Rule of St. Benedict into Old English and composed an Old English account of King Edgar's sponsorship of the monastic revival. In the hands of Aelfric and Wulfstan the vernacular was to become a literary instrument of considerable power. Ethelwold did not neglect Latin, the traditional language of religion and scholarship. In addition to the *Regularis Concordia* he may also have composed poetry in Latin. He certainly encouraged the production of Latin works. His pupil

Wulfstan, the precentor of Winchester—not to be confused with Wulfstan of York—composed verses in praise of Winchester's St. Swithun, another biography of Ethelwold, and apparently a work, now lost, on music.

Revived monastic life and learning demanded large quantities of books. It is no doubt due to the accident of survival that there now exist far more tenth-century manuscripts from Canterbury than from other intellectual centers. However, enough that originated in Winchester, Abingdon, Peterborough, and Thorney have come down to us to show that Ethelwold was a very influential figure in English book-production. He was perhaps the most important agent in the dissemination in England of the continental script known as Caroline or Carolingian minuscule, a handsome script whose letterforms are essentially those we still use today: the first securely dated example comes from Abingdon in 961. He encouraged the artists who decorated manuscripts in the style known as the "Winchester school," of which the earliest dated example comes from 966. Shortly after this the most sumptuous of late Anglo-Saxon illuminated manuscripts was produced for Ethelwold's personal use, the famous "Benedictional of St. Ethelwold" now in the British Library. Its artist was Godeman, monk of Winchester and later first abbot of Thorney.

This does not exhaust the roll call of Ethelwold's cultural activities. He was a great builder, at Abingdon, Ely, Thorney, and above all at Winchester. Although none of his work at Winchester still stands, architectural historians have been able to get a fair idea of what he built through careful study of the written sources and through the excavations that took place between 1961 and 1970. In 971 the body of St. Swithun was moved or "translated" to a new shrine and a major remodelling of the cathedral began. It was extended both to the east and to the west, the most novel feature of the new west end being the addition of a monumental "west-work" analogous in style to several German churches of the ninth and tenth centuries. Before the works at the cathedral, Ethelwold had carried out certain rebuilding operations at all the monastic communities in the town; after them he laid out a new bishop's palace for himself and his successors. We know less than we should like to about the decoration of these buildings. It is certain that the cathedral church was adorned with monumental sculpture and ceramic tiles. There were probably wall-paintings, textile hangings, and

plenty of gold and silver candelabra; perhaps too some exotic curiosities of the sort that Bishop Leofric was to leave to Exeter a century later. Nowadays we keep our cathedrals spick and span and
sparsely furnished, and maintain a reverent hush when we visit
them. We insufficiently appreciate the gaudiness, bustle, and clut-
ter of the surroundings in which the Anglo-Saxons worshipped.

Ethelwold's artistic patronage was not designed, we may guess,
only to the glory of God. It may have had diverse motives. The re-
designing of the cathedral at Winchester may have been occasioned partly by new liturgical needs. For example, the *Regularis
Concordia* provides our first evidence from anywhere in western
Christendom for the performance of an Easter play—a significant
episode in the prehistory of modern drama—and the demands of
this could have influenced the design of the remodelled cathedral.
There is also a sense in which Ethelwold's buildings were a sort of
architectural manifesto of the reform movement: a splendid new
cathedral and an imposing episcopal palace in the royal city of
Winchester—potent reminders, in their lavish grandeur, that the
conjoint authority of king and bishops was what mattered most in
the English church.

Ethelwold was the first of the reforming triumvirate to go. He
died on 1 August 984.

The *Regularis Concordia* has been edited and translated by Dom T.
Symons, 1953. For an introduction to Ethelwold's artistic patronage see F. Wormald, *The Benedictional of St. Ethelwold,* 1959,
and T. A. M. Bishop, *English Caroline Minuscule,* 1971. M. Bid-
dle and others, *Winchester in the Early Middle Ages,* 1976, is an
absorbing study of the city's development.

ST. OSWALD (*d.* 992), bishop of Worcester and archbishop of
York, was together with Dunstan and Ethelwold a member of the
trio of ecclesiastical reformers who dominated English church life
in the second half of the tenth century. Like the other two men
Oswald was well-connected: Archbishop Oda of Canterbury was his
uncle. Oswald was probably a native of the eastern Danelaw. He received a good education, though we do not know where. His uncle
Oda's patronage enabled him to buy—yes: a strong whiff of an unreformed church—a minster church in Winchester among the
community of clergy attached to which he settled. He could hardly

have failed to make the acquaintance of Dunstan and Ethelwold who were both much at court in this the first city in the kingdom and recipients of the patronage of Bishop Elfheah of Winchester. After some time Oswald desired to go abroad to learn the true principles of the monastic life. Oda advised him to go to the celebrated monastery of Fleury, on the Loire, where he himself had adopted the monastic habit, probably in 936. Fleury, recently reformed under the influence of Cluny, was at the height of its renown as a model monastic house following the Rule of St. Benedict, whose mortal remains, removed from Monte Cassino to Fleury in the seventh century, were a focus of pilgrimage. Dates in Oswald's early life are nonexistent. He probably went to Fleury in the first half of the 950s, when he was perhaps aged about thirty.

After some years at Fleury Oswald decided to return to England to teach true monastic observance there. On his arrival back in his native land Oswald found that his uncle Oda had just died (2 June 958), so he addressed himself instead to Oscytel, archbishop of York (956–71), who was another kinsman. Oscytel brought him and Dunstan together. It was Dunstan who was responsible for Oswald's promotion to the bishopric he had recently vacated, Worcester, in 961.

Oswald remained bishop of Worcester for the rest of his life. To it he added the archbishopric of York in 972, holding the two sees in plurality for twenty years. Much of his energies went into monastic foundations. The first monastery he established was at Westbury-on-Trim, in the extreme south of his diocese, in 963. It was followed by several more in the diocese of Worcester over the next few years—Evesham, Pershore, Winchcombe, and perhaps Deerhurst. At Worcester itself Oswald gradually transformed his cathedral chapter into a monastic priory, as Ethelwold had done at Winchester in 964. Outside the diocese his most famous foundation was at Ramsey in the Fens in 968: the initial endowments were provided by Ethelwine, alderman of East Anglia from 962 to 992, one of the sons of Athelstan Half-King. Oswald was probably involved in the refoundation of Crowland—formerly the hermitage of St. Guthlac—whose first abbot was another kinsman. He may have tried, though unsuccessfully, to reestablish Northumbrian monastic life at Ripon. At several of these houses the influence of Fleury can be detected. Germanus, an Englishman who had been at Fleury with Oswald, was the first prior of Ramsey and went on to become the first abbot of Winchcombe. Abbo, a prominent monastic reformer and intellectual, later to be abbot of Fleury from 988 to 1004, spent two years teaching at Ramsey (985–87) where he composed his life of St. Edmund, the East Anglian king killed by the Danes in 870. (Abbo was murdered by the monks of La Réole in Gascony who were reluctant to accept his reforms: a reminder that the career of a tenth-century monastic reformer could be dangerous.) Monks from Fleury advised in the drawing-up of the document known as the *Regularis Concordia,* commissioned by Ethelwold of Winchester, which laid down the rule of life to be observed in the reformed English monasteries.

A large number of documents, for the most part leases of land, issued by Oswald while bishop of Worcester, has survived. They are of great interest for their information about the tenure of land in later Anglo-Saxon England. They also testify to Oswald's efficiency as a man of business in the administration of Worcester's endowments. Comparable documents from York have not survived, though a few estate-surveys and memoranda about endowments suggest that Oswald was equally careful in the management of his northern diocese. Byrhtferth of Ramsey, his earliest biographer, laid stress on Oswald's energetic diocesan administration.

Oswald was a man of aristocratic temper. He was a lavish spender on his journey to Rome in 971, like Dunstan ten years beforehand. He showered gifts of books, vestments, plate upon his monasteries. At Ramsey he would feast "royally" with plenty of wine drunk from horns chased with gold and silver to wash down the banquet. Of the gorgeous trappings of this great prelate's life little now remains. The magnificent Ramsey Psalter, now in the British Library, was probably made for him (and one of its artists, interestingly, also worked at Fleury). But we must try to be aware of these trappings. The reformers of the tenth century may at heart have been holy and humble men of God. But they moved through their world like princes. To lose sight of this is to miss more than just the style of the late Anglo-Saxon church.

Oswald's career, not surprisingly, had many features in common with those of Dunstan and Ethelwold. We can sense the presence of a group of kinsmen about him: Archbishop Oda, Archbishop Oscytel, Abbot Thurcytel of Crowland, and numerous relatives who feature as beneficiaries of or witnesses to the series of

Worcester leases. Oswald was sustained by a group of kinsmen and in his turn sustained them. The same sense of a small, close-knit clique emerges from study of his network of connection among the highest circles of church and state: Dunstan, Ethelwold, Alderman Ethelwine, and of course King Edgar who promoted Oswald to Worcester and York and actively encouraged the establishment of the new monasteries.

Wealth, might, and magnificence: powerful family clans; the forceful support of the king. This is what we can read in and sometimes between the lines of our sources. These sources were uniformly favorable to the reformers. It is always useful to ask the question, what do they *not* tell us? They drop barely any hints that the reform was not plain sailing through unruffled waters. But was there any opposition? It is easy enough to see who gained by it. Who lost?

The essential point to grasp is that the tenth-century reform was not just about monastic observance but about property-rights and patronage as well. The unreformed religious communities were for the most part closely integrated into local aristocratic society—their inmates the members of prominent local families, these families in varying degrees the beneficiaries of a legal interest in the communities' endowments. For its victims reform was often an attack on entrenched property-rights, family expectations, and local sentiment. Ethelwold's expulsion of the secular chapter from Winchester in 964 was an act of expropriation without legal justification. Dunstan's mastery of the art of patronage must have disappointed expectations not just of ecclesiastical office but of material gain. Oswald's kin from eastern England who received lands on the Worcester estates in the west displaced existing tenants drawn from local gentry families. Many people suffered from the reform movement. It is not surprising that there was an antimonastic reaction after Edgar's death.

However, the three leaders were survivors. Not for them the grim fate of Abbo of Fleury. Oswald survived the longest of them. He died on 29 February 992.

E. John, *Orbis Britanniae*, 1966, contains a collection of stimulating essays mainly focused on the tenth-century reform, and some specifically on Oswald's part in it.

ST. EDWARD THE MARTYR (*c.* 963–78) was king of England from 975 until his murder in 978. When King Edgar died in 975 he left two young sons. Edward, the son of his first marriage, was aged about twelve; Ethelred, the son of Edgar's second marriage (to Aelfthryth), was about nine. There was a dispute about the succession, just as there had been on the death of King Eadred in 955. The faction that supported Ethelred was led by the queen-dowager Aelfthryth, and may have included Bishop Ethelwold of Winchester. Edward's supporters were led by Archbishop Dunstan of Glastonbury. It was the latter party that came out on top.

Edward's short reign is ill-documented. We are left with what a distinguished historian of Anglo-Saxon England has called "a vague impression of disorder." There was trouble of an unspecified kind in the north: Earl Oslac of Deira was banished. Farther south, in Mercia, Alderman Aelfhere attacked some of the monasteries that had been so closely associated with the policies of King Edgar. They were defended by the noble families whose members were their patrons. In parts of the country a state of something approaching civil war between different aristocratic factions seems to have ensued. In 976 there was a serious famine, which must have intensified distress and discontent. Meanwhile the young king was growing up into an unattractive personality, given to outbursts of rage, which struck terror into his household. (His tutor, Bishop Sideman of Crediton, possibly a restraining influence, died in 977.)

On 18 March 978 King Edward was murdered by Ethelred's retainers. Who was responsible? The murder took place while Edward was staying at Corfe in Dorset, an estate belonging to his stepmother Aelfthryth, while Ethelred and his household were also staying there. The beneficiary of the crime was his stepbrother Ethelred, who became king. The perpetrators of it were Ethelred's associates, and they were never punished. It has been irresistibly tempting to attribute the murder to the machinations of Aelfthryth in the interests of her son Ethelred. But the matter is by no means clear. The earliest sources implicate neither Aelfthryth nor Ethelred. It is quite possible that Ethelred's retainers acted on their own initiative. Edward's murder remains one of the unsolved mysteries of English history.

Whatever the truth about Edward's killing, there can be no doubts about the rapid growth and diffusion of his cult. In 979 his body, which had been hastily interred at Wareham, was moved to the nunnery of Shaftesbury at the instance of Aelfhere of Mercia, the senior alderman in the kingdom. In 1001 his remains were transported on the king's orders to a more fitting shrine inside the abbey church. Byrhtferth of Ramsey, composing his biography of Archbishop Oswald about the year 1000, made it clear in the text that he took Edward's sanctity for granted. So did Adelard of Ghent in his life of Dunstan composed about the same time. The anonymous compiler of the *Anglo-Saxon Chronicle* referred to Edward as a "heavenly saint." Miracles were being claimed at the tomb by 1001 at the latest. Shortly afterwards the nuns of Shaftesbury commissioned a suitably edifying account of Edward's death. Early in the reign of Canute his cult was given official recognition: it was decreed that his feast day should be celebrated throughout England. Surviving evidence shows that it was. Edward's name occurs in eleventh-century ecclesiastical calendars, such as the one contained in the very splendid Missal of Robert of Jumièges, now at Rouen but written and illuminated in England, perhaps at Winchester, before 1023. There also survive hymns, prayers, and masses for his feast day of eleventh-century composition.

C. E. Fell, *Edward: King and Martyr,* 1971.

ETHELRED II (*c.* 966–1016), king of England 978–1016, remembered by his countrymen as Ethelred the Unready, presided over England during a time of national misery and humiliation for which he himself must bear a heavy weight of responsibility. Ethelred was the third son of King Edgar, born in about 966. When his half brother Edward was murdered in 978 the twelve-year-old Ethelred succeeded him. Whether or not the young man was implicated in the crime, none may say. However, there hangs over his reign an atmosphere of suspicion and distrust in the governing circles of England; and the king's actions, as time went on, seem to have intensified this.

Our records of Ethelred's reign are dominated by the Danish attacks on England. They began shortly after his accession, reached a crescendo in the years 1009–13, and culminated in the conquest of England by the Danish rulers Sweyn and his son Canute in the years 1013–16. In 980 Danish fleets attacked Hampshire, Kent, and Cheshire; in 981, Devon and Cornwall; in 982, Dorset. In 988 Devon was visited again. In 991 it was the turn of Kent, Suffolk, and

Essex. In the last year named a very important development occurred. On the advice of the archbishop of Canterbury the decision was taken to raise a levy of taxation amounting to £10,000 to pay the Danes to go away. This was the origin of the tax famous—or infamous—in English history under the name Danegeld.

It is important to be clear that this was not an initiative without precedent. Ninth-century rulers in both England and Francia, including Alfred, had on occasion bought peace from the Vikings. King Eadred, who died in 955, had left a large sum of money in his will for precisely this purpose. Neither should we condemn the policy out of hand. The Danish forces were big and well-equipped. Their mastery of the sea enabled them to strike at will and suddenly against any part of England's long and vulnerable coastline. Against an enemy so swift, so ruthless, and so unpredictable it was exceedingly difficult to muster effective defense. (The analogy with modern international terrorism, though not exact, is a useful one.) In the circumstances it seemed sensible to treat with the attackers. Only time was to show

> That if once you have paid him the Dane-geld
> You never get rid of the Dane.

The tax devised was unique in the western Europe of its day and is one of the most weighty indications of the sophistication of late Anglo-Saxon government. Our knowledge of its workings is derived in the main from the record of the Domesday survey conducted for William the Conqueror in 1086, but there is no reason to believe that in its essentials the system had been different in Ethelred's time a century beforehand. Danegeld—often simply termed geld—was a tax on land. Land was assessed for taxation in units called by different names in different parts of the country, the most widespread being the term *hide*. Each county was assessed for tax in large round figures of assessment-units. Within each county this fiscal obligation was shared out among the hundreds, the administrative subdivisions of the shire. Thus, for example, Northamptonshire was assessed at 3,200 hides and was subdivided into 22 hundreds, 4 hundreds-and-a-half, and 2 double hundreds, assessed respectively at 100, 150, and 200 hides—which makes up a total of 32 hundreds, i.e., 3,200 hides. Within each hundred the obligation was further shared out among the estates of individual landowners. Thus we know from documents of Ethelred's reign that Ardley in Oxfordshire was assessed at 5 hides, or that Risborough in Buckinghamshire was assessed at 30. The government would decide to levy a tax at a certain rate, anything between 2 and 20 shillings on the hide. The system of assessment was flexible in other ways. Areas that had experienced economic dislocation, for instance, through devastation in war, could have their burdens temporarily reduced. Favored courtiers could also obtain unrealistically low assessments (a phenomenon known as "beneficial hidation"). Tax had to be paid in current coin of the realm under the system instituted by King Edgar at the great recoinage of 973. There were stringent penalties for failure to pay. Very large sums of money were raised. Recorded receipts—which are not of course necessarily total receipts—between 991 and 1018 amounted to at least £240,500. While it is not possible to offer precise modern equivalents for this sum, we can be certain that it represents many hundreds of millions of pounds in the values of today. The England of King Ethelred II was taxed with breathtaking efficiency.

We know about assessment and yield. The processes about which we know hardly anything are those of collection and accounting. Local royal officials were presumably charged with collection: that is to say, in each county the shire-reeve, or sheriff, and whatever subordinates he may have commanded. Since it is impossible to conceive how so elaborate a fiscal system could have been operated without some central accounting mechanism, it seems permissible to infer its existence despite the absence of any references to it; though this is an inference that not all historians would accept. What is fairly clear is that the system as a whole demanded officials who were both numerate and literate for its workings. Like the monetary system it simultaneously presupposed and generated a reserve of administrative skills. You cannot have taxation without bureaucracy.

Rudyard Kipling's lines quoted above proved all too true in Ethelred's England. The Danes were back in 992. In 993 they attacked Northumberland, Yorkshire, and Lincolnshire. In 994 it was the turn of London, Essex, Kent, Sussex, and Hampshire; the Danes wintered in England and were paid £16,000 in geld. In 997 a Danish force ravaged the lands on either side of the Bristol Channel and then the south coasts of Devon and Cornwall. In 998 it turned to Dorset and then settled on the Isle of Wight, exacting supplies from Hampshire and Sussex. In 999 it laid Kent waste before departing to friendly bases in Normandy. The year 1001 brought the Danes back to Sussex and Devon. In 1002 they took a geld of £24,000. (Note how the figures steadily increase.) Exeter was sacked in 1003 and the Danes penetrated far inland to ravage in Wiltshire. In 1004 they turned their attention to East Anglia: Norwich and Thetford were sacked and burned, and after fierce fighting the marauders returned to Denmark in 1005. In the following year they were back. Sandwich was occupied and the southeast was raided. The Danes wintered again on Wight and around Christmas 1006 raided from there right through Hampshire into Berkshire. In 1007 £36,000 was paid to them in Danegeld. The year 1008 was peaceful, but in 1009 a bigger army than ever before arrived in England led by, among others, King Sweyn of Denmark and Thorkell the Tall. Sussex, Hampshire, Berkshire, Kent, Essex, Buckinghamshire, Oxfordshire were attacked in 1009. East Anglia suffered in 1010, and great raids were sent deep into West Saxon territories such as Wiltshire. In 1011 Canterbury was captured and Archbishop Aelfheah held as a hostage; he was murdered in the following spring. A geld of £48,000 was paid over in 1012. King Sweyn reappeared in 1013, this time intent on conquest. A campaign that swept through a wide zone of territory in the midlands and the south gave him all he wanted. By the end of the year he was master of the country. King Ethelred, who had spent most of the year in the safety of London, left to pass Christmas on the Isle of Wight and then fled overseas to Normandy.

"And when they were in the east, the English army was kept in the west, and when they were in the south, our army was in the north." It was in such passages as this that an anonymous contemporary chronicler lamented the humiliation and suffering of the English during these dreadful years. He had no doubts about where to lay the blame. It was the fault of the king and his counsellors, especially the evil Eadric Streona, alderman of Mercia. But the truth may have been less straightforward than this. Ethelred was not a consistently ineffective ruler. He was capable of taking intelligent measures to counter the Danish peril. For example, his marriage to the Norman princess Emma in 1002 was part of a treaty between the English and Norman courts designed to prevent Danish use of Norman ports as bases for attacks on England. Or again, two years previously in 1000, Ethelred led an expedition to the northwest and devastated Strathclyde. The background to this campaign is obscure; it is likely that it was connected with Hiberno-Norse raids from Ireland, which received Cumbrian help: it shows that the king was capable of effective military action. Yet again: in 1008 the king commissioned the building of a navy to counter the Danes, and we know that the job got done, for a contemporary tells us that in 1009 these ships "were ready, and there were more of them than ever before had been in England in any king's time." And yet once more: Ethelred was as alive as his predecessors to the importance of providing strong-points—*burhs*—where local defense could be concentrated. One of his burghal foundations, at Cadbury in Somerset, has been excavated. It was not an ineffectual ruler who brought into being a fleet far larger than Alfred's, who raised huge sums of money in taxation, who founded towns, who maintained a well-managed currency of good weight and fineness, and who conducted an intelligent foreign policy.

So what *was* going wrong in Ethelred's reign? For a clue we should return to the king's nickname. Though not recorded in the surviving sources until long after his death, it was probably coined during his lifetime. The modern English adjective "unready" is an adaptation of the Old English *unraed*, meaning "no-counsel." The name Ethelred is formed from the Old English words *aethel* and *raed*, meaning "noble counsel." The king's nickname originated in a play upon words: "noble counsel, no counsel." It indicated that he lacked judgment, listened to bad advice, and in consequence ruled unjustly. There is evidence to suggest that these were indeed Ethelred's failings. He seems to have ridden roughshod over property rights. A charter of 998 restores land "which in the time of my youth at the instigation of certain people I stole from the bishopric of Rochester." There are others like it. They may be compared with other documents in which the king adopted a suggestively defensive tone in stressing the legality of the way in which he had acquired the lands to which they refer. Excessive taxation was another form of interference with property rights, since forfeiture of property was one of the penalties for failure to pay up. Archbishop Wulfstan of York was one very influential contemporary who considered Ethelred's taxation unjust; there were probably other prominent men of like mind. There were worse crimes than this. In 1002 Ethelred had a number of prominent Danes who were resident in England murdered. In 1006 he engineered the murder of the alderman of Northumbria and the blinding of his two sons. In 1015 he connived at the murder of two other prominent noblemen. It is no wonder that Ethelred could not inspire loyalty, that we hear so frequently of treachery and desertion. We begin to understand the reasons for the atmosphere of suspicion and distrust.

This background may help us to understand the tone of the king's legislation. Ethelred issued several codes of law. So we term them: but they have more the character of manifestos of government policy than of lawmaking as we normally understand it. They also have a strongly Christian, exhortatory, homiletic character. This is not surprising, for all of them were probably drafted by ecclesiastics, and about half of them certainly by Wulfstan. They show us how churchmen wanted the king to rule, and their bulk and repetitiveness strongly suggest the ways in which he was disappointing ecclesiastical expectation. Churchmen did not regard Ethelred as a satisfactory ruler.

The most interesting evidence of this occurs toward the end of his reign. Shortly after Ethelred's flight his victorious enemy Sweyn died (February 1014). A deputation of lay and ecclesiastical leaders crossed to Normandy and invited Ethelred back to England—but on terms. He had to promise to govern his people "more justly than he did before . . . to be a gracious lord to them and reform all the things which they hated." It was a constitutional pact of a kind that was to have a long and distinguished future. But Ethelred's restoration was no happier than what had gone before. There is some evidence to suggest that the king failed to mend his ways; there was discord in the royal family; and there was no let-up in the Danish assault. In the spring of 1015 Ethelred's son Edmund Ironside rebelled against his father and brought out northern England behind him. In the summer Canute returned, overran Wessex, and received the allegiance of the treacherous Mercian alderman Eadric. Ethelred was by now a sick man. He spent the winter of 1015–16 in London, whose citizens had been consistently loyal to him, and there he died on 23 April 1016.

Ethelred II's reign presents a sorry spectacle. Yet it was also a time of positive attainment. It is a doleful thing to remember a king because he instituted tax, but the Danegeld did register a remarkable advance in the science of government. Above all it was a time of notable cultural achievement. It has left us the prose of Aelfric and Wulfstan; the poem commemorating the heroic stand of Byrhtnoth at the battle of Maldon; some fine architectural monuments such as the exquisite little church at Bradford-on-Avon in Wiltshire, once thought to have been the work of St. Aldhelm but now convincingly redated to *c.* 1000; such superlative manuscripts as the Bosworth Psalter, the Sherborne Pontifical, and the Eadui Gospels; outstanding metalwork and sculpture such as the Brussels Cross or the walrus-ivory crozier now in the Victoria and Albert Museum. Ethelred II's reign lies at the center of that "golden age of Anglo-Saxon art" so splendidly displayed at the British Museum exhibition in 1984. It is comforting to be reminded that great artistic achievement can occur in a period of political turmoil and national degradation.

The most recent account of Ethelred's reign is contained in the important, if sometimes difficult, study by S. Keynes, *The Diplomas of King Aethelred "the Unready," 978–1016,* 1980, especially ch. 4.

BYRHTNOTH (*d.* 991) owes his enduring fame to his death in battle against the Danes at Maldon. Before that he had had a distinguished career as a prominent servant of successive English kings. Byrhtnoth came of wealthy and aristocratic stock: it is possible that he was descended from the royal dynasty that had once ruled independent Mercia. He was born probably about 925–30. He married a lady named Aelflaed, the daughter of Aelfgar, alderman of Essex; Aelflaed's sister Aethelflaed was the second wife of King Edmund. Byrhtnoth was made alderman of Essex in 956 and held the office until his death. His sphere of authority seems to have embraced more than the county of Essex. It apparently included Huntingdonshire and Cambridgeshire and may toward the end of his life have extended even farther northward. Sufficient documentation has survived to show that Byrhtnoth was a man of enormous landed wealth, accumulated partly through inheritance, partly through his marriage, partly through royal grant. Most of his landholdings were concentrated in the eastern counties of Essex, Suffolk, and Cambridgeshire, but he held estates elsewhere as far afield as Worcestershire and Oxfordshire. He probably held land on an even ampler scale than his contemporary Wulfric. Byrhtnoth stood high in the favor of the kings he served: "my well-beloved earl" was how Edgar referred to him in 964. He was closely associated with Edgar's policy of reviving monastic life and was a generous benefactor of the monasteries of Ely and Ramsey, founded respectively by Ethelwold and Oswald in the late 960s. The first abbot of refounded Ely shared a name with our Byrhtnoth and may have been a relation. Byrhtnoth was a strong upholder of the monasteries in the so-called antimonastic reaction in the reign of King Edward the Martyr.

Byrhtnoth was killed fighting against the Danes at the battle of Maldon in 991. His last fight was commemorated in a celebrated Old English poem. Both the battle and the poem have generated controversy among historians and students of literature. Byrhtnoth and Maldon have proved capable of sustaining a modest academic light industry—nothing on the scale of the vast multinational conglomerate represented by *Beowulf* studies, but respectable nonetheless—over the last fifty years or so. For example, it has been claimed that there were two battles of Maldon, not one; that it (or they) was (or were) fought not as was for long believed about the causeway linking Northey Island to the mainland in the Blackwater estuary, but somewhere else; that the poem was composed very soon after the event; that the poem was composed about forty or more years later; that the poem is a reliable source of historical information; that the poem is almost completely devoid of historical value; that the poem is an archaistic work harking back to the warrior-ethic of the pagan heroic age of the ancient Germans; that the poem is a work of deep Christian conviction, probably the composition of a learned monk, embodying a forward-looking attitude to the place of warfare and patriotism in a Christian society; and so on, and so forth. The greatest tribute to the poem is that it rises above such pedantic wranglings. Read it and see.

For a recent verse-translation see M. Alexander, *The Earliest English Poems*, 1966.

ETHELWEARD (*d. c.* 999) was an English nobleman of exalted rank, prominent in public affairs, a patron of religion and scholarship, and the author of a Latin chronicle. He was a member of the West Saxon royal family, a descendant of King Ethelred I (the elder brother of King Alfred), and probably a brother of Queen

Elfgifu, the wife of King Eadwig. Between 973 and 998 his name features in the witness-lists of royal charters as an alderman; it is assumed that he died shortly after the latter date. His aldermanry lay in the west country: it certainly included Dorset and may have embraced the whole of the southwestern peninsula. By virtue of his rank and office he was among the more important of the counsellors of King Ethelred II, a man entrusted with political tasks at the highest level, as, for instance, the negotiation of a treaty with the Danes in 991.

Ethelweard was also a man of very considerable wealth, some of which he laid out in monastic foundations. He and his son Ethelmaer founded the monastery at Cerne in Dorset in 987, and after his father's death Ethelmaer founded Eynsham in Oxfordshire. Cerne—now Cerne Abbas—and Eynsham were the houses in which Aelfric spent much of his working life. He was one of the three scholars—the others being Wulfstan of York and Byrhtferth of Ramsey—whose literary works are among the glories of late Anglo-Saxon culture. Ethelweard was one of Aelfric's patrons. Aelfric translated six books of the Old Testament into Old English at his request, and some of his *Catholic Homilies* and *Lives of the Saints* were dedicated to Ethelweard.

Ethelweard's *Chronicle* is a most remarkable document. It is the only surviving Latin work composed by an English layman before the fourteenth century. And Ethelweard's was no ordinary Latin. He wrote in the extraordinarily convoluted Latin style that modern scholars term "hermeneutic." Revived in the tenth century on the model of the writings of St. Aldhelm, it had been much cultivated in the circle of Bishop Ethelwold of Winchester, under whose influence Ethelweard had perhaps received his literary training. It is clear that Ethelweard was a man of advanced education. How unusual was he, in this respect, among his lay contemporaries? Historians debate this point inconclusively. It is probable that a knowledge of Latin was a very rare accomplishment among tenth-century laymen, but it may well be that vernacular literacy was more widespread than scholars have generally been prepared to concede. After all, King Alfred—a realist if ever there were one— had considered lay education a practical goal. Indeed, it is hard to see how the advanced governmental institutions of late Anglo-Saxon England could have functioned properly—and we know that they *did*—without reasonably widespread literacy. References to books in lay people's wills of this period are suggestive, though we all know that to possess a book is not necessarily to read it.

Ethelweard's *Chronicle* is a Latin version of a set of annals, now lost, in Old English. It traces the history of the English from their origins, settlement in England, and conversion to Christianity down to the reign of King Edgar, laying special stress on the great deeds of the kings of Wessex, to whom, as we have seen, Ethelweard was related. So was the lady for whom the work was composed: Matilda, abbess of Essen in Germany, the granddaughter of the emperor Otto I and his English consort Edith, the sister of King Athelstan. This dedication is one of several indications of contact between England and Germany on the part of the aristocracy and clergy in the late tenth and early eleventh centuries. It is likely that such contacts were a good deal more dense than the surviving evidence allows us to see. Anglo-German communication may have been as close and fruitful for both sides as Anglo-Frankish links had been in the eighth and ninth centuries. There was nothing insular about late Anglo-Saxon culture. Ethelweard, like Wulfstan, lived in a big world. He was a cosmopolitan.

The Chronicle of Ethelweard has been edited and translated by A. Campbell, 1962.

WULFRIC (*d. c.* 1004) was the founder of the monastery of Burton-on-Trent, the northernmost house established in the course of the English monastic revival of the tenth century. Wulfric was a nobleman of the northern region of Mercia, rich, devout, and loyal to the house of Wessex—a significant combination of qualities. His loyalty is attested by his subscriptions to royal charters between *c.* 970 and 1002. (Such subscriptions usually indicate that the witness in question was in attendance at the royal court and among the king's counsellors, or *witan*, "wise men.") We have in addition the evidence of a grant of land to him by King Ethelred II in 995 made "on account of the most faithful obedience with which he has served me." Wulfric was a reliable king's man.

His loyalty was worth having, for he was a man of enormous landed wealth and therefore influence and power. We can gauge the extent of his territorial resources owing to the fortunate survival of his will, drawn up between 1002 and 1004. He disposed of about eighty separate landed estates scattered over a dozen counties ranging from Yorkshire in the north to Gloucestershire in the south and from the Wirral peninsula in Cheshire to the west across to the Lincolnshire Wolds in the east. The greatest concentration lay in Derbyshire, Staffordshire, and Leicestershire. Some of these estates were of modest size, but others were huge, such for example, as the estate of Conisbrough in Yorkshire. Conisbrough means "king's fortress." The magnificent twelfth-century castle keep, which still stands there, serves as a reminder of the strategic importance of the place, commanding the crossing of the river Don on the main route from south to north. It must have been an important strong-point in the fighting between the West Saxon kings and the Danes of Northumbria in the second quarter of the tenth century. It is likely, though we cannot prove it, that Conisbrough had been granted to Wulfric's family by one of the kings of Wessex. Some of Wulfric's estates were certainly acquired by royal grant. But the bulk of them seem to have been inherited from his father (whose name is unknown) and his mother Wulfrun.

Wulfric had no son. His only child, a daughter who may perhaps have been an invalid, received a few small bequests. His brother Aelfhelm, alderman of southern Northumbria from c. 993 to 1006, received much, and so did Aelfhelm's sons. So too did his sister's family. But in the main his generosity was directed at his monastic foundation at Burton-on-Trent, which received no less than forty-eight estates together with much livestock and movable goods. Burton was the most notable, though not the only, manifestation of Wulfric's piety. Its first abbot was a monk of Winchester. This is significant. Winchester was the home of the reformed monasticism established by Bishop Ethelwold and King Edgar. Wulfric's foundation was not simply an act of personal piety designed to secure the salvation of his soul: it was also a means by which West Saxon cultural, and indeed political, influence seeped into a region hitherto largely immune from it. In this context it is noteworthy that Wulfric made it clear in his will that he looked to the king and the archbishop of Canterbury, as well as to his brother, to be the patrons of his monastery after his death.

Wulfric's career and connections, in so far as we can make them out from his will and other records, have something to tell us about the process by which West Saxon authority was made effective over the Danelaw and a unified kingdom of England emerged in the tenth century. These documents also reveal something of the sheer wealth of the aristocracy, and that not just in land: the amount of gold that Wulfric disposed of is remarkable. The Danes who systematically plundered England during Ethelred II's reign were correct in their assessment of it as an extremely rich country. Documents of a slightly later date have another lesson to teach. For reasons unknown, Wulfric's family fell foul of the king not long after his death. His brother Aelfhelm was killed in 1006 and his two sons blinded. Morcar, the husband of Wulfric's niece, was killed in 1015 and his brother with him. Much of the family property was confiscated by the king. The family monastery at Burton also suffered. Its endowments as recorded in Domesday Book (1086) were less than half those listed in Wulfric's will of eighty years earlier. The history of the family and of the monastery in the eleventh century illustrate the fragility of landed power at that period and the fluidity of late Anglo-Saxon society.

P. H. Sawyer has edited *The Charters of Burton Abbey*, 1979, with an important introduction on Wulfric and his family.

ST. AELFHEAH, ALPHEGE, or **ELPHEGE** (*d.* 1012) was archbishop of Canterbury from 1005 to 1012, and the first of the five holders of that office who have met their deaths by violence. After a monastic training, probably at Glastonbury, Aelfheah became abbot of Bath about 968–70. In 984 he was promoted to the bishopric of Winchester on the death of Ethelwold, and in 1005 moved on to Canterbury. In 1008, alongside Archbishop Wulfstan of York, he was responsible for drawing up one of the legal ordinances of King Ethelred II. Practically nothing else is known of his archiepiscopate.

His grisly death, however, is well-documented. In September 1011 a Danish army under Thorkell the Tall and possibly Sweyn Forkbeard took Canterbury and sacked it. The archbishop and several other prominent people were captured. Aelfheah remained a prisoner in Danish hands during the winter. In April 1012 the Danes were camped outside London at Greenwich awaiting the payment of the colossal sum of £48,000, which they had exacted from the English government in Danegeld. The money was paid over shortly after Easter, which fell on 13 April. The Danes demanded that an additional sum of £3,000 should be paid as a ransom for the archbishop. Aelfheah courageously refused to permit this and, despite the protests of Thorkell the Tall, was lynched by a mob of drunken Danes on 19 April. They pelted him with bones and then finished him off with an axe.

Aelfheah was immediately acclaimed as a martyr. His tomb in St. Paul's rapidly became the focus of a cult and it was believed that miracles were performed there. Relics were big business in the eleventh century. The success of Aelfheah's cult was too much for his own monks of Canterbury to contemplate from a distance. In 1023 they had the relics of Aelfheah moved to Canterbury, much to the fury of the clergy of St. Paul's and aided by King Canute who laid on the necessary armed escort for the occasion. Aelfheah's cult continued lively for the remainder of the Middle Ages and is attested by a number of church-dedications.

EMMA (*d.* 1052) was queen-consort of England, wife successively of Ethelred II and Canute. Emma was a daughter of Duke Richard I of Normandy (*d.* 996). Her marriage to Ethelred in 1002 arose from the course of Anglo Norman diplomacy. Relations between England and Normandy had been strained in the recent past, despite a treaty in 991, by the habit of Danish raiders on England using Norman harbors as their bases, as, for example, in the summer of 1000. (It should be borne in mind that the duchy of Normandy had originated as a Danish colony only about ninety years before.) Emma's marriage to Ethelred was almost certainly part of a wider settlement of outstanding grievances between the English and Norman courts. Of her life in England over the next eleven years we know practically nothing save that she bore the king three children. The eldest, Edward—later to be better known as Edward the Confessor—was born probably in 1005. In the winter of 1013, when Sweyn Forkbeard was completing his conquest of England, the royal family went into exile. They found a refuge at the court of Emma's brother, Richard II of Normandy. Emma may have accompanied Ethelred back to England in 1014 and remained there until his death in 1016: we do not know. She was certainly in Normandy in 1017.

It was in this year that she was approached by Canute, the conqueror of her husband's kingdom, with an offer of marriage. This she accepted. This was a hard-headed bargain on both sides. Canute wanted to neutralize the potential hostility of the Norman duke, who might have made trouble by promoting the interest of

Emma's sons—his nephews, refugees at his court—by her first marriage. Emma was able for her part to insist that only Canute's sons
by her should have a right to the English crown; thus doing all she
could to debar Canute's offspring by his earlier consort, Aelfgifu of
Northampton, from the succession. Emma has been much blamed
by later historians for thus abandoning her children by Ethelred.
This is unjust: she had little room for maneuver, and by her course
of action she did at least secure their safety. Nevertheless, it is obvious that the person who profited most from the marriage was
Emma herself.

Emma and Canute were married in 1017. She bore him two
children, Harthacnut (king of England 1041–42) and Gunnhildr
(who married the emperor Henry III of Germany in 1036). Her
most important public role beside childbearing was probably assisting in the projection of an image of royal piety, which Canute (or
his advisers) thought it politic to foster. In 1023 she attended the
translation of the body of St. Aelfheah from London to Canterbury. She collected relics. She was a generous patron of churches
and monasteries such as Winchester, Ely, and Ramsey. Her generosity extended to churches abroad, such as Bremen in Germany
and Poitiers in France, and doubtless those of her native Normandy as well. A contemporary manuscript now in the British Library depicts her and her husband presenting a big golden cross
to the New Minster at Winchester (later Hyde Abbey): onlooking
monks raise their hands in gratitude, while hovering angels direct
the royal couple's eyes to the heavens, whence Jesus, Mary, and St.
Peter look down approvingly. This was precisely the image which
Emma and Canute sought to project.

But there was a good deal more than piety to Emma's character. The adroitness of her maneuvers in 1016–17 should prepare us
for her actions some twenty years later. On Canute's sudden death
in November 1035 a struggle for the succession ensued between
factions supporting his son by Aelfgifu, Harold, and his son by
Emma, Harthacnut. Naturally, Emma upheld the claims of the latter. The details of the conflict cannot be fully reconstructed, but it
is clear that Emma lost the first round. By 1037 Harold had made
himself king of England, assisted by the fact that Harthacnut had
been detained in Denmark. Emma was forced into exile in Flanders where she was joined by Harthacnut. From there she con-

ducted a vigorous propaganda campaign against Harold. It was during this period (1031–40) that she commissioned the work known as the *Encomium Emmae* ("In Praise of Emma"), a political tract by a monk of the Flemish monastery of St. Bertin designed to glorify Emma and to support the claims of Harthacnut. When Harold died in 1040 Emma and her son crossed to England and Harthacnut made himself king. Shortly afterwards, in 1041, he invited his half brother Edward to return to England. On Harthacnut's early death in 1042 Edward ascended the throne, which he was to occupy until 1066.

Emma had fought hard for Harthacnut's succession and his sudden death at the age of only about 23 must have been a severe blow to her. Worse was to follow. Late in 1043 the new king, her firstborn son Edward, turned up at Emma's residence at Winchester accompanied by a posse of his leading counsellors and deprived her of her estates and treasure. The event has never been satisfactorily explained. Contemporary chroniclers reported that Edward had long resented his mother's neglect of him. This may well be true, but the participation of the king's chief ministers in Emma's disgrace surely indicates that political as well as domestic issues were at stake: precisely what these were we cannot now tell. What is certain is that Emma was now eclipsed. She was allowed to reside at Winchester, suitably provided for, but she played no further role in politics. And it was at Winchester that she died, and was buried beside Canute, in 1052.

Emma was a forceful, ambitious, and unscrupulous woman: a survivor, who for forty years played a leading role at the highest level of English political and social life. Hard, even ruthless, as she emerges from contemporary record, it is difficult to believe that she could have done what she did without more endearing characteristics. Charm is a quality that often eludes the historian. Paradoxically—for one so determined to make her mark—her significance in English history is owing more to chance than to design. The marriage of a Norman princess into the English royal family in 1002 entwined the fortunes of two dynasties. When Emma's son Edward died in 1066 her great-nephew, Duke William of Normandy, at once began to finalize the preparations for the invasion that would give him the kingdom to which he believed he had a right.

The best treatment of Emma's career is to be found in the intro-
duction to the edition and translation of the *Encomium Emmae
Reginae* by A. Campbell, Camden Society, 3rd series, vol.
LXXII: Royal Historical Society, 1949.

EADRIC STREONA (*d.* 1017) was alderman of Mercia in the
reign of Ethelred II and became notorious for his treachery. Eadric owes his unsavory reputation to the anonymous monk of
Abingdon who edited the annals that deal with Ethelred's reign in
what is known as manuscript "C" of the *Anglo-Saxon Chronicle*. It
should be noted that these annals were composed between 1017
and 1023. The author wrote after Eadric's fall and with the advan-
tages of hindsight.

Our first certain knowledge of Eadric comes from the year
1007 when he was entrusted with the aldermanry of Mercia. The
governance of all the lands between the Thames and the Humber,
which this office entailed, made Eadric one of the most powerful
men in the kingdom of England. This appointment must have
been preceded by earlier stages in a rise to prominence, but the
details of these cannot be recovered. But about one incident that
immediately preceded his promotion we may be reasonably confident. It is likely that it was Eadric who was responsible in 1006 for
the murder of Aelfhelm, alderman of Northumbria (the brother
of Wulfric), and the blinding of his two sons. The tissue of intrigue
and feud among the ruling elite that must have lain behind this
outrage can only be surmised, not reconstructed. It has been plausibly argued that there was "something approaching a palace revolution among the principal lay associates of King Ethelred" in the
years 1006–7. Eadric and his faction came out on top. He was the
king's principal counsellor for the next eight years: as one of our
sources puts it, he "presided over the whole kingdom like a subking." Matrimony consolidated his power: at some point he married the king's daughter Edith.

These years were of course a time of demoralization and defeat for the English in their struggle against the Danes. Eadric was
blamed for this. For instance, there was an occasion in 1009 when
the king could have attacked the Danes but, says the Abingdon
chronicler, "it was hindered by Alderman Eadric, as it always was."
He seems to have preferred paying Danegeld to fighting. He per-
petrated acts of violence: in 1015 two more prominent Northum-

brian noblemen were killed, apparently while being entertained by him at Oxford. Finally he was guilty of the most heinous of all crimes, treachery to his lord: in 1015 he went over to Canute. But this was not all. The year 1016 was dominated by fighting between Edmund Ironside and Canute. When Edmund seemed to be gaining the upper hand in the late summer Eadric abandoned Canute and went over to him. Finally, at the battle of Ashingdon in October Eadric "did as he had often done before: he was the first to start the flight and thus betrayed his liege lord and all the people of England." Canute's victory on that occasion gave him most of England; Edmund's death shortly afterwards, all of it. Canute restored Eadric to control over Mercia but evidently did not trust him. Late in 1017 the king had Eadric murdered—"very rightly," comments one of our sources.

Eadric's treasonable career is not a pleasant one to contemplate. But moralizing reflection should be resisted. There were other prominent men who acted likewise. The historian should try to understand something of the forces that shaped such a career. Two factors may be significant. Firstly, what we call "politics" were at this period very largely propelled by rivalries and feuds among the ruling aristocratic elite. Eadric's vendetta against the principal Northumbrian family is a case in point. Edmund Ironside's mother had been Northumbrian, not inconceivably connected with this family; the lady whom Edmund married in 1015 had just had her first husband butchered by Eadric. Relations between Edmund and Eadric must have been strained, to say the least, in 1015–16. Canute's first English consort was a lady named Aelfgifu. Her father had been the alderman of Northumbria killed in 1006 and her brothers the two men blinded then, probably at Eadric's instance. Her first cousin had been married to one of the men killed by Eadric in 1015. Did she encourage, even demand, Eadric's death in 1017?

The second point arises from Eadric's nickname: "Streona" means "acquisitor." Eadric was greedy for wealth and enriched himself at other peoples' expense. It has been suggested that one means by which he did so was connected with the payment of Danegeld. The burden of taxation laid on the country in the reign of Ethelred was a heavy one. Many people must have found difficulty in paying their share. Those who could not pay forfeited their land either to those who could come forward with the money and pay the tax due in their place, or to the king, whose local officials could then dispose of it to other purchasers. As one of the king's first ministers Eadric would have been a man whose will it would have been difficult, perhaps dangerous, to resist. He would also very probably have been a man who would have enjoyed the artificially low tax assessments of a favored courtier. Furthermore, the bulk of his estates lay in western Mercia, an area less subject than other parts of the country to the raiding and warfare that had such a debilitating effect on the economy. Eadric was very rich and he could use the tax-law of the time to enrich himself even further. As a later eleventh-century writer observed, "he joined estate to estate at will." No wonder he preferred paying tax to fighting.

THORKELL THE TALL was one of the Viking leaders prominent in English affairs late in the reign of Ethelred II and early in that of Canute. A native of Denmark, possibly connected with the Danish royal family, his early career is shrouded by legend. He emerges into the light of history as the leader of what a contemporary chronicler described as an "immense raiding army," which landed in Kent in the summer of 1009. Between 1009 and 1012 Thorkell's forces ravaged and plundered much of midland and southern England. It was his men who murdered Archbishop Aelfheah of Canterbury at Greenwich in 1012, though Thorkell had tried in vain to prevent them. After the payment of Danegeld to them the Danish forces dispersed and Thorkell with a fleet of forty-five ships (indicating a manpower of about 3,500) entered the service of King Ethelred. He fought with Ethelred against Sweyn Forkbeard in 1013 and remained loyal to Ethelred throughout 1014. At some subsequent point he went over to Canute. It is assumed, though it cannot be proved, that Thorkell changed sides with Eadric Streona toward the end of 1015. At any rate, Canute had sufficient confidence in his loyalty to make him earl of East Anglia in 1017. During Canute's absence in Denmark in 1019 Thorkell seems to have acted as the regent of England. Then there came a sudden reversal in his fortunes. Toward the end of 1021 Thorkell was outlawed and banished by Canute; we know nothing certain about the background to this quarrel. Thorkell retired to Denmark but apparently remained powerful and a potential menace to Canute. This brought the king back to Denmark in 1022. Thorkell was evidently strong enough to exact terms of reconciliation favorable to himself: Canute entrusted him with the government of Denmark. Nothing is heard of him subsequently and it is assumed that he died shortly after 1023.

UHTRED was earl of Northumbria from *c.* 1006 until his murder, which gave rise to a celebrated feud, in 1016. Uhtred was descended from a family that had governed Bernicia, the northern half of Northumbria, in virtual independence of the Wessex-based kings of England, from at least the last years of the ninth century. His vigorous defense of Northumbria from the Scots in about 1006 led King Elthelred II to add Deira, that is Yorkshire, to his earldom. Uhtred held the office of earl of all Northumbria from then on. In 1013 he submitted to Swcyn Forkbeard but in the confused period following Sweyn's death in 1014 he went over to Edmund Ironside, with whom he was campaigning early in 1016 in the midlands. Canute managed to slip into Uhtred's Yorkshire territories, forcing Uhtred to hasten back and submit to him. However, when the two men met, Uhtred was murdered at the instigation of Eadric Streona by another Northumbrian nobleman named Thurbrand. Both in its background and in its consequences there was more to this crime than meets the eye.

Uhtred had been thrice married. His first wife was a daughter of the bishop of Durham; his second wife the daughter of a man prominent in Yorkshire; his third wife one of the many daughters of King Ethelred. (Uhtred was thus the brother-in-law of Eadric Streona who had him killed.) As a condition of his second marriage Uhtred had promised his father-in-law that he would kill an enemy of his, Thurbrand. As we have seen, Thurbrand struck first. But Uhtred's blood had to be avenged. His son by his first marriage, Ealdred, became earl of Northumbria in about 1019. At some date unknown Ealdred avenged his father by killing Thurbrand. The feud was inherited by Thurbrand's son Carl. For some time Carl and Ealdred sought to ambush one another, but friends intervened to reconcile the two families. Peace was patched up and Carl and Ealdred even pledged themselves to go on pilgrimage to Rome in brotherhood. But for reasons unknown the strife flared up again. In about 1038 Carl killed Ealdred at Rise, near Beverley. Ealdred left five daughters but no son. One of these girls married Siward, earl of Northumbria, and their son Waltheof inherited the feud. He managed to corner Carl's sons and grandsons while they were feasting at Settrington, near Malton, and massacred all but two of them.

The story of this three-generation feud survives in a few paragraphs of a short tract composed at Durham about the year 1100. The author, whose main concern was with certain properties of the church of Durham transmitted through the bishop's daughter who was Uhtred's first wife, tells it casually, as though there was nothing specially unusual about it. It has been said that the story indicates how violent life was in a part of England which had experienced heavy Scandinavian influence. This is doubtful, for similar feuds can be traced in parts of early medieval Europe that received no Viking settlers. In any case, there is every likelihood that more than family honor was at stake. Uhtred's family was Bernician, Thurbrand's Deiran. It was a contest for local influence between rival networks of kinsmen and retainers. The chance survival of this document affords us a precious glimpse of the realities of regional power-struggles in later Anglo-Saxon England.

C. R. Hart, *The Early Charters of Northern England and the North Midlands,* 1975, contains a translation of the text.

EDMUND IRONSIDE was briefly king of England between April and November 1016. He was the third son of King Ethelred II and his first wife Aelfflaed, daughter of Earl Thored of Northumbria, and was born in about 990. Edmund first comes into prominence in 1015 when, in effect, he rebelled against his father who had been recently restored to the kingdom of England after the death of Sweyn Forkbeard. We are told that he abducted the widow of a prominent Northumbrian nobleman and married her against his father's wishes. He then went to the territory of the Five Boroughs (Stamford, Leicester, Lincoln, Nottingham, and Derby) where "the people all submitted to him." Early in 1016, in alliance with Earl Uhtred of Northumbria, he devastated the northwest Mercian territories of Eadric Streona. The background to these events is not known. A plausible guess is that Edmund was apprehensive of the designs of his stepmother Emma, who may have been trying to supplant the children of Ethelred's first marriage and secure the succession to the throne upon her son Edward (later to be known as Edward the Confessor).

When Canute gained power in Northumbria and had Uhtred murdered, Edmund fell back upon London where he joined his father. Ethelred died in April 1016 and Edmund was acclaimed king. He devoted the following six months to a courageous but finally unsuccessful struggle to prevent Canute from gaining mastery of England. In the course of this Edmund may have been sustained by an alliance with one or more of the Welsh princes. No less than six battles were fought during these months. The last of them, at Ashingdon in Essex in October, proved a decisive defeat for the English forces. Edmund and Canute met shortly afterwards on an island in the river Severn near Deerhurst in Gloucestershire and agreed on partition: Edmund was left with Wessex, Canute took the rest of the country, including London. Such a partition would in all likelihood have proved unworkable, but, in the event, Edmund died soon after it had been agreed and Canute became sole king of England. It was most convenient for Canute that Edmund should have died at precisely this juncture, but there was no contemporary suggestion of foul play. Edmund's nickname "Ironside" was probably contemporary and referred to his bravery.

SWEYN FORKBEARD (d. 1014) was successively king of Denmark and, by conquest, of England. Sweyn (properly Swegen) displaced his father Harold Bluetooth and made himself king of the Danes in about 988. He devoted much of his reign to attacking England and exacting tribute, the famous Danegeld, until he finally turned to conquest in 1013. Very little is known of the institutions of tenth-century Denmark, but it is clear that her kings were able to execute large-scale public works such as the great military camps at Fyrkat, Trelleborg, and elsewhere, or the causeway at Ravning, and it is likely that some means of raising fleets by means of a royal ship-levy existed. Sweyn's forces were big and well-equipped, bent on the systematic exploitation of the vulnerable England of King Ethelred II.

Sweyn's own part in the campaigns of the years 991–1013 is difficult to elucidate owing to the meagerness of our sources. It is probable that he campaigned in England before his first recorded appearance there in 994, and it is just possible that he was one of the Danish leaders at the battle of Maldon, where Byrhtnoth fell, in 991. In 994 he attacked London unsuccessfully, ravaged in southeast England, and wintered at Southampton, exacting a geld of £16,000. He returned to Scandinavia in 995 by way of the Irish Sea. During the years 995–1000 he was apparently detained in the north by troubles about which we are ill-informed with the Swedes and the Poles. It is likely that his marriage to a sister of Duke Boleslav of Poland was connected with these obscure goings-on. The child of this union was Canute (or Cnut), born in about 996. Sweyn may have been back in England in 1001–2, when a geld of £24,000 was levied. He was certainly there in 1003, when he sacked Exeter and ravaged Wiltshire, and in 1004, when East Anglia was the target: Norwich and Thetford were sacked and a fierce but in-decisive battle was fought against Ulfcetel of East Anglia. The year 1005 found Sweyn back in Denmark, but he probably returned to England in 1006 when the Danes ravaged in Kent and Sussex and settled on the Isle of Wight for the winter: about Christmas they raided through Hampshire into Berkshire and defeated an English army; £36,000 was forthcoming as geld in 1007. We lose sight of Sweyn again in 1008. It is likely that he was the commander of one of the several Danish armies that were operating in England dur-ing the years 1009–12, which exacted a geld of £48,000 and mur-dered Archbishop Aelfheah. After this he seems to have returned to Denmark by way of the Irish Sea—as in 995—surviving ship-wreck off the coast of Pembrokeshire on the voyage home.

In 1013 he came intent upon conquest and his tactics were dif-ferent. He landed at Gainsborough on the Trent, in the northern Danelaw where he could count on the sympathy of the Anglo-Dan-ish aristocracy. He then systematically laid waste the country in a wide arc through Oxford and Winchester to London. After this display of force, as the *Anglo-Saxon Chronicle* records, "all the nation regarded him as full king." Ethelred fled to Normandy and Sweyn returned in triumph to his fleet at Gainsborough. But disaster struck in his moment of glory. He died suddenly on 3 February 1014, bequeathing his ambitions to his son Canute.

CANUTE, properly **CNUT,** king of Denmark, England, and Nor-way, was born the son of Sweyn Forkbeard and his Polish wife in about 996. While still only a youth he accompanied his father on the expedition that led to the Danish conquest of England in 1013. After Sweyn's untimely death early in 1014 and the return to England of King Ethelred II, Canute withdrew to Denmark. He returned in 1015 and after fierce fighting against the forces of Ethelred and his son Edmund Ironside won his way after the latter's early death in November 1016 to sole power as king of England. The first of the eleventh-century conquests of England had been accomplished.

During the years 1017 and 1018 Canute remained in England to consolidate his conquest. In 1019 he led an expedition to Denmark to enforce his authority there following the death of its ruler, his brother Harold. During his absence England was left in the charge of Thorkell the Tall, Canute's leading magnate. Subsequently, in 1021, Canute and Thorkell quarrelled, and Thorkell was banished. He took himself off to Denmark where he remained menacing. This brought Canute back to Denmark in 1022–23, and a settlement was reached under the terms of which Thorkell was to govern Denmark as Canute's viceroy. After Thorkell's death, probably shortly afterward, he was succeeded in this office by Canute's brother-in-law Ulf. But Ulf in his turn proved unreliable. In 1026 he joined a coalition of the kings of Norway and Sweden directed against Canute, whose attempts on a third return visit to Denmark to deal it a decisive blow resulted in a serious defeat for himself at the battle of the Holy River (off the coast of Scania in what is now southern Sweden). In 1027 Canute journeyed on pilgrimage to Rome where he attended the coronation of the Emperor Conrad II of Germany. The year 1028 found him back in Scandinavia. Canute had already had Ulf murdered to retrieve his position in Denmark. Now an Anglo-Danish fleet overawed the Norwegians, whose king fled without fighting a battle. Canute was at the height of his power, Lord of Denmark, England, and Norway. He managed to hold this precarious empire together until his death at the age of only about forty in 1035.

Such, in brief outline, is the narrative framework of Canute's career. It focuses attention upon the difficulty the king experienced in holding on to his far-flung territories. (Norman and Angevin rulers were to experience comparable difficulties.) Canute's empire was a personal creation and did not survive his death. In so far as we may infer any overall political strategy— which is not very far—Canute seems to have thought of England as a source of wealth, manpower, and skills on which he could draw for the prosecution of his ambitions in Scandinavia.

England around the year 1000 was a rich country: thickly set-tled, intensively exploited, able to sustain a superstructure of church, aristocracy, and towns. A line of gifted rulers from Alfred to Edgar had developed institutions of government of remarkable sophistication; most formidably, the ability to cream off surplus wealth in the form of taxation—the Danegeld or simply geld, which bulks so large in the records of Ethelred II's reign. Canute grasped this inheritance eagerly. The geld that he exacted in 1018 was quite possibly the heaviest levy of taxation to which this coun-try has ever been subjected. Anglo-Saxon kings commanded the means of raising armies and navies; Canute could use these forces in his Scandinavian campaigns, as in 1028. Another way in which Canute could exploit England was by handing out its land to re-ward his followers. For example, a certain Orc, one of Canute's housecarls—privileged military retainers—received lands in Dorset from the king, which he used later on to endow the monastery of Abbotsbury. The passage of these lands into the hands of the church and thereby the preservation of records relating to them are the only reasons why we hear anything of Orc; it follows that there may have been others like him of whom we hear nothing. Some of Canute's followers received very extensive grants of land: Tofi the Proud, for instance, held estates in Norfolk, Essex, Hert-fordshire, Surrey, Berkshire, and Somerset. It is true that the wholesale dispossession of the native English aristocracy, such as was to happen in the reign of William the Conqueror, did not occur under Canute. Nevertheless, almost every shire in the coun-try can show evidence of land grants to his Danish followers.

But Canute did not rely solely on his Danish henchmen in the government of England. The continuity of administrative practice attested in fiscal and judicial matters depended on the coopera-tion with the new regime of the agents of government both secular and ecclesiastical (as was also to be the case after 1066). The adhe-sion of bishops such as Wulfstan of York was an important factor in the stability of Canute's rule. There were also new men who came to the fore, prepared to serve him and eager to reap the rewards of his patronage. Two examples may suffice: Godwin, who had be-come earl of Wessex before the end of 1018, and the priest Sti-gand, who was given charge in 1020 of the minster church founded by Canute at Ashingdon.

Institutional continuity and the ordered exploitation of England by the king should not blind us to the fact that Canute's conquest was a fairly brutal affair. The English hostages whose hands, ears, and noses he cut off in 1014 could have testified to this effect. There were executions, confiscations of property, banishments, extortionate taxation, and many acts of injustice. In some ways Canute looks like a barbarian conqueror from the heroic age of Scandinavia. It is of interest in this connection that the Old English epic *Beowulf,* which celebrates just such a warlord, survives in a manuscript copied, probably, during Canute's lifetime; some scholars have gone so far as to suggest that the work was actually composed in his honor. In 1965 there was excavated at Winchester a fragment of stone sculpture depicting part of a scene from the Scandinavian legend of Sigmund and the wolf. It has been suggested that this frankly secular scene with its pagan overtones should be associated with Canute; the sculpture probably formed part of a frieze that could have adorned his tomb.

The pagan past was not far away. One of the rune-stones at Jelling in central Denmark proclaims that Canute's grandfather, King Harold Bluetooth, had "made the Danes Christian." So, in a formal sense, he had. But Christianity took a long time to penetrate their hearts and minds. The young Canute was presumably brought up a Christian of sorts; but his religion was probably only skin-deep. Yet in England he acquired a reputation as a devout Christian monarch famous for his extravagant piety. How did this come about? The most plausible answer is that this was an image carefully nurtured by his leading ecclesiastical advisers, the bishops. Canute was presented with this model and urged by them to conform to it. They for their part could ensure that this was how Canute would appear to posterity.

In the latter task they were completely successful. Take, for example, the famous story of Canute and the waves (which is recorded for the first time about a century after his death). The point of the tale is the king's Christian humility: his failure to stem the tide demonstrated to his flatterers the weakness of his power compared with that of God. Strictly contemporary evidence shows that Canute took his Christian and royal obligations very seriously. His piety was lavish and ostentatious. He staged the translation of the body of St. Aelfheah to Canterbury in 1023. He was instrumental in building up the monastery of Bury St. Edmunds. Many cathedrals and monasteries both at home and abroad were grateful for his generosity. Bishop Fulbert of Chartres, one of the most distinguished churchmen of his day, praised Canute's piety and munificence. Canute's pilgrimage to Rome in 1027 advertised on a European stage his penitential devotion. His coinage bore Christian symbolism and his charters were replete with devout phraseology. The laws issued in his name, drafted by Archbishop Wulfstan of York, were in a sense manifestos of the king's Christian intentions.

It is an impressive record, as it was intended to be. Yet the extent to which Canute was genuinely tamed and civilized by his bishops remains debatable. He murdered his brother-in-law. His harsh taxation was regarded by churchmen such as Wulfstan as unjust. The most revealing evidence of Canute's practice is furnished by what we know of his marriages. Soon after his arrival in England in 1015 he had formed a liaison with a lady named Aelfgifu of Northampton. She came of distinguished lineage—her father had been alderman of Northumbria and her uncle was Wulfric the founder of Burton abbey—and Canute's association with her was probably intended to gain her family's support. In 1017 he married Emma, the widow of Ethelred II, another match that clearly had a political motive. But marriage to Emma did not mean that Aelfgifu was set aside. Canute publicly maintained two consorts. His son by Aelfgifu, Harold, succeeded him as king of England from 1035 to 1040; his son by Emma, Harthacnut, from 1040 to 1042. Pious though he may have been, Canute set a something less than perfect example of Christian matrimony.

Canute's career and reign are poorly documented. There is much that will always remain mysterious about their public course as well as about the recesses of the king's character. We know just enough to sense a formidable warrior who wrought great deeds in a short life and moved vigorously if at times uncertainly toward acceptance of the values and customs of Christendom, which had meant little to his Scandinavian and Slavonic ancestors. We can also appreciate in these sparse records the wealth and order of the late Anglo-Saxon state. The kings of the tenth century had done their work well. Canute realized that he had every interest in maintaining in good repair the fabric that they had erected. It was the appreciation not just of an opportunist but of a statesman too.

WULFSTAN, archbishop of York 1002–23, was the most distinguished intellectual figure of the late Anglo-Saxon church and a statesman of the first rank under Ethelred II and Canute. He was probably a native of the eastern Danelaw and received his early training as a monk, perhaps at Ely where he was later buried. He became bishop of London in 996 and was promoted to York in 1002. Like several other tenth- and eleventh-century archbishops of York he held the see of Worcester in plurality with York for part of his archiepiscopate (until 1016).

Wulfstan was a prolific writer. He and his friend Aelfric were the most commanding figures of the intellectual revival that grew out of the movement of ecclesiastical reform initiated by Dunstan, Ethelwold, and Oswald. But while these three churchmen had been mainly concerned with the regular religious life of monastic communities, Wulfstan's concerns were wider. He addressed himself to the proper ordering of Christian society as a whole, secular as well as ecclesiastical, and in particular to the conduct and obligations of bishops and kings. This preoccupation was given intensity by the troubled times in which he lived. Wulfstan interpreted the Danish attacks on England during the reign of Ethelred as a punishment inflicted by God upon an erring people. The point was made vehemently in his best-known work, the *Sermo Lupi ad Anglos* (The sermon of the wolf to the English), composed probably in 1014. (*Lupus,* "the wolf," was a literary alias used by Wulfstan in a play upon the first syllable of his name.)

> Understand well also that now for many years the devil has led astray this people too greatly and there has been little loyalty among men. . . . If we are to experience any improvement we must then deserve better of God than we have previously done. For with great deserts have we merited the miseries which oppress us, and with great deserts must we obtain relief from God if henceforward things are to start to improve. For lo! we know full well that a great breach will require much repair, and a great fire no little water if the fire is to be quenched at all; and great is the necessity for every man that he keep henceforward God's laws eagerly. . . .

Wulfstan's message was bleak. Like Gildas, whom he quoted, he indulged to the full what Gibbon once unforgettably described as "the natural pessimism of sacred oratory."

Wulfstan's works were for the most part written in the vernacular, rather than Latin, in order to reach as wide an audience as possible. His prose style, of which the above is a sample, was distinctive. By using stylistic criteria scholars have been able to identify a large number of works as his. They may be roughly classified into two groups, the legal and the homiletic. But these are not rigid categories, for the two genres overlap and interpenetrate. The legal writings possess to a striking degree the character of homilies, while the sermons are much concerned with the legal and customary obligations of Christian people. The two strands come together in Wulfstan's most ambitious work, the *Institutes of Polity, Civil and Ecclesiastical*, on which he was working toward the end of his life. It embodies his mature reflections on the duties of the different groups of people who together constitute the society of Christians. As such, the *Institutes of Polity* is heir to a long tradition of political and social thought that reaches ultimately back to St. Paul. But its more immediate ancestry is to be sought in the writings of the Carolingian period, and it has analogies with the works of his continental contemporaries, especially the bishops of Germany and northern France.

Wulfstan was a man of wide intellectual cultivation who was steeped in the works of the leading thinkers of the Carolingian age, such as Alcuin and Bishop Theodulf of Orléans (*d.* 821). That age had been remarkable for the definitive articulation by churchmen of a body of theory designed to guide secular rulers such as Charlemagne, Louis the Pious, and Charles the Bald along what they called "the royal road" to *sapientia,* "wisdom." Wisdom was regarded not as an abstract intellectual quality but as a disposition and a technique for the right guidance of a community in harmonious accord with God-given standards of public and private morality. For Wulfstan such guidance was a task at once urgent and somber. The kings he served left much to be desired. Ethelred was an unjust as well as an ineffective ruler who needed correction. Canute was a barbarian conqueror who needed schooling in the basic disciplines of Christian rulership. Wulfstan's concerns find vivid expression in the legal texts that he drew up for these kings. He was responsible for at least three of the legislative enactments of Ethelred's later years, in 1008, 1009, and 1014. In 1018 he drafted legislation for Canute and in 1020–22 was responsible for drawing up Canute's definitive law-code, the most comprehensive piece of legislation issued by any ruler of the Anglo-Saxon period.

The clergy also needed guidance. Wulfstan composed tracts on the duties of bishops. Some of his sermons are pastoral letters to the clergy of his diocese, and he also commissioned two pastoral letters from Aelfric. Another sermon is devoted to the conduct of communities of canons, largely drawn from the Carolingian author Amalarius of Metz. He composed a tract on the examination of candidates for ordination to the priesthood. The so-called "Northumbrian Priests' Law" is a set of directives to the clergy of the diocese of York.

Wulfstan was not just a theorist who told kings and clergy what they ought to be doing. He was an active diocesan bishop as well. He restored monastic life at Gloucester. He was vigilant in his care for the well-being of his churches: surveys of the archiepiscopal estates of York and annotations in his own hand in a register of Worcester documents testify to this. A collection of penitential letters shows him imposing the disciplinary procedures of the church upon erring members of his flock at both London and York. He enlarged the libraries at York and Worcester.

Wulfstan was not an original thinker. He looked mainly to the past, and his overriding concern was to proclaim and enforce the law of God as it had come down to him. It was a concern shared by other English bishops among his contemporaries; but because they have left no body of writings behind them, their thoughts and aspirations are not accessible to us as Wulfstan's are. The readiness of the leading English clergy to shoulder the burden of proclaiming moral and legal norms during a time of trouble was a tribute to their training, their corporate spirit, and their courage. It was also an important condition for the stability of English social and political institutions.

AELFRIC (*d. c.* 1012), abbot of Eynsham, was one of the most accomplished writers of Old English prose in the late Anglo-Saxon period. He received his education at the hands of Bishop Ethelwold of Winchester, where he became a monk. He became associated with the family of Ethelweard the chronicler: patrons who were distinguished by rank, wealth, and literary interests. When in

987 Ethelweard and his son Ethelmaer founded the monastery of Cerne in Dorset, now Cerne Abbas, Aelfric went there to take charge of the teaching. Later on, in 1005, Ethelmaer established another monastery at Eynsham in Oxfordshire, and Aelfric became its first abbot. He spent the rest of his life there and died at some date unknown, perhaps about 1012.

The chronology of his many writings has been approximately established as follows. Between 989 and 992 he composed, or at least completed, two books of sermons, the *Catholic Homilies*. Between 992 and 999 he translated six books of the Old Testament into Old English (the so-called *Hexameron*) and composed a series of *Lives of the Saints*. The *Hexameron* was commissioned by Ethelweard, and some of the sermons and saints' lives were also dedicated to him. During the same period Aelfric wrote two textbooks for the instruction of his pupils in Latin, the *Grammar* and the *Colloquy*. In the early years of the eleventh century we find him composing pastoral letters for Archbishop Wulfstan of York and Bishop Wulfsige of Sherborne. After his move to Eynsham he composed a Latin life of his master Ethelwold, probably completed in 1006, and a brief treatise on the Bible written at the request of an Oxfordshire landowner named Sigeweard of Asthall.

Aelfric's *Colloquy* was cast in the form of a conversation between master and pupils about everyday matters, the object being, of course, to practice Latin grammar and enlarge vocabulary. It thus provides some interesting vignettes of Anglo-Saxon life. Here, for example, is an interview with one of the king's huntsmen.

"Have you been hunting today?"
"Not today, for it is Sunday, but yesterday I was out hunting."
"What did you take?"
"Two stags and a boar."
"How did you take them?"
"I captured the stags with nets and I killed the boar."
"How did you come to slay the boar?"
"The hounds drove him toward me; I was standing in his path and could quickly spear him."
"You must indeed have been brave."
"A huntsman cannot be timid."
"What do you do with the game you have taken?"

"I give to the king whatever I take, because I am his huntsman."
"What does he give you in return?"
"He clothes me well and feeds me, sometimes he gives me a
horse or a ring."

Apart from the Latin textbooks and the biblical translations,
Aelfric's works, like Wulfstan's, were designed for the moral guidance of clergy and laity alike in a time of trouble. He held up to his
audience the saints of a distant Christian past, and also the example of more recent heroes:

> In England also kings were often victorious through
> God, as we have heard say; just as King Alfred was, who
> often fought against the Danes, until he won the victory
> and protected his people; similarly Athelstan, who
> fought against Olaf and slew his army and put him to
> flight, and afterwards lived in peace with his people.
> Edgar, the noble and resolute king, exalted the praise
> of God everywhere among his people, the strongest of
> all kings over the English nation; and God subdued for
> him his adversaries. . . .

Aelfric's thoroughgoing royalism is a further illustration of the
close connections between the reforming churchmen of the tenth
century and the royal house. His works are an important source
for our understanding of the political ideas of the period.

> No man can make himself king, but the people has the
> choice to choose as king whom they please; but after he is
> consecrated as king he then has dominion over the
> people, and they cannot shake his yoke from their necks.
>   When there is too much evil in mankind, councillors
> should investigate with wise deliberation which of the
> supports of the throne has been broken and repair it at
> once. The throne stands on these three supports: those
> who work, those who fight, those who pray . . . On these
> three supports the throne stands, and if one is broken
> down it falls at once.

Aelfric was a man of wide intellectual cultivation, abreast of recent theological developments as well as steeped in the accumulated learning of the past. He was a fine stylist, writing an English prose that was rich, supple, and vigorous. In his life and works he was a monument to the achievements of the ecclesiastical revival of tenth-century England.

M. McC. Gatch, *Preaching and Theology in Anglo-Saxon England: Aelfric and Wulfstan,* 1977.

BYRHTFERTH (*d. c.* 1015?) was a monk of Ramsey and an important figure in the intellectual life of later Anglo-Saxon England. Ramsey had been founded in 968 by Oswald, bishop of Worcester and archbishop of York, who had received much of his intellectual and religious training in France, at the renowned monastery of Fleury. Oswald was determined that Ramsey should be a center of learning in the same mold. Once the new house had become established Oswald invited Fleury's most learned inmate, Abbo, to take up residence there for a time as a teacher. Abbo of Fleury was at Ramsey during the years 985–87 and Byhrtferth undoubtedly came under his influence.

Abbo's intellectual interests lay particularly in history, logic, mathematics, and astronomy. Byrhtferth's concerns reflected those of his mentor. He was more of a scientist than a pastoral theologian or homilist like his contemporaries Aelfric and Wulfstan. His most important scientific work was his *Enchiridion,* or *Manual,* which he completed in about 1011. It is a textbook guide to the science of what was known as *computus,* that is to say, the understanding of the ecclesiastical calendar. It was written partly in Latin and partly in Old English so that it could be understood by those whom the author slightingly referred to as "ignorant rustic priests." It was not a work of any originality: the *Manual* reflects the learning of Fleury and looks back to Bede, for whom Byrhtferth had the greatest respect. However, it was learned, comprehensive, and designed for practical use, to meet a need. It would be very interesting to know how widely the *Manual* really did circulate in the English secular church, but we have no means of telling.

The canon of Byrhtferth's historical works has not yet been fully established but in the present state of research looks roughly as follows. He composed a Latin life of St. Egwin (*d.* 717), an early bishop of Worcester, probably commissioned by Oswald (composition therefore presumably preceded Oswald's death in 992). Probably in the 990s he compiled a chronicle of Northumbrian history. He wrote a Latin life of Oswald about the year 1000, which is a historical source of great importance for our understanding not only of the tenth-century monastic revival but also of the reigns of Edgar and Edward the Martyr. Finally, it has recently been claimed that he was the compiler of one version—the so-called "B" manuscript—of the vernacular annals known as the *Anglo-Saxon Chronicle*. If these attributions are correct, Byrhtferth emerges as the most notable English historian since Bede.

Byrhtferth's work has suffered some neglect, partly because *computus* is a subject without much appeal to modern readers, partly because his Latin style was prolix and difficult. He was a man of ample learning and of some influence as a teacher. Above all, perhaps, he is testimony to the diversity of intellectual cultivation that was fostered in England by the tenth-century revival of religious life and study.

GODWIN (*d.* 1053) was earl of Wessex and the most powerful man in England after the king from 1018 until his death. His origins and rise to prominence are obscure. He was evidently well-connected, for he received a bequest from the eldest son of King Ethelred II in 1015. He must have been one of the earliest and most dependable supporters of Canute, for he was given the earldom of Wessex early on in the Danish conqueror's reign, certainly by 1018. Wessex was the richest portion of England; it contained the royal city of Winchester and the archiepiscopal city of Canterbury; it overlooked the English Channel from the North Foreland to Land's End: whoever governed Wessex was a man in whom the king reposed special trust. A further indication of Godwin's prominence is the marriage he made in 1019. His bride was Gytha, the sister of Earl Ulf of Denmark (who was himself married to Canute's sister Estrith). No other English magnate attained so exalted a place as Godwin in Canute's regime.

Godwin maintained this position, not without difficulty, during the reigns of Canute's two short-lived sons, Harold (1035–40) and Harthacnut (1040–42). In 1036 he was responsible for the murder of Alfred, the brother of Prince Edward (later to be known as Edward the Confessor), who had landed in Wessex in a bid for the throne. The extent of Godwin's culpability is not clear. He claimed later that he had been acting on King Harold's orders. This episode almost certainly poisoned relations between him and Edward, but it did not lead to his displacement after Edward's return from exile to become king of England in 1042. Indeed, Godwin consolidated his position by marrying his daughter Edith to the king in 1045.

Godwin and Gytha had a large family, six sons and at least three daughters. (It is significant of Godwin's allegiances that five of them were given Scandinavian names.) Godwin was ambitious for his sons and as far as we can see they were able, pushing men. Small wonder that this jostling, upstart clan—the Kennedys of the eleventh century, as it were—should have dominated English political life during the reign of Edward the Confessor. Sweyn, the eldest son, got an earldom in 1043; Harold in 1044; Tostig in 1055; Leofwine and Gyrth in 1057. It has been calculated that the territorial wealth of the sons of Godwin on the eve of the Norman conquest was only a little less than that of the royal family itself.

Godwin's position did not go unchallenged. The king harbored grievances against him, he had enemies at court, and there were arguments over patronage and policy. Relations between King Edward and Godwin's family deteriorated in the late 1040s. The eldest son Sweyn disgraced himself by seducing an abbess and subsequently murdering his cousin: he was exiled in 1049. In 1051 Edward struck against the whole family. Seizing as his pretext Godwin's failure to punish an affray at Dover and subsequent armed resistance to the royal commands, Edward scattered the clan in exile and confined his queen to a monastery. It was a moment of crisis in Godwin's career even more alarming than the tricky period betwen 1035 and 1042. A contemporary commented:

> No-one in England would have believed that such a remarkable thing could happen, for Godwin had been raised so high that he ruled the king and all England, his sons were earls and royal favorites, and his daughter was married to the king.

Godwin was down but not out. He and his sons gathered a fleet and an army and in September 1052 returned to England prepared if necessary to fight their way back to power. The threat of force was enough. Edward saw that the game was up. Godwin and his family were reinstated. He ended his life in April 1053 in secure possession of his earldom of Wessex.

Godwin was an able and ambitious man who was at the center of English political life for thirty-five years. It is hard to detect redeeming features in his character: though some there must have been, for he was well-liked in Wessex. He was remembered as a despoiler of the church, and his ecclesiastical cronies seem for the most part to have been worldly men such as Stigand. His wife Gytha was more devout. She refounded a religious community at Hartland in Devon and ended her days after the Norman conquest in the nunnery of St. Omer in Flanders.

SIWARD (*d.* 1055) was a Danish follower of Canute who was rewarded with an earldom in Northumbria. From about 1032–33 he was earl of Deira (Yorkshire); to this was added Bernicia (the northern half of Northumbria) in about 1042. Very little is known of his tenure of office. He seems to have governed a restive province with fair success. He may have been responsible for extending English rule across the Pennines into Cumbria, where British, Norwegian, and Scottish princelings had been ruling and squabbling since the early tenth century. Siward is best remembered—thanks to Holinshed and Shakespeare—for his exploits against the Scots. The most famous of these occurred in 1054 when he led an army into Scotland, defeated Macbeth, and replaced him as king of Scots with Malcolm Canmore. In the following year Siward died and was buried at York in the church he had founded and dedicated to St. Olaf (now St. Olave's). He was succeeded as earl of Northumbria by Tostig Godwinson.

W. E. Kapelle, *The Norman Conquest of the North,* 1979, may be used, with caution, for all that relates to the north of England in the eleventh century.

MACBETH (*d.* 1057) was king of Scotland from 1040 until his defeat by Earl Siward of Northumbria in 1054 effectively removed him from power. Before his accession Macbeth had been *mormaer* of Moray. This is a Gaelic term meaning "great steward," in theory indicating some degree of subordination to the king. However, the *mormaers* of Moray were pretty independent men with regard to the rulers who called themselves kings of the Scots whose seat of power lay mach further to the south. In attempting to bring Macbeth to heel King Duncan I (1034–40) was defeated and killed. Macbeth took the kingship and Duncan's sons fled into exile.

Scottish history before *c.* 1100 is pathetically ill-documented. Macbeth's reign is no exception. We know that, like his slightly elder contemporary Canute in 1027, Macbeth went on a pilgrimage to Rome in 1050, where "he scattered money like seed to the poor"; readiness to leave the country might indicate a degree of confidence about the stability of his rule. We are told that he was a generous benefactor to the religious community on St. Serf's Island in Loch Leven. We hear that he fought against the English on at least one occasion before 1054, though we know nothing of the circumstances. Siward's invasion of 1054 led to a hard-fought battle in which Macbeth was defeated but managed to escape to the north. Siward installed Malcolm, son of Duncan I, as king; his authority presumably ran only over southern Scotland. Three years later, in 1057, Macbeth was cornered at Lumphanan, about twenty miles west of Aberdeen, where he was defeated and killed.

Macbeth's wife was a lady with the unlovely name of Gruoch. Nothing to the discredit of the real Lady Macbeth is told in the reliable sources; but then, practically nothing of any kind at all is told of her. Macbeth's evil reputation is owed entirely to the imagination of fourteenth- and fifteenth-century chroniclers.

A. A. M. Duncan, *Scotland: The Making of the Kingdom,* 1975.

"Lady" GODIVA, properly **GODGIFU,** famous in legend for her ride through Coventry, flourished in the middle years of the eleventh century. She was married to Leofric, who was earl of Mercia from about 1025 until his death in 1057 and a leading figure in the reigns of Canute and Edward the Confessor. Godiva outlived her husband and may have survived until as late as about 1080. Leofric and Godiva were generous patrons of the church. In 1043 they founded the monastery of Coventry. About 1053–55 they founded the minster of Stow in Lincolnshire, where the magnificent church built under their patronage still stands. They were also generous benefactors of Leominster, Wenlock, Worcester, Evesham, and Chester. According to the legend first recorded in the thirteenth century Godiva rode naked through Coventry at the whim of her husband in a kind of ordeal, as a result of which he agreed to free the people from tolls levied at their market. The story, preposterous as it stands, may contain some garbled memory of a privilege granted to the monastery of Coventry by the founders. The legend has inspired many artistic and literary treatments. Tennyson's handling of it in his poem Godiva is a quintessentially Victorian version; one of many indications that the nineteenth century is in some ways more remote from us than the eleventh.

ST. EDWARD THE CONFESSOR (1005?–66) reigned as king of England from 1042 until 1066. He was the eldest child of the second marriage of King Ethelred II, to Emma of Normandy. His childhood was overshadowed by the Danish assault upon England for which his father's reign is chiefly remembered. When Canute had completed his conquest of England in 1016 Edward went into an exile that was to last for twenty-five years. His mother Emma returned to England to marry Canute in 1017: it may be that Edward never forgave her for this. His exile lasted half his adult life and must have been a formative experience. It is a pity that we know so little about it. Norman writers—who had William the Conqueror's axe to grind—were later to stress his indebtedness to the dukes of Normandy; but it is likely that Edward spent time at other princely courts in northern France besides the Norman one. After Canute's death in 1035 Edward led a raid on England. The circumstances of this episode are obscure. If it was a half-hearted attempt upon the English throne it seems to have been bungled. In 1040 Harthacnut, the son of Emma and Canute, became king of England and in the following year he recalled Edward from exile. Precisely what was involved in this *rapprochement* is not clear. All we know is that upon Harthacnut's sudden death in June 1042 Edward became king.

Edward's most recent biographer has likened him to Charles II. Although we know a good deal about his reign it is not easy to form any very distinct impression of his personality. (The saintly King Edward is a myth got up by the monks of Westminster in the twelfth century; Edward's canonization in 1161 was largely a political job, as royal canonizations tend to be.) Like Charles, Edward may well have been clever, idle, and a shade cynical; we may be sure that he did not want to go on his travels again. The first ten years of his reign were years of insecurity that culminated in a sharp political crisis in 1051–52. The ensuing thirteen years were more tranquil, though increasingly dominated by the question of the succession to the throne, until another political crisis flared up in 1065 and Edward's life and reign ended in misery and anxiety.

Canute had run England—which was only a part, we should remember, of a widespread northern empire—by delegating power to a small number of earls each of whom was entrusted with responsibility for the administration of a block of shires. This had reinforced a tendency for more and more local power to become concentrated in fewer and fewer hands. Edward, the returning exile, had no choice but to accommodate himself to these circumstances. For at least the first ten years of his reign English political life was dominated by the three great earls: Godwin of Wessex, Leofric of Mercia (the husband of Godiva), and Siward of Northumbria. Of these, Godwin was the most formidable and the most intimately connected with the king. His daughter Edith was married to Edward in 1045. His earldom of Wessex was the heartland of the kingdom. His landed wealth was colossal. His able and ambitious sons were acquiring earldoms elsewhere in the country, Sweyn on the Welsh border in 1043 and Harold in East Anglia in 1044.

The ascendancy of Godwin and his family was the most important fact of English political life in the 1040s. There are signs that Edward resented it. Another constraint upon him was the need to reward those who stood by him during his exile, such men as Leofric who was given the bishopric of Exeter in 1046. This might mean conflicts with the Godwin faction over patronage, for Godwin too had clients who expected rewards. Edward's promotion of the Norman Robert Champart to the see of London in 1044 was probably pushed through in the face of opposition. His further promotion of Robert to Canterbury in 1051 ran counter to Godwin's wishes and gave rise to a political crisis.

The crisis of 1051–52 is well-documented in the contemporary sources though certain crucial episodes remain obscure. In September 1051 Godwin staged a rebellion against the king that misfired. Edward seized the opportunity to banish the earl and his sons. The Godwin faction broken, Robert Champart became Edward's leading minister. Possibly under Robert's influence—though it is very difficult to see who (if anyone, apart from the king) was pulling strings behind the scenes—Edward seems to have made an offer of the succession to the throne to Duke William of Normandy in the winter of 1051–52. In the summer of 1052 Godwin and his sons returned from exile and staged a military *coup* that restored them to power in September and ousted Robert who fled to Normandy. Earls Leofric and Siward apparently counselled magnanimity and moderation. Godwin had got what he wanted, though he did not live long enough to enjoy it: he died in April 1053. Harold succeeded to the earldom of Wessex and his brother Tostig got Northumbria on Siward's death in 1055. Two other brothers were promoted in 1057, Gyrth to East Anglia and Leofwine to Kent and Essex. Between 1057 and 1065 all the earldoms in England save only Mercia were in the hands of Godwin's sons.

This should not be taken to mean that Edward had been reduced to powerlessness. In the second half of his reign Edward, by now an elderly man by the standards of his family and the day, presided successfully over a united kingdom. Edward's England enjoyed reasonably secure frontiers, a prosperous economy, a stable coinage, and the peace afforded by efficient governmental institutions. The king busied himself during these years with the rebuilding of Westminster abbey church on an immensely grand scale.

The only cloud on the horizon, and one that loomed ever more menacingly, was the question of the succession. We do not know by what date it had become clear that Edward and Edith were not going to have any children. Possibly acceptance of the fact that the marriage was and would remain barren was an element in the political crisis of 1051–52. The nearest claimant by blood was Edward, the son of the king's half brother Edmund Ironside, who had lived all his life as a refugee in Hungary and in consequence was known as Edward the Exile. His return to England, presumably to be groomed for the succession, was negotiated by an embassy led by Bishop Ealdred: unfortunately he died immediately after he had come back, in 1057. His son Edgar was an infant who was clearly unsuitable on grounds of age. The three most imposing claimants outside Edward's kin were Harald of Norway, Sweyn of Denmark, and William of Normandy. Harald's claim was based upon a treaty between his predecessor Magnus (1035–47) and Harthacnut by which if either were to die childless his dominions were to pass to the survivor; and Harthacnut had died childless. It was not a very persuasive claim but Harald pressed it vigorously and was to meet his end in 1066 in pursuance of it. Sweyn of Denmark, who was a nephew of the great Canute, put it about that Edward had promised him the succession to England in about 1048. It does not sound very likely but it cannot be ruled out. After all, promises are cheap. Perhaps Edward's promise to William was offered cheaply too; but it was taken very seriously indeed. Norman sources claim that William was offered the throne in 1051–52, which we can credit, and that Edward subsequently (1064?) sent Harold Godwinson to Normandy to swear allegiance to him, which we can believe only with reservations, because the story raises all sorts of difficulties. However, William believed that he had a legitimate claim and in this he was upheld by the pope in 1066.

It has been argued that Edward's most serious failure lay precisely in the lack of any clear directives about the succession. In justice to him it should be said that it is too easy to forget that the balance of political interests was exceedingly fragile; too much so, perhaps, for Edward to have been able to commit himself firmly to any one party. Uncertainty about his successor was Edward's strongest political card. He kept the suppliants waiting until the last possible moment.

That moment, when it did come, is surrounded by ambiguities. In October 1065 the Northumbrians rebelled against Tostig. Harold could not or would not help him, so the king had to concede to the rebels' demands and sacrifice his earl of Northumbria. Tostig went into exile, with effects that were to prove deadly to him and to three of his brothers in the following year. The Northumbrian revolt broke Edward's health. Although the medical evidence is far from clear, it is likely that the king had a series of strokes, losing his rational faculties in the course of them, which led to his death on 5 January 1066. Shortly before his death he made some sort of bequest of the kingdom of England to Harold. (Even the Normans conceded that this had happened.) Exactly what was said is not clear: one wonders whether the dying man knew what he was saying, or could render it intelligibly. Whatever it was, it was enough for Harold. He acted with haste. Edward was buried in his beloved new Westminster abbey on the day following his death, Thursday, 6 January 1066. On the very same day Harold was crowned king of England.

F. Barlow, *Edward the Confessor*, 1970.

ROBERT CHAMPART (*d.* 1053?) was a Norman monk who held the archbishopric of Canterbury for a short time in the troubled years 1051–52. He received his training as a monk apparently at the monastery of St. Ouen in Rouen, where he rose to be prior, and became abbot of Jumièges in 1037. Jumièges, originally founded in the seventh century, abandoned during the Viking invasions and refounded *c.* 940, was one of the most distinguished monasteries in Normandy, closely connected with the ducal family, a center of learning and ecclesiastical reform. Its enormous church, which was being built during Robert's abbacy, is one of the grandest monuments of Norman Romanesque architecture.

In 1041 Robert seems to have accompanied Prince Edward back to England. This in itself is rather odd. Why should the abbot of a famous Norman monastery have entered the household of a prince returning to his country after a long exile to claim an uncertain inheritance? We cannot tell, but there may have been more to it than meets the eye. After Edward's accession in 1042 Robert became one of his most favored counsellors. It quickly became clear that his main rivals were Earl Godwin and his kinsmen. In 1044 Edward promoted Robert to the bishopric of London, probably in the teeth of opposition. Late in 1050 the archbishopric of Canterbury fell vacant. The monks of Canterbury wanted one of their own number, Adric, who was a relative of Godwin, to be the next archbishop. The king overrode their wishes and in March 1051 gave the see to Robert. This appointment precipitated a severe political crisis.

Robert journeyed to Rome shortly afterward and stopped in Normandy on the way. It is likely that he conveyed an offer of the succession to the English throne from King Edward to Duke William. On his return he and Godwin quarrelled openly. In September Godwin attempted to rebel against the king, but the plot misfired and he and his sons were sent into exile. Robert's part in these events is not clear. He stood for a policy that Godwin opposed. He gained from Godwin's fall. He is said to have tried, though unsuccessfully, to get Edward to divorce the queen, Godwin's daughter. It was probably he who was instrumental in bringing William of Normandy to England in the winter of 1051–52 for the purpose of further negotiations about the English succession.

Whatever may have been Robert's role in the complicated events of 1051–52 it is clear that this was the high point of his influence with King Edward.

His triumph did not last long. In September 1052 Godwin and his sons staged a military *coup* that restored them to power in England. Robert fled the country, never to return, and the archbishopric of Canterbury was given to Stigand. Robert made his way to Rome to lay his case before the pope and then returned to Jumièges where he died shortly afterward.

Robert was one among several Normans who achieved prominence in England during the reign of Edward the Confessor; to name but two others, William who became bishop of London in 1051, and Richard FitzScrob who received lands on the Welsh Marches and gave his name to Richard's Castle in Herefordshire. Some historians have seen in these men a kind of fifth column whose members prepared the way for William's invasion in 1066. This is misguided. However, there *is* a sense in which Robert of Jumièges was instrumental (among many others) in bringing about the Norman conquest. His active pursuit of what might be called the Norman option in the question of the English succession strengthened the claims that William's propagandists were later to make on his behalf. His other contribution was less deliberate. Because Robert never resigned the see of Canterbury, Stigand was an intruder. Here once more William's propagandists could make political capital out of the circumstance, plausibly presenting him as an upholder of the law of the church bent on delivering England from the clutches of a scoundrel.

STIGAND (*d. c.* 1072) achieved notoriety as the last Anglo-Saxon archbishop of Canterbury. His name was Old Norse rather than Old English, and he was probably a native of Norwich; it is therefore likely that he was of Anglo-Scandinavian descent. He must have been born about 990, for he was already a priest by 1020. (According to the law of the church, not always observed in practice, a man might not be ordained to the priesthood before the age of thirty.) It is in the latter year that he first comes into view, as the king's priest who was granted the newly founded royal minster at Ashingdon in Essex. In other words, he had ingratiated himself rapidly with the new regime of the conqueror Canute and was doing well out of it. (The parallel with the secular career of Earl

Godwin is striking.) His progress during the remainder of Canute's reign was unspectacular, though his subscriptions of royal charters suggest that he remained close to the center of public affairs. Thereafter his rise was meteoric. King Edward promoted him to the bishopric of Elmham in 1043, onward and upward to Winchester in 1047, and finally to the pinnacle of Canterbury in 1052.

However, there were flaws in his position. First, he had been uncanonically intruded into Canterbury following the expulsion of the previous incumbent, Robert Champart. Second, he was a pluralist: he retained the see of Winchester after his move to Canterbury. Third, when in 1058 he acquired his *pallium*, the symbol of archiepiscopal authority, it was from the antipope Benedict X, himself in uncanonical possession of the see of Rome. These irregularities were ably exploited by William of Normandy who received papal support for his invasion in 1066 on the grounds that he would purge the church in England of its corrupt head.

It does not appear that Stigand himself was troubled by his neglect of proper form. He comes across from the records that have survived as an extremely worldly prelate. Canterbury and Winchester were the two wealthiest sees in England. He had jobbed his brother Ethelmaer into the bishopric of Elmham on his departure for Winchester in 1047. He was accused of prolonging vacancies in some of the richer abbeys such as Ely in order to divert their revenues into his own pocket. He acquired extensive estates, especially in East Anglia and Gloucestershire, not always by reputable means.

Stigand was immensely powerful as well as immensely rich. The archbishop of Canterbury was a key figure in the life of the state as well as of the church. Stigand was an able administrator who was one of the first ministers of Edward throughout his reign. By 1066 he had been at the center of English public life for nearly half a century. He knew everybody who mattered; he knew how everything worked. He was indispensable.

Perhaps it was for this reason that William the Conqueror was so slow to move against him. Stigand had crowned Harold in January 1066. After the battle of Hastings he had toyed with loyalty to Edgar Atheling, but like Archbishop Ealdred of York and others he had come round to William. In March 1067 Stigand was taken in honorable captivity to Normandy. On his return to England he was permitted to resume his archiepiscopal functions. But he must have known that the game was up. In the spring of 1070 a papal legate visited England and held a church council at Winchester at which Stigand was deposed. He must by then have been a very old man. He was permitted to live out the remainder of his days unmolested. He is said to have died in 1072.

F. Barlow, *The English Church, 1000–1066*, 1963.

EALDRED (*d.* 1069), archbishop of York from 1060 until 1069, was the most distinguished English ecclesiastic of the last generation before the Norman conquest. His career has much to tell us of the tone and style of the late Anglo-Saxon church. Ealdred was a native of Wessex and began his ecclesiastical career as a monk of Winchester. In 1027 he became abbot of Tavistock. In 1046 he was promoted to the episcopate as bishop of Worcester; between 1055 and 1058 he administered the bishopric of Ramsbury, and between 1056 and 1060 that of Hereford; in 1060 he added York to his sway. For a short time Ealdred governed an ecclesiastical empire even more vast, though a good deal less valuable, than that of Stigand. However, in 1061 the pope compelled him to cease holding Worcester and York in plurality.

In the late Anglo-Saxon church, nominations to bishoprics were generally made by the king. Bishops had important secular responsibilities, such as the administration of justice in the shire court, and were in some sense public servants. It is likely that Ealdred's career owed something to the patronage of influential courtiers, perhaps especially to Earl Godwin. It is certain that he distinguished himself in the conduct of the king's business. In 1049 we find him defending his frontier diocese against the Welsh. In 1050 he visited Rome on royal business. In 1054 he led an embassy to Germany to negotiate the return to England of Edward "the Exile," the son of Edmund Ironside, then regarded as a possible successor to the childless Edward the Confessor. In 1061 he again visited Rome.

Not all his travels were connected with official business. In 1058 he made a pilgrimage to Jerusalem, travelling overland through Germany, Hungary, and the Byzantine empire. He travelled, we are told by a contemporary, "in such state as none had done before him," and at the Holy Sepulchre he offered "a worthy gift, a golden chalice of very wonderful workmanship." Ealdred was a lavish patron of the arts. He sponsored building works at several religious communities, Gloucester, Southwell, Beverley, Ripon, and York. At Beverley he had the ceiling of the church painted and gilded, and furnished it with a pulpit and a big crucifix made of bronze, silver, and gold. This metalwork was German in style, and probably in workmanship. Germany was in the forefront of European culture in the eleventh century, and German influence can be detected behind other concerns of Ealdred. He is known to have brought books back from Germany in 1054. These probably included a manuscript, now surviving in a fragmentary state in the British Library, of an important liturgical work known as the "Romano-German Pontifical," previously unknown in England. It was also from Germany that Ealdred derived the impulse to reform the houses of secular canons in his diocese, such as Beverley, by insisting on a more regular communal life. He imported a monk from Flanders, Folcard of St. Bertin, to write up the life and miracles of the local saint, John of Beverley (d. 718), and incidentally to commemorate the doings of his patron Ealdred in suitably flattering terms.

Rich and well-connected; able and ambitious; courtier, diplomat, and man of the world; patron of artists and scholars: Ealdred, it has been said, "was the closest to a 'prince bishop' that England could produce." He embodied an ideal of sane and dignified churchmanship cooperating harmoniously with the secular power that was shortly after his death to be called in question by the intemperate reformers of the circle of Pope Gregory VII. However, it was political rather than ecclesiastical rancors that clouded Ealdred's last years. The revolt of the Northumbrians against Tostig in 1065 plunged his diocese into turmoil. On the death of King Edward in January 1066 Ealdred threw the weight of his influence behind Harold.

After Harold's defeat and death at Hastings, Ealdred was faced with a political choice of great difficulty. Though tempted to support the Anglo-Saxon claimant Edgar Atheling, the son of Edward the Exile, Ealdred seems to have grasped the decisive nature of William's victory and wisely decided to accept the Norman duke as king. It was Ealdred who officiated at William's coronation in December 1066. The adhesion to William of a man of Ealdred's standing was an essential condition for the continuity of English government, itself one of the most remarkable features of the Norman conquest. It also made it possible for Ealdred to try to moderate some of the worst excesses of Norman rapacity: a famous story, which may well be true, records how the archbishop cursed the new Norman sheriff of Worcestershire for his brutal treatment of the conquered.

Despite all his efforts, Ealdred ended his days at a moment of crisis and peril. In 1069 Northumbria rose in rebellion against William. Ealdred died in September. Had he lived a little longer he might have succeeded in tempering the terrible vengeance that the king wrought in the winter of 1069–70 in the harrying of the north.

J. M. Cooper, *The Last Four Anglo-Saxon Archbishops of York,* 1970.

LEOFRIC (*d.* 1072), bishop of Exeter from 1046 until his death, is chiefly remembered today for the book-collection he amassed and left to his cathedral library. Leofric was apparently a native of Cornwall, but he was brought up and educated in Lotharingia, that is, roughly speaking, the western parts of the Rhineland. At that period Lotharingian cathedral communities and religious houses were renowned as centers of learning, spirituality, and ecclesiastical revitalization. Bruno, bishop of Toul from 1027 to 1048, was not untypical of the sort of churchmen under whose influence Leofric may have come; as Pope Leo IX (1048–54) Bruno was to become a famous reformer. In addition to receiving a good education and becoming acquainted with the latest tendencies in continental church life, Leofric seems also to have met and entered the service of the exiled prince Edward (later to be known as Edward the Confessor). Leofric seems to have been in Edward's entourage when he returned to England in 1041. After his accession to the throne in 1042 Leofric was one of the "king's priests," i.e., an important minister and civil servant. He was rewarded with a bishopric in 1046.

The bishopric established at Crediton early in the tenth century by Archbishop Plegmund had responsibility for the whole vast area of Devon and Cornwall. At some point in the tenth century a separate diocese for Cornwall had been established, rather precariously, at St. Germans, just across the river Tamar from Plymouth. Leofric decided to concentrate the two, to fix the seat of the diocese at an important urban center, Exeter, and to reform the way of life of the cathedral community by introducing canons living according to the rule of Bishop Chrodegang of Metz (d. 766). (In the middle years of the eleventh century this was a cathedral constitution much favored by reforming churchmen in Lotharingia and Germany.) The approval of Pope Leo IX was secured in 1049 and of King Edward in 1050. Within four years of his appointment Leofric had carried out a major reform in his diocese.

He also made it his task to put the finances of his bishopric on a secure footing. This he did partly by consolidating and extending its landed endowments, partly by instituting regular arrangements for sharing the income therefrom between on the one hand the bishop and his household and on the other the community of canons who formed the cathedral chapter. This, again, was a common concern of ecclesiastical reformers of the period. It also displays the disciplined planning of the former civil servant. Like his contemporary Ealdred of York—though not on Ealdred's princely scale—Leofric undertook also to embellish his church by stocking it with treasures. These included vestments, bells, processional crosses, silver plate, carpets and other hangings; also such curiosities as three bearskins, a "fyrdwain" (or "army-cart"—whatever that might have been), and a silver pipe through which consecrated wine could be sucked from a chalice as through a straw (an instrument technically known as a fistula).

He also left to his church a very considerable library of over sixty volumes. About half of these were service books of one sort or another. Also represented were canon law, and some of the works of Pope Gregory I and Bede. Some of the books were in Old English. These included the translation of Boethius by King Alfred and "a big English book on various subjects written in verse." This volume, happily still where Leofric left it, is the manuscript known as the Exeter Book, one of the principal collections of Old English poetry. It contains, among much else, two of the poems of Cynewulf and such other deservedly famous pieces as *The Wanderer, The Seafarer, Widsith, Deor, The Wife's Lament,* and *The Ruin.*

After his death in 1072 Leofric was remembered as a good man and an active pastor. Bishops such as he give the lie to the Norman propaganda myth that the late Anglo-Saxon church was somehow "decadent." Nothing could be further from the truth.

F. Barlow and others, *Leofric of Exeter,* 1972, is a pleasing collection of essays. Nearly all the poems in the Exeter Book have been translated (into prose) by S. A. J. Bradley, *Anglo-Saxon Poetry,* 1982.

TOSTIG (*d.* 1066) was earl of Northumbria from 1055 to 1065. He was the third son of Earl Godwin and the younger brother of Harold. Tostig was probably born about 1025. We first hear of him in 1049 when he was active in naval operations against some Vikings from Ireland. In 1051 he married Judith, the sister of Count Baldwin V of Flanders; thereby becoming the brother-in-law of Duke William of Normandy. It was to Flanders that he accompanied his father when they were exiled in 1051–52. Three years after the family's restoration to the favor of King Edward, Tostig was promoted to the earldom of Northumbria. This can be seen simply as part of the aggrandizement of the house of Godwin. It can also be interpreted as a daring political initiative on the part of the king. Northumbria had never been governed by a man from southern England. Tostig was brave, shrewd, and hard. His appointment indicated Edward's intention of bringing a distant and unruly province under much firmer royal control.

Tostig tried hard for ten years but failed, and was ejected by a revolt, which set in motion a train of events that were to be fatal not only to Tostig himself but also to the Anglo-Saxon kingdom of England. In the first place, he failed adequately to defend Northumbria from the Scots. In 1057 King Malcolm had finally rid himself of Macbeth and brought all of Scotland under his sway. Enabled thereby to turn his attention southward, he started raiding into England in 1058–59. In 1061, when Tostig was absent on a pilgrimage to Rome, Malcolm again attacked. A contemporary writer favorable to Tostig tells us that he riposted "as much by cunning schemes as by martial courage and military campaigns"; another way of putting this would be to say that he did not fight back. We need not doubt Tostig's personal courage. There may have been good reasons for preferring diplomacy to force. The trouble was that the Northumbrians expected him to act with the martial heroism of an Uhtred or a Siward. Scottish raids caused destruction and suffering: captives, goods, livestock were being carried off; there may have been territorial losses too. By failing to meet force with force Tostig was falling short in one of his primary duties as earl of Northumbria.

He failed, secondly, to get on with the people who mattered in the north. For example, in 1056 he was instrumental in the choice of a certain Ethelwine for the important bishopric of Durham. Ethelwine was a southerner like Tostig and he was not welcome to his cathedral community. Tostig and his wife were generous benefactors of Durham. (The quality of the works of art they had to offer can be gauged from the superlative manuscript known as the "Gospels of Countess Judith," now in the Pierpont Morgan Library in New York, which she commissioned from a southern workshop, possibly Canterbury, between 1051 and 1065.) But generosity may not have outweighed the mishandling of ecclesiastical patronage. As far as the secular aristocracy was concerned, Tostig became involved—perhaps inevitably—in the violent feuds and faction-fighting of the sort that convulsed the families of Uhtred and Thurbrand. In 1063 he had two prominent Northumbrian noblemen murdered; another followed in 1064.

The rebels in 1065 had further grievances. Tostig had "unjustly laid a heavy tribute on the whole of Northumbria." It can be shown that Northumbrian tax-assessments were low in the eleventh century. It may be that Tostig simply tried to tax Northumbria as the remainder of the country was taxed. When King Edward was negotiating with the rebels in the autumn of 1065 they insisted that he "renew the law of King Canute." Is this an indication that Tostig had introduced new customs—West Saxon law to accompany West Saxon taxation—into his earldom? Possibly. It sounds very much the sort of thing the king may have had in mind in appointing Tostig.

In October 1065 rebellion broke out and Edward was compelled to sacrifice his minister. Tostig went into exile and spent the winter in Flanders. In the following year he attempted a military comeback, necessarily and tragically directed against his brother Harold, who had succeeded the old king in January. In May 1066 he appeared off the Isle of Wight with a fleet, raided the coastal parts of Sussex, and occupied Sandwich for a time. Afterward he made his way northward, harrying in Norfolk on the way, until he landed in northern Lincolnshire. There he was defeated by the English defense forces, and fled to Scotland where he spent the summer. It is likely that he had already entered into negotiations with Harald Hardrada, king of Norway, with a view to joining his projected invasion of England.

The Norwegian fleet appeared in English waters toward the end of the summer, and Tostig joined it. The sequel is well known. After a hard-fought battle at Fulford on 20 September Harald of Norway and Tostig occupied the city of York. They then withdrew to Stamford Bridge to await hostages. There they were surprised by Harold of England on 25 September. The invaders were decisively defeated. Both Harald and Tostig were killed.

HARALD SIGURDSSON, commonly called **HARDRADA,** "the Ruthless" (1016–66) was king of Norway from 1047 until his death in battle at Stamford Bridge in 1066. He was a descendant of Harald Fairhair (the father of Eric Bloodaxe) and a half brother of King Olaf Haraldson, better known as St. Olaf. Olaf was defeated and killed by his rebellious subjects at the battle of Stiklestad in 1030. Harald, who was fighting alongside his half brother, was wounded but managed to escape. He spent the following fifteen years in exile as a soldier of fortune, partly in the service of the princes of Russia, partly in the famous Varangian regiment of the Byzantine emperors: in the latter employment he saw service in Bulgaria, Sicily, Asia Minor, and Syria. During these years he amassed a fortune from booty, enjoyed all sorts of exotic adventures, earned a reputation as a commander famed for his bravery and ruthlessness, and acquired a loyal band of followers. Accompanied by them he returned to Scandinavia in 1045 to lay claim to Norway. His nephew Magnus, who had been ruling Norway since 1035, was overawed and agreed to share the kingdom with Harald. The death of Magnus in 1047 left Harald as sole king. His reign in Norway was largely taken up with long-drawn-out warfare against King Sweyn Estrithson of Denmark, which came to an end in 1064.

The peace made in 1064 freed Harald for a project he had long been meditating: an invasion of England. In 1038 Magnus of Norway and Harthacnut, the son of Canute who was at that time king of Denmark and claimant to the throne of England, had made a treaty that stipulated if either party should die without an heir his kingdom should pass to the other. Harthacnut had died childless in 1042. Magnus claimed both Denmark and England under the terms of the treaty and until his death in 1047 was regarded with apprehension by the English government of Edward the Confessor. Harald Hardrada persuaded himself that he had inherited Magnus's claim to England. In 1058 his son had raided England. Once peace had been made with Denmark Harald began to prepare a great invasion fleet, which he proposed to lead in person. It was just a question of when the blow would fall.

In the event it fell in the late summer of 1066. Harald, his forces enlarged by the adhesion of Tostig who had been sent into exile in the previous year, crossed the North Sea and after ravaging the coast of Yorkshire sailed up the Humber and the Ouse. The ships were left at Riccall and the Norwegian army advanced overland the remaining nine miles to York. A Northumbrian army that attempted to block the way was shattered at Fulford, just south of York, on 20 September. Harald and Tostig received the submission of York and then withdrew a few miles to the east, to Stamford Bridge at the crossing of the river Derwent, to await the delivery of hostages. There they were surprised on the following day by King Harold of England, who had dashed up from the south with astonishing speed after hearing of the invasion. The battle of Stamford Bridge was hard fought but ended in an overwhelming English victory. Both Harald Hardrada and his ally Tostig were killed. Of the three hundred or more ships which had brought the invaders a mere twenty-four sufficed to carry the survivors home to Norway.

M. Magnusson and H. Palsson, *King Harald's Saga*, 1966.

HAROLD II, who was the last Anglo-Saxon king of England, perished at the battle of Hastings in 1066. Harold, the second son of Earl Godwin of Wessex and his wife Gytha, was born in about 1022. He owed his advancement in the service of King Edward to his abilities as well as his birth. He became earl of East Anglia in 1044, and held that office until his family was temporarily broken in the political crisis of 1051. Harold spent his few months of exile in Ireland, rejoining his father and his brother Tostig for their triumphant return to power in 1052, after which he was restored to the earldom of East Anglia. On Godwin's death in April 1053 Harold succeeded him as earl of Wessex and the second man in the English kingdom.

Harold's chief claim to fame before 1066 rested upon his Welsh campaigns of 1063. In 1039 Gruffydd ap Llywelyn had become prince of Gwynedd and Powys (i.e., north and central Wales) and in 1055 he absorbed Deheubarth (i.e., southern Wales) as well, thus becoming in effect king of Wales. He was an able soldier and an inspiring leader, under whose direction attacks were launched upon England's western marches. Sometimes these raids had serious consequences: in 1056, for example, the newly appointed bishop of Hereford (formerly one of Harold's clerks) was killed. In the early 1060s Harold was charged with countermeasures. Accordingly, in 1063, he led a fleet from Bristol round to Anglesey to ravage the coastline while Tostig led an army overland from Chester into north Wales. Gruffydd was outmaneuvered and shortly afterward murdered by his own followers. The Welsh were cowed into submission. It was a well-conducted campaign over difficult country and it brought Harold renown as a general.

We should very much like to know when it first occurred to Harold that he might succeed Edward as king of England. Shortly after the death of the king's nephew, Edward the Exile, in 1057? Perhaps: we shall never know. What we do know is that Harold visited Normandy, most likely in 1064, as the emissary of King Edward. The episode was given prominence on the Bayeux Tapestry, one of whose central scenes is the famous representation of Harold swearing an oath to Duke William. But what was the oath about? This is the question that has never satisfactorily been answered, for the answer offered by the Norman sources is tendentious and the English sources, with one possible exception, do not mention Harold's mission at all. The exception is the contemporary author of the *Vita Edwardi Regis* ("Life of King Edward")—a fascinating and puzzling document—who observed casually at one point that Harold "was, alas, rather too free with oaths." Whether or not this is a covert allusion to Harold's Norman oath, it suggests a streak of duplicity in his character. Harold took oaths too lightly. Not so William, whose case in 1066 rested on the claim that Harold was guilty of perjury in seizing the throne of England.

In fact, of course, Edward had bequeathed the throne to Harold on his deathbed in January 1066, and Harold had made sure of getting ecclesiastical recognition by having himself crowned immediately after Edward's death. Designation and coronation were all very well, but Harold must have known that he would have to fight to hold on to the English throne. There were three immediate enemies: his brother Tostig, exiled in the autumn of 1065; King Harald Hardrada of Norway; and Duke William of Normandy. The first two of these joined forces in the summer of 1066 and landed in Yorkshire in September. Harold, who had been guarding the south coast of England against Norman invasion during the summer, hastened up to the north to confront the invaders. He inflicted an overwhelming defeat on them at Stamford Bridge on 25 September.

Only two days later the wind changed in the English Channel and William's army could embark. The Normans landed at Pevensey on the twenty-eighth. News of this seems to have reached Harold on 1 October, and he set off at once for the south. Scarcely credible though it is, he seems to have reached London on 5 October. He paused there for a week to give his troops some much-needed rest and to rally reinforcements. Then he marched down to Sussex to give battle on 14 October: with what results we know.

The apparatus of government apparently continued to function during his ten-month reign just as it had done under his predecessor King Edward. However, Harold was king for too short a time for us to gauge what sort of ruler he was or to guess what sort of ruler he might have turned into. We do not really know much about his character. He was brave and resolute, but also watchful and cautious. He knew his way round his world: he had travelled in France, Italy, Flanders, and Ireland. Like his father he was not a particularly devout man. He refounded a religious house at Waltham in Essex, but he was also remembered as a despoiler of the church. By a mistress named Edith Swan-neck he had at least four children; and there is no sign that Harold abandoned her—in this like his predecessor Canute—when he contracted a legal marriage to another Edith, the daughter of Earl Alfgar of Mercia and widow of his enemy Gruffydd of Wales.

Harold is most vividly brought before us in the embroidered scenes of the Bayeux Tapestry. Indeed, as has often been remarked—and this is really very odd in a work of art that celebrates William's conquest—Harold is in a sense the hero of the Tapestry's drama: the tragic hero, the great man brought low by the flaw of character that led him to perjure himself. That is one way of looking at Harold sympathetically. Another has grown out of nostalgia. To Harold attaches all the pathos and the glamor of the last Old

English king—in a potent national myth, the last representative of the golden, good old days before the Norman yoke was laid on English backs. But it does not do to romanticize Harold. He was an ambitious and none-too-scrupulous man who managed to make himself king of England by somewhat questionable means. It was his appalling ill-fortune to be attacked simultaneously on two fronts. He fought hard to maintain himself. He lost.

Exactly how he met his death is still debated. The evidence of the Bayeux Tapestry is crucial but ambiguous. Harold was struck down either by an arrow in the eye or by the swords of Norman knights. The latter seems the more likely of the two. But you can take your pick. You can even have your cake and eat it and opt for both successively.

D. M. Wilson, *The Bayeux Tapestry*, 1985. The *Vita Edwardi Regis* has been edited and translated by F. Barlow, 1962.

Bibliographical Note

The best route into any historical period is via the original sources and there can be no excuse for not taking it when the quantity of sources is manageable and they are readily available in reliable translations. For Roman Britain see J. C. Mann and R. G. Penman, *Literary Sources for Roman Britain*, 1977. For Anglo-Saxon England the best collection is to be found in the series *English Historical Documents*, a series under the general editorship of D. C. Douglas: volume I, edited by D. Whitelock, 2nd ed., 1979, spans the period from *c.* 500 to 1042; volume II, edited by D. C. Douglas and G. W. Greenaway, 2nd ed., 1981, runs from 1042 to 1189.

An excellent introduction to Roman Britain is provided by M. Todd, *Roman Britain, 55 B.C.–A.D.400: The Province beyond Ocean,* 1981. For much ampler treatment see the equally good work of P. Salway, *Roman Britain,* 1981. The Ordnance Survey map of *Roman Britain,* 4th ed., 1978, is an essential aid. The best way to keep abreast of recent work is through consultation of the journal *Britannia,* published annually (from 1970) by the Society for the Promotion of Roman Studies.

The most recent treatment of the obscure period that lies between the end of Roman rule and the emergence of the Anglo-Saxon kingdoms is J. N. L. Myres, *The English Settlements,* 1986. F. M. Stenton, *Anglo-Saxon England,* 3rd ed., 1971, is the standard work on its subject; first published in 1943 and subsequently undergoing only minor revisions, it is a work that has worn extraordinarily well and on many topics remains authoritative. Inevitably, however, recent research and subtler shifts of attitude and expectation among historians have rendered Stenton's work in some respects outdated. The best introduction to recent work is to be found in P. H. Sawyer, *From Roman Britain to Norman England,* 1978, and above all, in the collaborative work edited by J. Campbell, *The Anglo-Saxons,* 1982: the latter work is outstandingly good; easily the best introduction to its subject at present available. There are two admirable Ordnance Survey maps, *Britain in the Dark Ages,* 2nd ed., 1966, which charts the period from *c.* 410 to *c.* 870, and *Britain before the Norman Conquest,* 1973, which does the same for *c.* 870 to 1066. More ambitious is the exceedingly useful *Atlas of Anglo-Saxon England* by David Hill, 1981. Annual bibliographies of recent work appear in the journal *Anglo-Saxon England,* 1972 onward, and summaries of current archaeological research in the journal *Medieval Archaeology,* published annually (from 1957) by the Society for Medieval Archaeology.

The text of this book was completed early in 1986, but publication has been delayed for reasons beyond the author's control. I should like to draw attention to two in particular among several new works devoted to this period: James Campbell's *Essays in Anglo-Saxon History,* 1986, is a distinguished collection by a leading scholar; the posthumously published work of J. M. Wallace-Hadrill, *Bede's "Ecclesiastical History of the English People": A Historical Commentary,* Oxford, 1988, supplements, though it does not replace, the earlier commentary by Plummer.

Glossary

Alderman. A nobleman who exercised local authority on the king's behalf within a shire or group of shires, such as **Athelstan Half-King,** pp. 161–62. After the Danish conquest under **Canute,** pp. 202–06, the term was gradually superseded by the Anglo-Scandinavian word *earl.*

Bretwalda. An Old English term meaning either "wide ruler" or "ruler of Britain," attested in only one ninth-century source but assumed to have been at an earlier date the vernacular word used to describe a king who enjoyed overlordship over other kings, such as **Aelle,** p. 17, or **Ethelbert,** pp. 26–28.

Burh. A fortified town such as those constructed by **Alfred,** pp. 123–24, and **Edward the Elder,** pp. 147–51.

Charter. The formal written record of the conveyance of property or rights from donor to beneficiary: charters were introduced into England in the wake of Christianity in the seventh century, probably in the time of **Augustine,** pp. 30–31, certainly by the time of **Theodore,** pp. 41–45.

Computus. The science of the ecclesiastical calendar; in particular, the skills required for the calculation of the principal movable feast of the Christian year, Easter. Among Anglo-Saxon scholars, **Bede,** pp. 68–80, and **Byrhtferth,** pp. 212–13, were distinguished computists.

Danegeld. A tax on land initially levied to buy off Danish attackers in the reign of **Ethelred the Unready,** pp. 181–87.

Danelaw. That region of England (principally East Anglia, the East Midlands, and Yorkshire) that received Danish immigration in the latter part of the ninth century under such leaders as **Halfdan,** pp. 120–22, as a result of which it developed social and legal peculiarities that served to distinguish it from the remainder of England.

Fyrd. The military force raised by means of the obligation of free men to serve an Anglo-Saxon king as soldiers in case of need.

Hagiography. The writing of the lives of saints: for a brief indication of the features of this distinct literary genre, see the entry for **St. Cuthbert,** pp. 58–60.

Hide. Originally denoted the amount of land needed to support a family; later—almost certainly by the time of **Bede,** pp. 68–80—the term was used as a notional unit in the assessment of land for services and taxes, and continued to be so used throughout the Anglo-Saxon period and beyond it.

Housecarl. A military retainer of the Anglo-Danish kings of the eleventh century such as **Canute,** pp. 202–06.

Hundred. The administrative subdivision of a **shire,** first attested in an ordinance probably issued by **King Edmund,** pp. 155–56, though likely to have originated somewhat earlier.

Minster. A church served by a community of clergy (not necessarily monastic in character).

Pallium. A white woollen stole decorated with dark purple crosses, given by the pope to an archbishop in token of his archiepiscopal status.

Paschal Controversy. The dispute about the manner of calculating the date of Easter, which exercised many of the churches of western Christendom in the seventh century.

Penitential. A handbook for confessors, offering guidance as to the appropriate penances for various sins: the earliest one produced in Anglo-Saxon England was attributed to **Archbishop Theodore,** pp. 41–45.

Peregrinatio. The Latin term for pilgrimage, in the sense of ascetic renunciation of home and kin for a life of Christian exile, as practiced, for example, by **Columba,** pp. 23–24, or **Egbert of Iona,** pp. 80–81.

Rule. A written code laying down the daily observance of a monastic community.

Scriptorium. The room in a religious community set apart for the writing and decoration of manuscripts.

Sheriff. Derived from *shire-reeve,* the official who represented the king in the routine administration of a **shire;** deputy of the alderman or earl; traceable from *c.* 1000 onward.

Shire. Derived from the Old English word *scir,* which meant originally a "bit" or "part," the shire was the main territorial subdivision of Wessex for the purposes of local administration, probably by the time of **King Ine,** pp. 61–63, certainly by the reign of **Alfred,** pp. 123–24; from Wessex the institution was extended to other parts of England in the tenth century.

Synod. A council of the church.

Thane. The privileged follower of a lord.

Tithe. The render of a tenth part of the annual produce of land to the church, payment of which was made compulsory by **King Edgar,** pp. 164–69.

Translation. The transference of the mortal remains of a saint from one resting-place to another, as, for example, the translation of **St. Aelfheah,** pp. 192–93, from London to Canterbury in 1023.

Wapentake. Derived from the Old Norse *vapnatak,* the brandishing of weapons to indicate assent, wapentake was the word used in the **Danelaw** for the subdivision of the **shire** elsewhere called a **hundred.**

Witan. The counsellors of an Anglo-Saxon king; by extension, a meeting of such counsellors: often rendered *witenagemot,* which means literally "meeting of wise men."

Index

Acca, Bishop of Hexham, 84; commissions biography of Wilfrid, 50

Aelfheah, St., Archbishop of Canterbury, 192–93

Aelfric, Abbot of Eynsham, 209–12; connection with Ethelweard the chronicler, 189; on King Edgar, 166; on St. Ethelwold, 174; on St. Swithun, 115

Aelle, King of Deira, 24–25

Aelle, King of Sussex, 17; *imperium* of, 25

Agilbert, Bishop of Dorchester and Paris, 39–40; briefs Archbishop Theodore on English conditions, 41; ordains and consecrates Wilfrid, 51

Agricola, Gnaeus Julius, governor of Britain, 6–7; manuscript of biography of, 103

Aidan, St., Bishop of Lindisfarne, 36–37; Bede's attitude to, 77; patron of Hilda, 46

Alban, St., 9; monastery dedicated to him founded by King Offa, 109

Albert, Archbishop of York, 104–5; Alcuin a pupil of, 105; books requested from, 102

Albinus, Abbot of Canterbury, 80; informant of Bede, 31, 76; pupil of Hadrian, 46

Alcuin, Abbot of Tours, 105–7; and Albert, 104; on Aldfrith, 60; biographer of Willibrord, 82; diffuses Bede's work abroad, 79; influence on Wulfstan, 208; poem on York, 93; on Wilfrid, 55; on Willehad, 103

Aldfrith, King of Northumbria, 60; friend of Ceolfrith, 68; quarrel with Wilfrid, 53

Aldhelm, St., Bishop of Sherborne, 63–65; on English church councils, 43; influence on Boniface, 86; and King Aldfrith, 60; literary influence of in tenth century, 189; Lul requests works of, 102; pupil of Hadrian, 46; on the school of Canterbury, 44

Alfred, King of Wessex, 123–34; accompanies father to Rome, 118; and Asser, 136–38; and Grimbald, 141–42; and John the Old Saxon, 142–43; and lay literacy, 189; and Plegmund, 139–40; praised by Aelfric, 211; translates works of Bede, 79; translates works of Gregory I, 29; translation of Boethius in library of Bishop Leofric, 227; wars with Guthrum, 135; and Werferth, 140–41; his will, 119

Ambrosius Aurelianus, 15–16

Arthur, 17–18

Asser, Bishop of Sherborne, 136–38; on Ealdorman Ethelred, 143; on fortresses, 127; on Grimbald, 141; on John the Old Saxon, 142; records Ethelwulf's generosity to the see of Rome, 118

Athelstan, King of Wessex, 151–55; and Haakon of Norway, 157; navy of, 166; and Oda, 159; possessed copy of Bede's *History*, 170; praised by Aelfric, 211

Athelstan Half-King, 161–62

Augustine, St., Archbishop of Canterbury, 30–31

Bede, St., 68–80; on Aelle of Deira, 24; on Aelle of Sussex, 17; on Aidan, 36, 77; on Augustine, 31; biography of Cuthbert, 58–59, 153; on Caedmon, 47–48; on Ceawlin of Wessex, 25; on Ceolfrith, 67–68; and Ceolwulf, 84; connections with Acca, 84; and Daniel, 85; on Edwin of Northumbria, 32–33, 77; on Egbert Archbishop of York, 92, 95; on Egbert of Iona, 81; on Ethelbert of Kent, 26; on Ethelfrith of Northumbria, 25; on Gregory I, 29; influence on Byrhtferth, 212; links with Chad, 41; on Ninian, 19; on the notion of 'the English people', 43, 79; possible influence on Dunstan, 170; on Redwalf of East Anglia, 31; represented in the library of Bishop Leofric, 227; reticence about Frankish ecclesiastical influence, 40, 78; translated for King Alfred, 132; unforthcoming on paganism, 35, 78; on Wilfrid, 50, 54, 55, 78; on Willibrord, 82; works requested by Lul, 102

Benedict Biscop, Abbot of Monkwearmouth-Jarrow, 56–57; accompanies Theodore to England, 41;

and King Aldfrith, 60;
receives endowments from
King Ecgfrith, 50; travels on
the Continent with Wilfrid,
·50
Birinus, St., Bishop of
Dorchester, 37; succeeded
by Agilbert, 39
Boadicea, 5–6
Boniface, St., Archbishop of
Mainz, 86–91;
correspondent of Nothelm,
80; and Cuthbert
Archbishop of Canterbury,
95; dealings with Willbrord,
82; diffuses Bede's work
abroad, 70; and King
Ethelbald of Mercia, 98–99;
and Leoba, 99; and Lul,
101; possible influence of
Wilfrid on, 55; and
Willibald, 101
Byrhtferth, 212–13; on King
Edward the Martyr, 181; on
Oswald Archbishop of York,
178; on York, 158
Byrhtnoth, 187–88

Cadwalla, King of Wessex,
60–61; compared with
Guthlac, 66; compared with
King Ine of Wessex, 61–62
Caedmon, 47–49; Bede's
approval of, 70
Caesar, Gaius Julius, 1–3
Canute, King of England,
202–6; and cult of Edward
the Martyr, 181; and Eadric
Streona, 197; invasion of

England, 186; marriage to
Emma, 193; patron of Bury
St. Edmunds, 123, and
Thorkell the Tall, 198–99;
and translation of St.
Aelfheah, 193; and Uhtred,
199
Caratacus, 4
Carausius, 9–10
Cassivellaunus, 3
Ceawlin, King of Wessex, 25
Cedd, St., Bishop of the East
Saxons, 40
Ceolfrith, Abbot of
Monkwearmouth-Jarrow,
67–68; appointed Abbot of
Jarrow, 56; early monastic
life of, 39
Ceolwulf, King of
Northumbria, 84
Cerdic, King of Wessex, 22
Chad, St., Bishop of York and
Lichfield, 41; friend of
Egbert of Iona, 80; quarrel
with Wilfrid, 52
Claudius, Tiberius Nero
Germanicus, Roman
Emperor, 3–4
Cogidubnus, Tiberius
Claudius, 5
Coifi, 34–35
Columba, St., Abbot of Iona,
23–24; missionary impulse,
38, 82
Constantinus (Constantine I),
Flavius Valerius, Roman
Emperor, 10–11; Ethelbert
of Kent compared to, 28;

his sword presented to King
Athelstan, 153
Constantine III, usurping
Roman Emperor, 12–13
Cunobelin, 3
Cuthbert, St., Bishop of
Lindisfarne, 58–60; final
resting place at Durham,
170; and King Athelstan,
153; opposes King
Ecgfrith's attack on Ireland,
50; reluctance to become a
Bishop, 43; travels of his
relics, 121
Cuthbert, Archbishop of
Canterbury, 94–96; and
Boniface, 89
Cuthbert, Abbot of
Monkwearmouth-Jarrow,
96; books sought from, 102
Cynewulf, 111–13; work
represented in the Exeter
Book, 227

Daniel, Bishop of Winchester,
85–86; advice on
missionary tactics, 34, 88;
one of Bede's informants,
76
Dunstan, St., Archbishop of
Canterbury, 169–72; and
Archbishop Oda, 160; and
Athelstan Half-King, 161;
exiled by King Eadwig, 163;
and King Eadred, 157; and
King Edgar, 164; and King
Edmund, 156; and the Life
of St. Edmund, 123

Eadbert, King of
Northumbria, 93–94
Eadred, King of Wessex and
England, 156–57
Eadric Streona, 196–98
Eadwig, King of England,
162–64
Ealdred, Archbishop of York,
224–26
Ecgfrith, King of
Northumbria, 49–50; and
Benedict Biscop, 56–57; his
death revealed to Cuthbert,
58; quarrel with Wilfrid, 53
Edgar, King of England,
164–69; and Athelstan Half-
King, 161; and Byrhtnoth,
188; collaboration with
Dunstan, 171–72;
collaboration with
Ethelwold, 173;
collaboration with Oswald,
179; during reign of
Eadwig, 162–63; praised by
Aelfric, 211; and seapower,
129
Edmund, St., King of East
Anglia, 122–23; Abbo's Life
of, 178
Edmund, King of Wessex,
155–56; at battle of
Brunanburh, 152
Edmund Ironside, King of
England, 200–1; and Eadric
Streona, 197; rebels against
his father, 186
Edward the Elder, King of
Wessex, 147–51;
collaboration with his sister

Ethel-flaed, 146; defeats
Danes in 893, 125
Edward the Martyr, King of
England, 180–81
Edward the Confessor, King of
England, 217–20;
attempted invasion, 213;
dealings with Godwin and
his sons, 214–15; dealings
with his mother Emma,
195; dealings with
Northumbria, 228–29
Edwin, King of Northumbria,
32–33; chapel founded in
memory of, 104; naval
power of, 49
Egbert of Iona, Bishop, 80–81;
opposes King Ecgfrith's
attack on Ireland, 49;
persuades monks of Iona to
observe Roman Easter, 73;
and Willibrord, 81
Egbert, Archbishop of York,
91–93; and Albert, 104; on
Archbishop Theodore, 45;
Bede's letter to, 36, 76–77;
and Boniface, 88
Egbert, King of Wessex,
113–14
Emma, Queen-consort,
193–96
Eric Bloodaxe, King of York,
157–59; wars with King
Eadred, 156–57
Ethelbald, King of Mercia,
96–99; and Boniface, 89;
and Cuthbert Archbishop
of Canterbury, 94; and
Guthlac, 66

Ethelbert, King of Kent,
26–28; conversion of, 30;
influential in conversion of
King Redwald, 31, 33
Ethelflaed, Lady of the
Mercians, 145–47;
collaboration with her
brother King Edward,
147–48; fortification of
Worcester, 141; marriage to
Ealdorman Ethelred, 143;
translates relics of St.
Oswald, 36
Ethelfrith, King of
Northumbria, 25–26
Ethelred, Ealdorman of
Mercia, 143–44; defeats
Danes at Buttington, 125;
fortification of Worcester,
141
Ethelred the Unready, King of
England, 181–87; dealings
with Wulfric's family,
191–92; marriage to Emma,
193; patron of St.
Frideswide's minster, 85
Ethelweard, 188–90; brother-
in-law of King Eadwig, 163;
patron of Aelfric, 189
Ethelwold, St., Bishop of
Winchester, 172–76;
granted abbacy of
Abingdon, 157, 160; and
King Eadwig, 163; and King
Edgar, 164–65; promotes
cult of St. Swithun, 115
Ethelwulf, King of Wessex,
117–20

Frideswide, St., 85
Fursey, St., 37–38; Bede's
    treatment of, 77

Germanus, St., Bishop of
    Auxerre, 13–14
Gildas, 21–22; possible
    reference to Vortigern, 14;
    quoted by Wulfstan, 208;
    refers to Ambrosius, 15;
    refers to Mount Badon, 18
Godiva, 216–17
Godwin, 213–15; rise to
    prominence under Canute,
    204
Gregory I, St., Pope, 28–30;
    Bede's knowledge of his
    works, 69; biography of
    composed at Whitby, 47;
    encounter with Anglian
    slave-boys, 24–25, 27; his
    work translated by King
    Alfred, 131; missionary
    concern of, 82; Paulinus
    sent to England by, 33;
    possible influence on
    Wilfrid, 51; relations with
    Augustine, 30; represented
    in the library of Bishop
    Leofric, 227
Guthlac, St., 66
Guthrum, King of East Anglia,
    134–35; coinage struck by,
    123; wars with King Alfred,
    124–25

Hadrian, Abbot of
    Canterbury, 45–46;
    Aldhelm his pupil, 64;
    declines see of Canterbury,
    41
Hadrianus (Hadrian), Publius
    Aelius, Roman Emperor,
    7–8
Halfdan, King of York,
    120–22; campaigns with
    Guthrum, 135
Harald Hardrada, King of
    Norway, 230–31
Harold II, King of England,
    231–34
Hengist, King of Kent, 16–17
Hilda, St., Abbess of Whitby,
    46–47; and Caedmon, 48
Honorius, Flavius Augustus,
    Roman Emperor, 13

Ida, King of Northumbria, 24
Ine, King of Wessex, 61–63;
    and Boniface, 86; and King
    Wihtred, 67
Ingimund, 144–45

John the Old Saxon, Abbot of
    Athelney, 142–43

Kenelm, St., 111

Leoba, St., Abbess of
    Tauberbischofsheim,
    99–100
Leofric, Bishop of Exeter,
    226–28
Lul, St., Archbishop of Mainz,
    101–3; corresponds with

Abbot Cuthbert of Monkwearmouth-Jarrow, 96; corresponds with Archbishop Cuthbert of Canterbury, 95; diffuses Bede's work abroad, 79, 96; succeeds Boniface, 90

Macbeth, King of Scotland, 215–16
Magnus Maximus, usurping Roman Emperor, 11

Nennius, 110–11; on Ambrosius, 16; on Arthur, 17–18; on Ida, 24; on Penda, 38; on Vortigern, 14–15
Ninian, St., 18–19
Nothelm, Archbishop of Canterbury, 80; his advice sought by Boniface, 88; informant of Bede, 31, 76

Oda, Archbishop of Canterbury, 159–61; annuls King Eadwig's marriage, 163; and Edward the Elder, 150; negotiates a peace, 155; Scandinavian ancestry of, 122; translates Wilfrid's relics to Canterbury, 56; uncle of Archbishop Oswald, 176
Offa, King of Mercia, 107–10; founder of Winchcombe Abbey, 111; laws doubtfully attributed to, 130;

possessed a copy of Bede's *History*, 79
Oswald, St., King of Northumbria, 35–36; and Birinus, 37; tomb embellished by King Offa, 109
Oswald, St., Archbishop of York, 176–79; and Byhrtferth, 212–13; at Fleury, 160, 173; and King Edgar, 164–65; promotes cult of St. Edmund, 123; refounds Winchcombe Abbey, 111
Oswy, King of Northumbria, 38–39; appoints Chad Bishop of York, 41; appoints Hilda Abbess of Whitby, 46

Patrick, St., 19–21; missionary vocation of, 29; possible connection with Germanus, 14
Paulinus, Bishop of York, 33–34; baptizes Hilda, 46
Pelagius, 11–12; British followers of, 14
Penda, King of Mercia, 38
Plegmund, Archbishop of Canterbury, 138–40
Pytheas, 1

Ragnar Lothbrok, 115–17
Redwald, King of East Anglia, 31–32
Robert Champart, Archbishop of Canterbury, 221–22

Septimius Severus, Lucius,
　Roman Emperor, 8–9
Siward, 215; involved in
　Northumbrian feud, 199
Stigand, Archbishop of
　Canterbury, 222–24; friend
　of Earl Godwin, 215; rise to
　prominence under Canute,
　204
Sweyn Forkbeard, King of
　Denmark, 201–2; invasion
　of England, 184, 193; and
　the murder of Archbishop
　Aelfheah, 192
Swithun, St. Bishop of
　Winchester, 115; cult
　promoted by Bishop
　Ethelwold, 175

Theodore of Tarsus, St.,
　Archbishop of Canterbury,
　41–45; entertained by
　Agilbert, 39; quarrel with
　Wilfrid, 52–53, 55
Thorkell the Tall, 198–99; and
　the murder of Archbishop
　Aelfheah, 192–93
Tostig, 228–30

Uhtred, 199–200

Vortigern, 14–15

Werferth, Bishop of
　Worcester, 140–41; and the
　restoration of London, 139
Wihtred, King of Kent, 67

Wilfrid, St., Bishop of York,
　50–56; and Acca, 84; and
　Boniface, 87; and Ceolfrith,
　67; consecrated by Agilbert,
　39; contends with Chad for
　the see of York, 41; expels
　Cuthbert from Ripon, 58;
　plans to accompany King
　Oswy to Rome, 39;
　promotes cult of Oswald,
　35; quarrel with King
　Ecgfrith, 49; quarrel with
　Theodore, 44; relations
　with Cadwalla, 61; relics
　translated to Canterbury,
　160; at synod of Whitby, 39;
　and Willibrord, 81
Willehad, St., Bishop of
　Bremen, 103
Willibald, St., Bishop of
　Eichstätt, 101–2
Willibrord, St., Archbishop of
　Utrecht, 81–83; dealings
　with Boniface, 86–87;
　encourages cult of Oswald
　on Continent, 35; pupil of
　Egbert of Iona, 81; pupil of
　Wilfrid, 55; related to
　Alcuin, 105
Wulfric, 190–92
Wulfstan, Archbishop of York,
　207–9; and Canute, 204; as
　drafter of royal legislation,
　140, 186, 192, 206; on King
　Ethelred's taxation, 185
Wystan, St., 114